THE PRAYER OF THE FAITHFUL FOR WEEKDAYS

THE

PRAYER OF THE FAITHFUL

FOR WEEKDAYS

A RESOURCE BOOK

Edited by ELTIN GRIFFIN O.Carm.

BLACKFRIARS PUBLICATIONS
DOMINICAN PUBLICATIONS
COSTELLO PUBLISHING COMPANY INC.

The Prayer of the Faithful for Weekdays
Copyright © 1985

Blackfriars Publications
Oxford

Dominican Publications
42 Parnell Square
Dublin I

ISBN 0-907271-64-2

Costello Publishing Company Inc.
Box 9
Northport
Long Island
NY 11768

Nihil obstat Arthur McCrystal, B.A., S.T.L., D.Phil.
Imprimatur Mgr D. Leonard, V.G.
Birmingham, 16 October 1985

Approved by the Australian Episcopal Liturgical Commission

This August 2012 reprint printed in Ireland by
Gemini International, Damastown, Dublin 15

CONTENTS

FEASTS AND SOLEMNITIES

Including feasts of our Lord which are not holy days, feasts of our Lady, feasts of founders of religious families, and national propers from Australia, England, Ireland, Scotland, and Wales.

COMMONS

MASSES FOR SPECIAL OCCASIONS

SUPPLEMENT FOR THE UNITED STATES OF AMERICA

INTRODUCTION

The editing of this work has been a labour of love. All the more so, when most of the people I contacted wrote back immediately to say yes to the invitation to contribute. All of them are busy people and I would like to thank them for their willing cooperation and for the excellence of their work.

This is a book which I hope will be used widely across the English speaking Church. It fills a huge pastoral vacuum. At times our weekday Eucharists come dangerously near ritualism. I am always a bit fearful of the lay person who claims that Father X is great; he gets us out in twelve minutes past the hour or half-hour. There is an extraordinary fidelity to the Eucharist among certain laity coupled with an equally extraordinary desire to get through with it as quickly as possible. The Liturgy of the Word for many is still a non-event and sadly, for some priests. The Old Testament readings are omitted on the plea that they do not make sense especially when it comes to bloody battles, to dividing up land or to some strange sounding names. It doesn't take a great deal of imagination to transpose the happenings of the Old Testament into contemporary life and into the local community. Vatican II succeeded in opening up the liturgy to a much richer fare of Scripture. Indeed the fare is so utterly rich that it becomes almost embarrassing.

INTERCESSORY PRAYER

The Prayer of the Faithful is part of the ministry of the Word. The people have listened to the Word and presumably, have been challenged by it. They respond to the Word by praying in the light of the Word for the needs of the Church, of all humankind and for the local community. The Prayer of the Faithful opens out the Word to the world, praying for its healing, enlightenment and guidance. Intercessory prayer is costly prayer. It demands that we extend the horizons of concern beyond ourselves and our petty preoccupations to the more universal concerns of the Church, of all humanity and of the society to which we belong. Intercessory prayer belongs to that category of praying which John McQuarrie calls 'compassionate thinking.' There is more to it than just expressing our concern in prayer. The way we focus our interceding challenges our consciences and provides a response from us in our lives to the needs of others.

This calls for a very creative approach to the composition of the Prayer of the Faithful. Indeed such prayers should be freshly minted for every celebration. Pre-packaged bidding prayers can fall very flat if they are announced without much sense of involvement.

Intercessory prayer calls for what Confucius terms 'humanheartedness', an ability to grasp and to embrace the ills of others and to extend the horizons of our expectation for them.

THE CONTRIBUTORS
These particular bidding prayers have been composed by quite a variety of persons. Some of them are noted liturgists from England and from Ireland. Other contributors, both men and women, are distinguished by the excellence of their pastoral work in parishes, chaplaincies, retreat houses and third level institutes. Two of our contributors represent our separated brethren in Ireland. Our prayer traditions are somewhat different, but their particular contributions to this volume represent a very neat fusion of both traditions.

The strength and weakness of this work may be in the diversity of styles that are presented. How this will affect the average worshipper is difficult to surmise. Today's young worshippers will be tomorrow's leaders in prayer. May they emulate the best elements in this collection.

GUIDELINES
Certain guidelines were supplied to all contributors. by and large they were followed. One had to respect the viewpoints of a few who gave reasons for direct address to the Lord either in the introduction to the bidding prayer or in the intercessions themselves. One has to respect the viewpoint of people of academic distinction or of academic weight. One is always fearful, however, of prayer degenerating into pietism which is much more easily encouraged by direct address to the Lord. However, the canons for suitable language in public prayer by and large have been honoured.

In the end none of the contributions can pretend to be more than guidelines or models which are always capable of being re-written and adapted to the capacity of the particular celebrating community.

CONTENTS
As will be obvious from the book itself, we have supplied Prayers of the Faithful for the thirty-four weeks in ordinary time as well as for all the weekdays in the major seasons. Solemnities which are not holy days are also catered for, as are the feasts of Mary. As for saints' days, we decided to include founders of religious families, and a series of commons for the rest, as in the breviary. Special occasions, such as church unity octave and the anniversaries of the dead, have been taken into account. The national propers for

Ireland, England, Wales, Scotland, and Australia are partially included.

May those who use this book find it stimulating for themselves and for the people they serve.

Eltin Griffin, O.Carm.

NOTES ON USING THIS BOOK

1. INTRODUCTION AND CONCLUDING PRAYER
The president of the assembly should introduce and conclude the Prayer of the Faithful.

2. INTENTIONS
It is the function of the deacon to present the intentions. Where a deacon is not available ideally a layperson should take on this role. Apart from the theological implications this arrangement makes for contrast in voices which stimulates attention.

3. RESPONSES
One should prevent the response getting into a rut such as the predictable 'Lord, graciously hear us'. At the same time an unfamiliar response or one that is too involved can make people feel embarrassed. One can distinguish two kinds of variations.

(a) General Variations
Let us pray to the Lord: Lord, hear our prayer.
Lord, in your mercy: Hear our prayer.
Lord, have mercy: Lord, have mercy.
Lord, hear us: And grant us your peace.
Lord, hear us: And fill us with your love.

(b) Seasonal Variations
Advent
Let us pray to the Lord: Lord, may your kingdom come.
We pray to the Lord: Come, Lord Jesus, come.
Lord, hear our prayer: Lord, come and save us.

Christmas
We pray to the Lord: Glory to God in the highest.
Lord, hear us: And grant us your peace.

Epiphany
We pray to the Lord: Lord, may your light come upon us.

Lent
We pray to the Lord: Lord, have mercy on us.
Lord, give strength to your people.
Create a new spirit in us, O Lord.
Jesus, Son of David, have mercy on us.
Lord, save your people.
Lord, have mercy on your people.

Eastertide
We pray to the Lord: Risen Lord, hear us.
                     Lord of life, save us.
                     Stay with us, Lord Jesus Christ.

Pentecost
Send forth your Spirit, O Lord: And renew the face of the earth.

4. SUNG RESPONSES
There is an abundance of these available. They seem to heighten the
prayer and involve people more fully. One of the simplest and most ·
successful is the Byzantine melody, to be found in the Mass of Our
Lady of Lourdes published by the Dublin Diocesan Pilgrimage.
Lucien Deiss offers quite a variety in his *Biblical Hymns and
Psalms* and *More Biblical Hymns and Psalms* both published by
the World Library of Sacred Music, Cincinatti.

5. WEEKDAYS IN ORDINARY TIME
Where the term *Year 1* or *Year 2* occurs over a particular intention
the reader should confine the intention to that particular year. One
contributor distinguishes the two years in his introductions. (Week
5 of Ordinary Time).

6. SPECIAL INTENTIONS
Special intentions such as the name of a deceased person whose anniversary occurs should be added to the intentions for a given day
unless there is already a petition for the dead in the series. In that
case the name of the deceased should be included in that particular
intercession. Otherwise the one leading the intercessions should add
something like the following:
    For those who have gone before us in Christ and especially for
    . . . that they may rest in Christ.
    For our loved ones departed and especially for . . . that they
    might find rest in the Lord.
    For all whom the Lord has called out of this life and especially
    for . . . whose anniversary occurs today. May (s)he enjoy the
    light of life eternal.
Particular intentions concerning the local community, personal
intentions or special occasions should be included at the end of the
intercessions and in some appropriate formula like the following:
    For the sick, the dying and especially for . . .
    For those who hunger and thirst after justice and especially
    for . . .
    Mindful of all the blessings that have come from him who is the

source of all good gifts we return thanks. We pray especially
for . . . who celebrates today the . . .

7. ADAPTATION

The prayer will sound all the more convincing if the president and
those who are engaged with him in the planning of the liturgy will
have internalised the content beforehand. Formulas straight out of
a book may fail to stimulate prayer among the participants. The
formulas given here should be adapted to the intelligence, to the
age and to the needs of those taking part. The idea is to re-draft
a Prayer of the Faithful that will vibrate with this particular
celebrating community and will at the same time respect the canons
of tradition and orthodoxy.

Many of the formulas supplied will naturally reflect the
spirituality of those who composed them. This may not necessarily
be in tune with the spirituality of the celebrating community. To a
group of people, for instance, whose social awareness may not be
so highly developed, pastoral sensitivity should dictate gradual
initiation into the larger horizons of social awareness through
catechesis, preaching and through corresponding prayer. To present such a group with ready-made intercessions which echo very
radical thinking may lead to inauthenticity in praying. It is not a
case of leaving people as they are, or where they are at, but of
gradually leading them to where they ought to be and should be.

CONTRIBUTORS

Paul Chandler, O.Carm. (Advent Weeks One and Two), is an Australian, and is studying for a doctorate in theology at the Gregorian University, Rome.

Aloysius Ryan, O.Carm. (Advent Weeks Three and Four), is on the staff of the Gort Muire Conference Centre, Ballinteer, Dublin.

Heber McMahon (Time after Christmas and after Epiphany) is a priest of Dublin diocese. He is curate at Artane, and is chairperson of the Dublin Diocesan Liturgy Commission.

Gerald King (co-author with Fr McMahon) is a student of theology at All Hallows College, Dublin.

Stephanie Brophy (Lent, Ash Wednesday and following days, and Week One) is a Sister of the Holy Rosary Congregation who is on the parish staff of the Pro-Cathedral, Dublin.

Donal Neary, S.J. (Lent, Weeks Two and Three), is attached to the Jesuit community at John Sullivan House, Monkstown, Co. Dublin. He specialises in spirituality and in vocations work.

Ernest Sands (Lent, Weeks Four and Five) is on the staff of Upholland Northern Institute, Lancs., England.

Seán O'Sullivan (Octave of Easter) is parish priest of Blackrock, Co. Dublin.

Placid Murray, O.S.B. (Weeks Two and Three of Easter), is a monk of Glenstal, a liturgist, and a leading Newman scholar.

Vincent Ryan, O.S.B. (Weeks Four and Five of Easter), is a monk of Glenstal, a liturgist, and author of several books.

Patrick Lynch (Weeks Six and Seven of Easter) is a priest of Achonry diocese, and is a curate at Culfadda, Ballymote, Co. Sligo.

Paul O'Brien, O.Carm. (Weeks One and Two Ordinary Time), is an English Carmelite who has recently been appointed to the Carmelite Retreat House, Williamstown, Mass., U.S.A.

Brendan Hoban (Weeks Three and Four Ordinary Time), a priest of Killala diocese, is curate at Beltra, Co. Sligo.

Gilbert Mayes (Week Five Ordinary Time), Dean of Lismore (Church of Ireland, Anglican Communion), is secretary of the Liturgical Advisory Committee of the General Synod of the Church of Ireland.

Maurice Carey (Week Six Ordinary Time), Dean of Cork (Church of Ireland, Anglican Communion), is very active in the ecumenical movement.

Conor O'Riordan, O.P. (Weeks Seven and Eight Ordinary Time), is involved in retreat work, residing in Cork.

Gabriel Harty, O.P. (Week Nine Ordinary Time, Feasts of the Presentation of the Lord and of the Rosary), is on the staff of Holy Cross Church, Sligo.

Gregory Ó Seanacháin, O.F.M. (Week Ten Ordinary Time, Holy Week), is involved in retreat work, and resides at the Abbey, Multyfarnham, Co. Westmeath.

Joseph Chalmers, O.Carm. (Weeks Eleven and Twelve Ordinary Time, St Teresa of Avila), specialises in Carmelite mysticism, and resides at Hazelwood Castle, Yorks, England.

Wilfrid McGreal, O.Carm. (Weeks Thirteen and Fourteen Ordinary Time), is chaplain at London University.

Martin Clarke (Weeks Fifteen and Sixteen Ordinary Time) is Director of the Catholic Youth Council, Dublin.

Patrick Kilgariff (Weeks Seventeen and Eighteen Ordinary Time) is parish priest at Newcastle-upon-Tyne. He is a former member of the Catholic Missionary Society.

Edward Matthews (Weeks Nineteen and Twenty Ordinary Time) is a priest of Westminster diocese who teaches at Allen Hall Seminary in London.

Brian Magee, C.M. (Weeks Twenty-one and Thirty-four Ordinary Time, St Vincent de Paul), teaches liturgy at the Mater Dei Institute of Religious Education, Dublin.

Fiona McGrory (Week Twenty-two Ordinary Time) is a student at St Patrick's College of Education, Drumcondra, Dublin.

Helena O'Donoghue, R.S.M. (Weeks Twenty-three and Twenty-four Ordinary Time), works as a parish sister in Shannon, Co. Clare.

Joseph Sheehan, O.Carm. (Weeks Twenty-five and Twenty-six Ordinary Time), belongs to the New York Province of the Carmelite Order, and is engaged in special education at Rochester, N.Y.

Patrick Jones (Weeks Twenty-seven and Twenty-eight Ordinary Time) teaches liturgy at Clonliffe College and at the Mater Dei Institute of Religious Education, Dublin.

Anne Kelly (Weeks Twenty-nine and Thirty Ordinary Time), married, with two children, is on the staff of St Patrick's College of Education, Drumcondra, Dublin.

P. J. Brophy (Weeks Thirty-one and Thirty-two Ordinary Time), formerly president of St Patrick's College, Carlow, is parish priest of Crosneen, Carlow.

Raymond Topley (Week Thirty-three Ordinary Time), a graduate of St Michael's College, Vermont, is involved in adult catechetics.

Christopher O'Donnell, O.Carm. (Common of the Blessed Virgin Mary, Our Lady of Lourdes, St Joseph), teaches systematic theology at the Milltown Institute, Dublin.

Thomas McCarthy, O.P. (Commons of Apostles, Martyrs, Virgins, Holy Men, Holy Women), is a patristics scholar who teaches systematic theology at St Mary's, Tallaght, Co. Dublin.

Edward McCarthy, O.Carm. (Proper for Scotland, Commons of Pastors, Doctors), is a student of philosophy at the Milltown Institute, Dublin.

Barbara Ellen Bowe, R.S.C.J. (Solemnity of Mary, Mother of God), is a doctoral student in New Testament at Harvard Divinity School, Cambridge, Mass.

Patrick Duffy, C.P. (St Paul of the Cross), is involved in retreat work and resides at Mount Argus, Dublin.

Bernard Treacy, O.P. (Transfiguration of the Lord), is an editor with Dominican Publications.

Vincent O'Hara, O.D.C. (Our Lady of Mount Carmel), is attached to the Avila Centre of Spirituality, Dublin.

Seán Collins, O.F.M. (Sts John the Baptist, Peter and Paul, Francis of Assisi), teaches sacramental theology at the Milltown Institute, Dublin.

Michael O'Donohue (All Souls, Anniversary of the Dead), is administrator of the Pro-Cathedral, Dublin.

Michael Winstanley, S.D.B. (St John Bosco), teaches Scripture at Ushaw College and at Durham University, England.

Declan Grogan, F.S.C. (St John Baptist de la Salle), is a student of history at University College, Dublin.

Raymond Moloney, S.J. (Sacred Heart, St Ignatius of Loyola, Novena of Grace) is a former president of the Milltown Institute and has been seconded to the new Jesuit Institute in Nairobi, Kenya.

Thomas Byrne, C.Ss.R. (St Alphonsus), is on the staff of St Clement's Retreat House, Belfast.

Linus Ryan, O.Carm. (St Therese of Lisieux), is on the staff of the Carmelite Church, Whitefriar St., Dublin.

Anselm Moynihan, O.P. (St Dominic), is a noted spiritual writer, and resides at St Saviour's, Dublin.

Gervase Corcoran, O.S.A. (St Augustine), is a patristics scholar who teaches theology at the Milltown Institute, Dublin.

Diarmuid Ó Murchú, M.S.C. (For the Evangelization of Peoples, for Peace and Justice, for the Starving People of the World, for the Sanctification of Human Work, for Refugees and Exiles) is chaplain at Holy Child Community School, Sallynoggin, Co. Dublin.

Patrick Lyons (Christian Unity) is curate at Balally, Dublin.

Diarmuid Ó Laoghaire, S.J. (Sts Brigid, Columban, and Naomh Colm Cille), teaches spirituality at the Milltown Institute, Dublin.

+**Joseph Duffy** (St Patrick, All Saints of Ireland) is Bishop of Clogher.

+ **Edward Daly** (St Columba) is Bishop of Derry.

Hugh Clarke, O.Carm. (Proper for England), is on the retreat staff at Allington Castle, Maidstone, Kent, England.

Stanley G. Luff (Proper for Wales) is parish priest at Llandovery, Wales.

Eltin Griffin, O.Carm. (Editor of this volume), teaches liturgy and spirituality at the Milltown Institute and at the Mater Dei Institute, Dublin.

SUPPLEMENT FOR THE UNITED STATES OF AMERICA

Kevin H. Donlon C.Ss.R. (St John Neumann) is editor of the monthly magazine, *Reality*.

Austin Flannery, O.P. (Thanksgiving Day) is editor of the journals *Doctrine and Life* and *Religious Life Review*, and managing editor of Dominican Publications, as well as being editor of *Vatican II: Conciliar and Post-Conciliar Documents* and of *Vatican II: More Post-Conciliar Documents*.

Bernard Treacy, O.P. (St Elizabeth Ann Seton, Independence Day, Labour Day, St Frances Xavier Cabrini) is assistant managing editor of Dominican Publications.

ADVENT

FIRST WEEK OF ADVENT: MONDAY

Introduction
At the beginning of our Advent journey, let us pray to the Lord who calls us to walk with hope on the paths of holiness and peace.

Intentions
1. That all Christians may grow daily closer to Jesus the Lord who alone has power to make us whole.
2. That our hope in the promises of the Lord and our faith in his presence will encourage us to work for a better world.
3. That all who are disabled in body or spirit will find compassion, courage and hope.
4. That leaders of nations will work for an end to war, and will strive for the peace that comes from justice.
5. That this Advent will be a time of grace for all the members of our parish, and especially for those who are estranged from the sacraments.

Concluding Prayer
Father, you promise to come to us with your Son and make your home with us. Hear our prayers, and with your Advent grace make our hearts a home where you can dwell. We ask this through Christ our Lord.

FIRST WEEK OF ADVENT: TUESDAY

Introduction
In the name of Jesus and the power of the Holy Spirit let us pray to the Father whose love for his people is without end.

Intentions
1. That the Church's living and preaching of the Gospel may be marked by the joy that comes from the Holy Spirit.

2. That all who exercise authority in society will use it with integrity and justice, especially towards those who are most poor and weak.
3. That we may learn to hear the call that comes to us from the little ones of the world.
4. That we will respect the creation of which we are a part, and see God's handiwork in all his creatures.
5. That all Christians may grow in the gifts of the Spirit: love and joy, peace and patience, kindness, goodness and faithfulness, gentleness and self-control.

Concluding Prayer
Father, you promise to come to us with your Son and make your home with us. Hear our prayers, and with your Advent grace make our hearts a home where you can dwell. We ask this through Christ our Lord.

FIRST WEEK OF ADVENT: WEDNESDAY

Introduction
Let us place our trust in the Lord who saves us, as we pray to him in the name of the whole Church.

Intentions
1. That the Church may be filled with a sense of the grandeur of God's plan and with a vision which gives hope.
2. May God give to all who are embittered by the sufferings and disappointments of life a healing of heart and spirit.
3. May God teach us compassion and to take up our responsibilities towards those who need us.
4. God bless the families of our parish and help us to open our hearts to one another.
5. That we may not waste our talents; may God help us to put ourselves at the service of the Gospel and of one another.

Concluding Prayer
Father, you promise to come to us with your Son and make your home with us. Hear our prayers, and with your Advent grace make our hearts a home where you can dwell. We ask this through Christ our Lord.

FIRST WEEK OF ADVENT: THURSDAY

Introduction
Let us pray to the Lord who is the strength of his people, and who challenges us to build our lives on him.

Intentions
1. For the whole people of God: that we may be more faithful in hearing his word and putting it into practice.
2. For all who long for the victory of justice and the coming of peace: that they will be sustained by the presence of the Lord.
3. For those who feel that life has no meaning: that they may sense the nearness of the Saviour who has made his home with his people.
4. For ourselves who are gathered here and for all in our parish: that we may open out hearts to Jesus and to one another.
5. For the unity of Christians: by building our lives more firmly on Christ may we come to find one another.

Concluding Prayer
Father, you promise to come to us with your Son and make your home with us. Hear our prayers, and with your Advent grace make our hearts a home where you can dwell. We ask this through Christ our Lord.

FIRST WEEK OF ADVENT: FRIDAY

Introduction
Our God makes all things new: he brings light from darkness and gives joy in sorrow. Let us pray to him with confidence, for he is coming to save us.

Intentions
1. May God open the eyes and ears of all Christians to hear his call and to see the path that he has marked our for them.
2. May God give us a greater sensitivity to the old, the sick, the disabled; and teach us to be grateful for his blessings.

3. May God help us to recognize our need for him, to admit your poverty and to put our trust in his mercy.

4. God has given us hope and healing: may he strengthen us to share his grace with one another.

5. God give us the gift of repentance and teach us to forgive those who sin against us.

Concluding Prayer
Father, you promise to come to us with your Son and make your home with us. Hear our prayers and with your Advent grace make our hearts a home where you can dwell. We ask this through Christ our Lord.

FIRST WEEK OF ADVENT: SATURDAY

Introduction
We do not have to search for God: he is always near and ready with his compassion. Let us pray to him with love and trust.

Intentions
1. May the Lord help our Church not to be closed in on itself: and remind us of our mission to the lost, the forgotten, the poorest.

2. May those who have lost their way on the road to God, especially those in our own families and parish, hear his voice guiding them back.

3. May God help us to accept bad times without bitterness, good times without selfishness, and to see his providence in all things.

4. May God send labourers into the harvest: giving us priests, religious and lay apostles who will spend themselves for the life of God's people.

5. Give to all who learn and all who teach a love of the truth.

Concluding Prayer
Father, you promise to come to us with your Son and make your home with us. Hear our prayers, and with your Advent grace make our hearts a home where you can dwell. We ask this through our Lord.

ADVENT: WEEK 2

SECOND WEEK OF ADVENT: MONDAY

Introduction
The Lord brings everlasting joy to his people. Let us pray to him with confidence, knowing that all we have comes from him.

Intentions
1. For the holy people of God: that we may follow more closely in the footsteps of the Lord.
2. For those whose hearts are paralyzed by evil, and for those who use their authority to do injustice: let us ask for the grace of conversion.
3. For the handicapped, the sick and the dying: that in the mystery of their suffering they may sense the closeness of Christ.
4. For ourselves: that our celebration of Advent may heal our hypocrisy and hardness of heart.
5. For the gifts of compassion and friendship: let us pray that we may be grateful in the receiving and generous in the giving.

Concluding Prayer
Father, giver of life and source of our hope, hear the prayers which we make in faith. Send your Spirit to open our hearts to the coming of your Son, who made himself one of us, and who is our Lord for ever and ever.

SECOND WEEK OF ADVENT: TUESDAY

Introduction
Let us pray to the Lord, who cares for his people as a shepherd for his flock.

Intentions
1. That we, who have ourselves known God's mercy, may share his love for the weakest and the most lost.

2. That we may never despair for the world, but that our hope in the coming of the Lord may be also a hope for the future of our world which he promises to make new.
3. That we may learn to pardon all who hurt us; that we may be healed of all bitterness.
4. That Christians who are alienated from the Church may stand again with God's people and use their gifts in the service of the Gospel.
5. For the dying: that as life fades their hope may flourish.

Concluding Prayer
Father, giver of life and source of our hope, hear the prayers which we make in faith. Send your Spirit to open our hearts to the coming of your Son, who made himself one of us, and who is our Lord for ever and ever.

SECOND WEEK OF ADVENT: WEDNESDAY

Introduction
Those who trust in the Lord and call on him find strength renewed. Let us to go him, then, knowing that he will share our burdens and give us rest.

Intentions
1. Let us pray for the Church throughout the world: that it may draw its strength from the word of God and its joy from faith in his presence.
2. Let us pray for those who have grown weary in doing good: that God will restore their vision, their enthusiasm and their hope.
3. Let us remember with love all those who have helped us become what we are: may the Lord bless them and teach us to be grateful for one another.
4. As we prepare for the celebration of Christmas, let us pray for a renewal of love in our families, especially those which are divided by misunderstanding and bitterness.
5. Let us pray for the unemployed and the homeless: that they may find work and shelter.

Concluding Prayer
Father, giver of life and source of our hope, hear the prayers which we make in faith. Send your Spirit to open our hearts to the coming of your Son, who made himself one of us, and who is our Lord for ever and ever.

SECOND WEEK OF ADVENT: THURSDAY

Introduction
The Lord is kind and full of compassion, slow to anger, abounding in love. With confidence we pray.

Intentions
1. We pray that we may truly take it to heart that the Holy One of Israel is our redeemer, that he will not desert his own.
2. We pray that we may take to heart the injunction to the Prophet, 'do not be afraid'; may he rid our lives of all needless anxiety and fear.
3. We pray that we may never lose sight of the hope that with his strength and his help we can transform the desert of our world today into a place of peace and plenty.
4. We pray that we may realise that the world is not conquered by violence, that we may empty our hearts of the violence that only destroys instead of building up.
5. We pray for the faith and for the courage of the Baptist to sustain us in times of crisis and of desolation.

Concluding Prayer
Father, giver of life and source of our hope, hear the prayers which we make in faith. Send your Spirit to open our hearts to the coming of your Son, who made himself one of us, and who is our Lord for ever and ever.

SECOND WEEK OF ADVENT: FRIDAY

Introduction
Jesus is the one sent to save his people from their sins. Let us pray to the Father that our hearts will be open to the gift of his Son.

Intentions
1. For the pilgrim people of God: that by his grace we may be firm in the faith, young in our hope and united in love.
2. For the young people of the world: that we may find in the Gospel the challenge to live a new life and build a new world.
3. For those who seek the truth without finding it: that their search will lead them to him who is truth and life.
4. For those who suffer from hunger, disease, violence and disaster: may the world find a new compassion for them.
5. For catechists and all who teach the Gospel: that through them the good news of salvation will be heard by all.

Concluding Prayer
Father, giver of life and source of our hope, hear the prayers which we make in faith. Send your Spirit to open our hearts to the coming of your Son, who made himself one of us, and who is our Lord for ever and ever.

SECOND WEEK OF ADVENT: SATURDAY

Introduction
The word of God is a light shining in the darkness. Let us pray that we may hear God's word and keep it in our hearts.

Intentions
1. In a world divided by misunderstanding and inequality, may God's Church be an instrument of reconciliation, justice and peace.
2. May the martyrs and prophets of our time teach us the heroism of Christian life.
3. For the grace to help refugees and exiles to build a new life in security and peace.
4. From the humility and poverty of Bethlehem, may we learn to see Christ in the poor and weak.
5. Let us pray for those who are old: that their wisdom and their prayers will be a strength for our community.

Concluding Prayer
Father, giver of life and source of our hope, hear the prayers

which we make in faith. Send your Spirit to open our hearts
to the coming of your Son, who made himself one of us, and
who is our Lord for ever and ever.

ADVENT: WEEK 3

THIRD WEEK OF ADVENT: MONDAY

Introduction
We who seek to recognise Christ, bring to the Lord all our
needs.

Intentions
1. We pray that the whole Church have clear vision of heart
to recognise and receive Christ when he comes.
2. That all civil leaders pave the way for his coming by
promoting authentic human and social values.
3. For all who are hungry, homeless and the victims of
injustice: that they may receive the peace of Christ through
practical compassion.
4. We pray for ourselves: that we accept without question the
authority of Christ and his Church.
5. That all preachers, teachers and catechists present Christ
with great authenticity and persuasion.

Concluding Prayer
Lord God, you so loved us that you sent your Son to be our
Saviour. Bless our needs and prepare our hearts that he may
be Lord of our lives. We ask this through Christ our Lord.

THIRD WEEK OF ADVENT: TUESDAY

Introduction
Though we are sinners we trust in God's mercy and bring to
him the needs of the Church, of the world and our own.

Intentions
1. For the Church, a sinful people, we pray that she never

lose hope or be afraid of drawing near Jesus, her head.

2. We pray for all in public authority, especially in our country: that they give hope and help to all who are broken and crushed.

3. That in this season of hope and peace there will be a united outcry from all people of good will against all forms of injustice and oppression.

4. That we ourselves in this parish will give encouragement to all who are in any kind of misery, especially the misery of sin, to allow themselves to be touched by the merciful Christ.

5. For all the dead, especially N.N.: that they be brought to the fullness of eternal light and peace.

Concluding Prayer
Lord God, you so loved us that you sent your Son to be our Saviour. Bless our needs and prepare our hearts that he may be Lord of our lives. We ask this through Christ our Lord.

THIRD WEEK OF ADVENT: WEDNESDAY

Introduction
Encouraged by the word of God, we bring all our needs to him.

Intentions
1. That the Church be always alert to the signs of Christ's coming and his presence in her midst, and continue his work of compassion.

2. That all leaders in civil society have great compassion for the sick, the helpless and the homeless, to lift them to their full dignity.

3. That we ourselves be moved by the plight of the needy in our parish and bring them Christ in practical ways of love and aid.,

4. That all who minister to the sick at home or in hospital be encouraged by the knowledge that through them Christ is among his loved ones.

5. That all the dead, especially N.N., be released from the bonds of sin to be with Christ.

Concluding Prayer
Lord God, you so loved us that you sent your Son to be our Saviour. Bless our needs and prepare our hearts that he may be Lord of our lives. We ask this through Christ our Lord.

THIRD WEEK OF ADVENT: THURSDAY

Introduction
As we prepare the way of the Lord, let us pray for the needs of his messengers.

Intentions
1. That the universal Church accept and welcome the prophets in her midst who prepare for the coming of the Lord.
2. That all leaders of society recognise and encourage prophets who call for justice and peace.
3. That there be many messengers who will untiringly help the poor, the sick and the oppressed, so that they too may receive the peace of Christ.
4. That our parish authority seek out and encourage those with special gifts so as to build up the body of Christ.
5. That all preachers and teachers of the word be gifted with wisdom, prudence, humility and persuasion.

Concluding Prayer
Lord God, you so loved us that you sent your Son to be our Saviour. Bless our needs and prepare our hearts that he may be Lord of our lives. We ask this through Christ our Lord.

THIRD WEEK OF ADVENT: FRIDAY

Introduction
We, a people who sit in darkness, ask our God for light.

Intentions·
1. For the Church: that confusion and the darkness of sin give way to the light, and that she may be a clear light to all nations.

2. That all who are called to serve in public office shed a ray of the light of hope to peoples who are in the darkness of wrong values.
3. We pray for all whose spirits are crushed and broken: that they may see the light of hope in many compassionate helpers.
4. For ourselves: that our eyes may be opened to see that Christ comes from the Father with the gift of saving mercy.
5. That all who have asked our prayers be blessed by God according to his wisdom and their needs.

Concluding Prayer
Lord God, you so loved us that you sent your Son to be our Saviour. Bless our needs and prepare our hearts that he may be Lord of our lives. We ask this through Christ our Lord.

WEEKDAYS OF ADVENT
FROM
DECEMBER 17-24

DECEMBER 17th

Introduction
We pray to Christ, divine wisdom in human form, that he will transform our lack of wisdom.

Intentions
1. We pray for the Church: that all her leaders open their hearts to be taught by Christ the true way of salvation.
2. For the leaders of our country: that they be blessed with wisdom and integrity so as to allow all the citizens to live in peace and harmony.
3. For all throughout the world who live in darkness and confusion and doubt: that they be led into the light of the truth which is Jesus Christ.
4. That all the members of our own parish be led to leave aside the values of the sinful world and live the values of Christ who is the way.
5. That all who are preparing for Christmas reflect on the true meaning of the coming of Christ.

Concluding Prayer
Lord God, our kind and loving Father, with sureness and confidence coming from Christ we bring you all our needs for your blessing. Out of your great love send us again Jesus, your Son and our Lord. Grant that we may welcome him with deep love. We ask this through Christ our Lord.

DECEMBER 18th

Introduction
We who know not the way, come to Christ who gave us his law to set us free.

Intentions
1. We pray that the universal Church, by accepting and preaching the law of Christ, be set free from all sin.
2. For political leaders, judges, civil servants and all others who make and administer the laws: that they be filled with such integrity as will set their peoples free from every bondage.
3. For all who are oppressed by unjust laws: that they be led to strong hope in practical help from our good God who loves them deeply.
4. That many modern prophets will be raised up from our midst to condemn unjust laws with the very strength of Christ himself.
5. We pray for ourselves: that, by living according to Gospel values, we will be set free from a life-style that is little better than slavery.

Concluding Prayer
Lord God, our kind and loving Father, with sureness and confidence coming from Christ we bring you all our needs for your blessing. Out of your great love send us again Jesus, your Son and our Lord. Grant that we may welcome him with deep love. We ask this through Christ our Lord.

DECEMBER 19th

Introduction
We ask Christ, set up as a sign of victory over sin for the whole world, to come to our aid.

Intentions
1. That the Church of Christ be fully cleansed and gifted with strong desire and urgent prayer for the reality of Christ's coming.
2. That the whole world be led to believe that Christ was raised up for it as a sign and source of full human living.
3. For all who preach and teach the Christmas message: that they instil in their listeners a sense of urgency and practicality about the coming of Christ.
4. For all who are hungry, homeless, deprived of justice: that, through practical help and compassionate helpers, they may see that Christ is coming to their aid.
5. We pray for all the dead, especially N.N.: that Christ may set them free with everlasting peace this day.

Concluding Prayer
Lord God, our kind and loving Father, with sureness and confidence coming from Christ we bring you all our needs for your blessing. Out of your great love send us again Jesus, your Son and our Lord. Grant that we may welcome him with deep love. We ask this through Christ our Lord.

DECEMBER 20th

Introduction
We who are held prisoners by the power of Satan ask Christ to set us free.

Intentions
1. We ask Christ who came to set us free to release the Church from all power of Satan, and thus to be her life.
2. We pray for the many peoples and nations dominated by the powers of darkness: that their leaders be blessed by God

with liberating desire and power.

3. For all who are in the slavery of fear, depression, anxiety or loneliness: that the Lord raise up many healers to set their spirits free.

4. We bring our own parish to the Lord and ask him to use us to set one another free, especially from sin.

5. For the ministers of the sacrament of reconciliation: that they learn its power to set free, and use it with great compassion, knowing that they too are sinners and weak.

Concluding Prayer
Lord God, our kind and loving Father, with sureness and confidence coming from Christ we bring you all our needs for your blessing. Out of your great love send us again Jesus, your Son and our Lord. Grant that we may welcome him with deep love. We ask this through Christ our Lord.

DECEMBER 21st

Introduction
We who often cannot see our darkness, ask Christ to come and enlighten us.

Intentions
1. That the entire Church, enlightened by Christ's coming, may see the areas of her darkness, and bring them to him to be set free and become the light of hope to the world.

2. We ask for the gift of true light for all civil leaders that they may honestly see and remedy all our problems.

3. For all who are so abandoned that they don't even see the possibility of help: that Christ will send helpers with the gifts of encouragement and persuasion.

4. For ourselves: that Christ will show us through our priests where we are in error and lead us out in the strength of freedom.

5. For all religious, especially those we know: that they will be untiring in fidelity to their way of life, and thus become a light for the Church.

Concluding Prayer
Lord God, our kind and loving Father, with sureness and confidence coming from Christ we bring you all our needs for your blessing. Out of your great love send us again Jesus, your Son and our Lord. Grant that we may welcome him with deep love. We ask this through Christ our Lord.

DECEMBER 22nd

Introduction
Since we have been created by God in his image and likeness we have confidence in bringing our needs to him.

Intentions
1. We pray for the Church, the Body and Bride of Christ: that he continue to form her in his likeness.
2. For all leaders of nations; that they rule their peoples with wisdom and let them know that they are God's children specially loved by him.
3. That all teachers and pupils bring the love of Christ into their families and in this way establish his kingship.
4. For all those, especially in the homeland of Christ, who have no peace: that through wise and compassionate negotiators, they too may experience his salvation.
5. That the great activities of preparing for Christmas will not overshadow Christ and the many gifts he wants to bring.

Concluding Prayer
Lord God, our kind and loving Father, with sureness and confidence coming from Christ we bring you all our needs for your blessing. Out of your great love send us again Jesus, your Son and our Lord. Grant that we may welcome him with deep love. We ask this through Christ our Lord.

DECEMBER 23rd

Introduction
Because Christ is God in our midst and knows all our needs, we have confidence in asking him to bless us.

Intentions
1. That the Church may more fully realise that she is the place of God among his people, and that she may radiate him to the whole world.
2. That civil leaders will always bring about conditions where the Church can flourish as Christ in each nation.
3. For the many oppressed by physical, psychological and spiritual needs: that they may experience through many channels that Christ has come.
4. For all who look after the sick, whether in hospitals or at home: that they may receive in full measure the peace of Christ and touch their patients with it.
5. That we ourselves become aware of the many ways Christ is in our midst and open our hearts fully to his life-giving power.

Concluding Prayer
Lord God, our kind and loving Father, with sureness and confidence coming from Christ we bring you all our needs for your blessing. Out of your great love send us again Jesus, your Son and our Lord. Grant that we may welcome him with deep love. We ask this through Christ our Lord.

DECEMBER 24th

Introduction
We bring all our needs to Christ that he may set us free to serve him in holiness and virtue.

Intentions
1. That the whole Church, by pondering the coming of Christ, be set free from all problems to serve him in holiness and virtue.
2. That this Christmas all leaders of civil society set their people free to welcome Christ and serve him.
3. That all afflicted with any misery at present be brought to the freedom of Spirit that comes from Christ.
4. Let us pray for our own parish: that Christ's special gift to us this year be service in practical holiness and virtue.
5. For the many people who have asked for our prayers: that

the Lord give them deep peace and all the other gifts they need at this time.

Concluding Prayer
Lord God, our kind and loving Father, with sureness and confidence coming from Christ we bring you all our needs for your blessing. Out of your great love send us again Jesus, your Son and our Lord. Grant that we may welcome him with deep love. We ask this through Christ our Lord.

CHRISTMASTIDE

OCTAVE OF CHRISTMAS (ALL DAYS)

Introduction
The Word came into our world a little child to draw us to the Father. May he be with us during these days of joy to sustain and guide us.

Intentions
1. For all who have come home for Christmas: may they treasure the love of relatives and friends and find the Lord in their loved ones.
2. For all who are without company at this season: may the Lord ease their loneliness and isolation.
3. For those who are without food and warmth: may they be sustained by concerned fellow Christians.
4. For ourselves: that we may give glory to God and be instruments of peace to others.
5. For all the children of the world, for their happiness and well being.
6. For those who have gone astray: may their hearts be moved by the mystery of the Word made flesh.

Concluding Prayer
Lord our God, as we celebrate the mystery of the word made flesh, grant that he may dwell in us and we in him, for you are Lord forever and ever.

JANUARY 2-5

Introduction
All the ends of the earth have seen the salvation of our God, may he remember in truth and in love the people he has chosen as his own.

Intentions
1. That during these days of grace we may live in Christ, full of confidence, that we may not turn from him in shame at his coming.

2. That we may realise more and more the love the Father has lavished upon us, letting us be called God's children.

3. That we may entertain the hope that when the future is revealed we shall be like him, because we shall see him as he really is.

4. That we may deepen our trust in him who is the Lamb of God, the one who takes away our sins.

5. That we may stay with him as his followers, in fidelity and in intimacy so that we may represent his presence to others along the road of life.

Concluding Prayer
Lord our God, as we celebrate the mystery of your Son's appearing, may we be penetrated with the light of his glorious presence and with the joy that he comes to bring to those who receive him in faith for he is Lord for ever and ever.

WEEKDAYS AFTER THE EPIPHANY

JANUARY 7th

Introduction
We trust and love our heavenly Father and so we are confident of his loving response as we ask for help in our lives.

Intentions
1. That the Church may always cherish the great light that has dawned in the coming of Christ in our lives and let it shine on all the people whose lives are filled with darkness.

2. That the leaders of the Church may reject all signs of domination and rather act as fathers leading us to full Christian maturity.

3. That, like Christ, the leaders of the world will have compassion on the sick and help them to health by re-directing funds from weapons so as to build up the kingdom of God rather than to destroy it.

4. For an increase in vocations to the priesthood and religious life so that the good news of Christ may be spread to the people of the world whose lives are so often filled with bad news.

5. For all the mentally handicapped; that the Lord will ever keep them close to his heart and show us his love through them.

Concluding Prayer
Father, we are nothing apart from you, and we know that you listen to our pleas for help. Grant us now our requests so that we can ever more be dedicated to you. Through Christ our Lord.

JANUARY 8th

Introduction
The Father has told us that we are his children, and so we turn to him with our prayers in a childlike spirit.

Intentions
1. That the Church will convince all people that God is love by giving them a concrete experience of his love and support.
2. That the pope will be a true prophet to the world, manifesting the countless ways by which God never ceases to pour out his compassion and love on us all.
3. That all men and women may, like Christ, be filled with a genuine feeling of pity for the less fortunate and be prompted to improve their lot.
4. For an increased spirit of thanksgiving in the world so that the gifts of God may never be taken for granted.
5. That all may be granted the gift of patience in order to appreciate the wonderful gift of prayer that has been given to us by the Lord.

Concluding Prayer
Father, we are nothing apart from you, and we know that you listen to our pleas for help. Grant us now our requests so that we can ever more be dedicated to you. Through Christ our Lord.

JANUARY 9th

Introduction
It is our Christian duty to pray for the needs of the world;
we know that God will respond out of love rather than
obligation as we put our needs in his loving hands.

Intentions
1. That the leaders of the Church will have courage and not
be afraid in the face of so much opposition to the truth of
Christ in the world of today.
2. For the leaders of all the world's dictatorships: that they
will allow their people their rightful freedom to love God and
to live as his children in service to their fellow man.
3. That all people will deepen their appreciation of Christ and
allow him fully into their lives as Lord of all they do.
4. For all who are retired: that they may enjoy this time and
find fulfilment, and not be left alone in a state of isolation
and uselessness.
5. For all who work on the land: that they may be blessed and
that their labours may produce sustenance for all.

Concluding Prayer
Father, we are nothing apart from you, and we know that
you listen to our pleas for help. Grant us now our requests
so that we can ever more be dedicated to you. Through Christ
our Lord.

JANUARY 10th

Introduction
Though we cannot see God, we believe; so we now make
these prayers to him in that firm conviction.

Intentions
1. That Church leaders, following the example of Jesus himself, will listen and serve, not dominate.
2. That all the leaders of the world's governments may
liberate those who are unjustly imprisoned and so further the
justice of the Lord.

3. For the deaf, the dumb and the blind: that despite their handicap they may have the love of Christ communicated to them through the loving concern of Christians.
4. That, like the wise men of the Epiphany, we may always recognize Christ in the simple things of life and give to him our best.
5. For all innocent victims of oppression: that in their pain they may hear the good news that, although deserted by men, Christ will never leave their side.

Concluding Prayer
Father, we are nothing apart from you, and we know that you listen to our pleas for help. Grant us now our requests so that we can ever more be dedicated to you. Through Christ our Lord.

JANUARY 11th

Introduction
God's Son listened to the cry of the leper; so we are confident that he will now listen to our cries.

Intentions
1. That the Church will always celebrate the sacraments of Christ with true faith and devotion, and recognize the Saviour's voice in the Holy Scripture.
2. That the political leaders of the world will co-operate with the leaders of the Church in the building up of a truly just and caring society.
3. That, like Christ, the ministers of the Church may always pity the sick and visit them, bringing them a real encounter with Christ through their compassion.
4. For all who are mentally ill: that they will not be rejected by their families and society but rather comforted in their anguish and isolation.
5. For those who work with the dying: that they will not be discouraged by the tragedies that they encounter but rather be filled with the hope that Christ offers and be empowered to communicate that hope.

Concluding Prayer
Father, we are nothing apart from you, and we know that you listen to our pleas for help. Grant us now our requests so that we can ever more be dedicated to you. Through Christ our Lord.

JANUARY 12th

Introduction
Our desire to pray is itself the gift of the heavenly Father, whom we ask to listen to our prayers and to forgive our pride for not always praying to him.

Intentions
1. That the Church and her leaders may not be tempted by the false gods of this world but be engrossed only in the worship of the true God.
2. That the leaders of governments will not tempt their peoples with false promises and empty ideals.
3. We pray that each of us will, like John th Baptist, desire that the Lord will occupy a greater place in our lives, and that our self-importance will diminish.
4. For all who are contemplating marriage: that they will embark on a path of real love and realize the dignity of their calling.
5. For all those who have rejected Christ: that their hearts may be softened by his love and their eyes opened to see him as their total fulfilment.

Concluding Prayer
Father, we are nothing apart from you, and we know that you listen to our pleas for help. Grant us now our requests so that we can ever more be dedicated to you. Through Christ our Lord.

LENT

Introduction
Let us pray that this lenten season will be a time of wholehearted and happy return to the Father.

Intentions
1. That the leaders of our Church may lead us even more faithfully in the worship of God and service of one another.
2. That Christians everywhere may turn to God our Father with renewed fervour.
3. That all people may hear God's appeal to be reconciled with each other in every circumstance.
4. That through fasting and almsgiving we may more generously share our goods and our time with the poor and lonely.
5. That the ashes we receive today may be an authentic sign that we will be faithful to the Gospel and to the living of our baptismal promises.

Concluding Prayer
God our Father, hear our prayers for a truly fruitful Lent. May our efforts in prayer and our deeds of mercy lead us to renewal, reconciliation and Easter Joy. Through Christ our Lord.

THURSDAY AFTER ASH WEDNESDAY

Introduction
Let us ask God to open our hearts and to give us the strength to seek life in him.

Intentions
1. Let us pray for the pope, our bishops and priests, that they may be strengthened in faith and be more effective in sharing with us the word of God.
2. For the leaders of our Church: that they may have the

courage to make difficult decisions according to God's will.
3. That the leaders of our country may be able to restore a sense of purpose to our nation.
4. For all who have turned away from God or who have grown careless in their faith: that Lent may be for them a time of new beginnings, awakened faith, renewed friendship with God and neighbour.
5. For young people, that they may accept the challenges of the present age as dedicated Christians.
6. That we ourselves may live as Christ has taught us, and recognise him in the daily crosses that come our way.

Concluding Prayer
Father, the source of all life, we are gathered here to share your word and your sacrament. May we choose always that which will lead us to eternal life. Through Christ our Lord.

FRIDAY AFTER ASH WEDNESDAY

Introduction
Conscious of the many blessings, both spiritual and material, that we have received, let us now ask for God's help.

Intentions
1. That the Church, by its own example of sacrifice and sharing, will help relieve the suffering of the world's poor, hungry and oppressed.
2. That during this lenten season Christians may understand better their responsibility towards God and man.
3. That we Christians may discover Jesus in those less fortunate, and that our conscience may be stirred to help the hungry and the poor throughout the world.
4. For the leaders of nations: that they may not be deaf to the cries of God's poor, but be attentive to the needs of the sick, the homeless, the unemployed.
5. That our lenten penances my lead us to share our goods with the less privileged of the world.

Concluding Prayer
Father, see our human weakness that drives us to enrich our-

selves without a thought for others. Help us to grow into people who can love as Christ loved, freely sharing with others the gifts of personality and skill that you have given us. Through Christ our Lord.

SATURDAY AFTER ASH WEDNESDAY

Introduction
God, in Christ, reconciles the world to himself. He does not hold our faults against us. Let us, then, with true sorrow for our sins become his people in Christ Jesus.

Intentions
1. That the Churches may acknowledge that they are ambassadors of reconciliation.
2. That those who lead their countries, their cities, their Churches, their families, be not complacent in their ruling, remembering that they too, are subject to the same failures that confront other people.
3. For those who have given their word but have broken it; for those who are suspicious, afraid, unable to trust the word of God or of other people.
4. For those who are faltering in their faith, or who are tempted to abandon it altogether.
5. For alcoholics and drug addicts and all who are emotionally crippled: that they will voluntarily seek the help the need.
6. That we, as a community, give ourselves in friendship to those who are lonely, shunned, unlikeable and yearning for human companionship.

Concluding Prayer
Hear our petitions, Father, and grant them through Christ our Lord.

LENT: WEEK 1

FIRST WEEK OF LENT: MONDAY

Introduction
The lesson for us in the word of the Lord today is that we

must obey God and treat others as we would Jesus himself. Let us ask for generosity as we respond.

Intentions
1. For the Church, its leaders and people: that we may have the courage to speak and struggle against all that would destroy human dignity.
2. For those who hold authority in the world: that, in the example of Christ, they may act with justice and compassion.
3. For all unrepresented people: that we will be aware of them and give them a fair hearing.
4. For those who suffer the effects of war, famine and hardship: that they will not yield to bitterness and violence, and with our help will find within themselves self-respect that will set them free.
5. That, by faith, we may see Christ in the people we want to ignore, bypass, disdain or despise.

Concluding Prayer
Father, in your generosity you sent your Son Jesus to teach us how to live and how to love. Help us to show this same generosity in helping others. Through Jesus Christ our Lord.

FIRST WEEK OF LENT: TUESDAY

Introduction
As the apostles asked Jesus to teach them how to pray, let us ask for the same gift, put aside the cares of the world, and draw closer to the Father.

Intentions
1. That our pope, our bishops and priests may grow in love for God through private prayer and public worship.
2. That Christians everywhere be more fervent in prayer during this lenten season.
3. For all the People of God: that they might open their hearts to the Holy Spirit and by his power learn to pray the words "Abba, Father".
4. For all those whose dedication to the word of God brings them insult and persecution: may the example of Christ and

our prayerful support keep them true to the faith we all share.
5. That we may leave behind our narrow self-centred prayers and dare to pray "Our Father" — that his will be done, his presence come, as he desires.

Concluding Prayer
God our Father, give us a deep sense of your fatherhood, that we may constantly address you in the way taught us by your Son, our Lord Jesus Christ, who lives and reigns for ever and ever.

FIRST WEEK OF LENT: WEDNESDAY

Introduction
Let us raise our hearts to the Lord, and ask his blessing on our prayers and penances this Lent.

Intentions
1. Let us pray for our holy Church: may we be faithful in prayer, sincere in our fast, generous in our alms, and sorry for our sins.
2. That people of every nation may experience the joy of God's presence which repentance brings.
3. For our towns and cities: that a lenten spirit may heighten our sense of communal love and concern.
4. That we may follow the example given to us by Jesus Christ, and conform to the will of God.
5. For ourselves: that our efforts this Lent may bring assurance of the new life that Jesus has promised us.
6. For ourselves: that in our praying and fasting we do not call attention to ourselves, but rather, grow in faith, in joy, and in openness to others.

Concluding Prayer
Father of all, you gave us the sign of Jonah to foreshadow the rising of your Son. As from all eternity you willed his resurrection, associate us with him forever. Through the same Christ our Lord.

FIRST WEEK OF LENT: THURSDAY

Introduction
Since the Lord himself reminds us to seek answers to our needs from the Father, let us, as Queen Esther did, approach him with all confidence and childlike trust.

Intentions
1. For the pope, our bishops and priests: that the liturgy may be a worthy sacrifice of praise, not an empty ritual, and that those who lead the community in worship may be people of true and deep prayer.
2. For all who work for the spread of Christianity in the world: that they may be inspired and encouraged in their work.
3. For those who are afflicted in mind and body: for the poor, the unemployed, the sick and the dying: that they may see their suffering as a means to growth in faith.
4. For all who have asked us to pray for them: that their needs may be answered.
5. For young people who are searching for ways to combine their desire for freedom with a mature sense of responsibility.

Concluding Prayer
Father, send us your Holy Spirit to voice in us our true needs, for we do not always know what we ought to ask. Through Christ our Lord.

FIRST WEEK OF LENT: FRIDAY

Introduction
There is so much bitterness and hatred among people, so much enmity and strife. Let us us ask God for the power to be true healers and reconcilers.

Intentions
1. That our country and our Church may seek justice, peace and unity.
2. That nations at war with each other may come to settle their differences.

3. For those in our society who are afflicted: may they not be crushed. For the perplexed: may they not despair. For the persecuted: may they not be forsaken. For the old and lonely: may they find friends.
4. May those who have gone before us in death know the refreshment of Christ's peace.
5. For our families and our whole parish: that we will live together in harmony and love.

Concluding Prayer
Almighty Father, grant our petitions. Help us to see and accept the individuality of each member of our community. Teach us to reach out to our neighbour, and together with them we shall truly be your people. Through Christ our Lord.

FIRST WEEK OF LENT: SATURDAY

Introduction
We eat and drink the Body and Blood of God's Son, given for us on the cross. We ask God to help us, in turn, to give ourselves to him by giving ourselves to others.

Intentions
1. That, through the mission of the Church, the love of Jesus for sinners may be in evidence among all peoples.
2. For those in every office of public service: that their role in society may serve justice and reflect the healing hand of God.
3. That national and international issues may not be clouded by the personal animosities of our leaders.
4. For those whose life is paralysed by fear, who are unable to laugh, or to be angry, to venture any risk, or to love: that they may experience the freedom which God's Spirit brings.
5. That all of us gathered here at the altar today will avail themselves of God's merciful forgiveness.

Concluding Prayer
Father, you promised us the eternal reward of heaven. Help us

to turn to your Son Jesus that we may find strength and faith to sustain us in our daily living. Through the same Christ our Lord.

LENT: WEEK 2

SECOND WEEK OF LENT: MONDAY

Introduction
Let us pray, my brothers and sisters, for the gift of compassion in our lives and that this spirit may be present in our people.

Intentions
1. Replace our selfishness with compassion for the struggles and sufferings of others.
2. Help us to see and hear beyond the faults of others to their sufferings.
3. May we know your compassion and forgiveness in our lives.
4. For those who are suffering through the harshness of others' judgements and greed.
5. May we not be afraid of suffering in our lives for it can make us compassionate.

Concluding Prayer
Lord God, hear us, we ask you. We need you in the weakness and fears of our lives. We need you to remind us and to help us to do good. Be present to us this day, we pray, companion in joy and in sorrow. Through Jesus Christ, our Lord.

SECOND WEEK OF LENT: TUESDAY

Introduction
Let us pray, my people, for the needs of our world and our Churches, and for ourselves.

Intentions
1. We pray that all of us may be sincere in doing what we

believe in the spirit of the gospel.
2. For leaders of all Churches: may they have the support of prayer and charity in fulfilling their ministry.
3. Forgive us for scandalising others with our weakness in spreading your gospel.
4. For the sick, the lonely and those who suffer through the harsh commands of others.
5. For those imprisoned in the cause of the gospel and their commitment to human justice.

Concluding Prayer
Lord God, hear us, we ask you. We need you in the weakness and fears of our lives. We need you to remind us and to help us to do good. Be present to us this day, we pray, companion in joy and in sorrow. Through Jesus Christ, our Lord.

SECOND WEEK OF LENT: WEDNESDAY

Introduction
Let us pray, my friends, in confidence to God our Father for the intentions close to our hearts and minds.

Intentions
1. For all our Churches: that we may see our role as servants of the gospel of peace and justice.
2. Heal us of all greed and pride that makes us want to be in control of others and their wishes.
3. For all mothers in their work of handing on their love and God's to their children.
4. For justice in our world based on a real awareness of the dignity of each person.
5. That we may be true followers of Jesus, the one who came to serve others.

Concluding Prayer
Lord God, hear us, we ask you. We need you in the weakness and fears of our lives. We need you to remind us and to help us to do good. Be present to us this day, we pray, companion in joy and in sorrow. Through Jesus Christ, our Lord.

SECOND WEEK OF LENT: THURSDAY

Introduction
Let us pray at this Mass for all in our world who suffer from famine or poverty, especially those who suffer through the greed of others.

Intentions
1. We pray for those who are hungry: bless the work of those working for them and help us to be grateful for what we eat and generous in sharing our resources.
2. For those who are homeless, cold, in want of shelter: we pray that efforts to house them may be blessed with success.
3. For those who are cold to the wants and needs of our brothers and sisters: forgive us.
4. For all who are working in the cause of justice and development of peoples.
5. That many young people may respond to the call to work for the poor and homeless in our world.

Concluding Prayer
Lord God, hear us, we ask you. We need you in the weakness and fears of our lives. We need you to remind us and to help us to do good. Be present to us this day, we pray, companion in joy and in sorrow. Through Jesus Christ our Lord.

SECOND WEEK OF LENT: FRIDAY

Introduction
Let us pray for the true gifts of Lent, renewal in our Church and in ourselves for the service of the gospel.

Intentions
1. Give us a deep sense of joy in the mystery of our calling to work with you in our world.
2. Give us too, Lord, a deep sense of our own inadequacy to open us to your saving power.
3. May we conquer some of our faults these weeks in true humility and for your service.

4. Send many workers into your vineyard as priests and religious in the joyful service of your gospel.
5. Give us the true spirit of forgiveness of those who have wronged us.

Concluding Prayer
Lord God, we pray our hopes to you because they are important to us and because we trust you. Be present to us, we ask you, and to all those for whom we pray. Through Jesus Christ our Lord.

SECOND WEEK OF LENT: SATURDAY

Introduction
Let us pray, my friends, to God the Father, who loves and forgives his people.

Intentions
1. That our Churches may be communities of forgiveness and reconciliation.
2. That peace and justice, founded on hope and reconciliation, may spread in our world.
3. For all whom we must forgive, that the Lord's grace may soften our hearts.
4. For peace and reconciliation between people of all Churches.
5. That we may deeply know the forgiveness of God in Jesus Christ.

Concluding Prayer
Lord God, we pray our hopes to you because they are important to us and because we trust you. Be present to us, we ask you, and to all those for whom we pray. Through Jesus Christ our Lord.

LENT: WEEK 3

THIRD WEEK OF LENT: MONDAY

Introduction
Let us pray, my brothers and sisters, in the name of Jesus for

the intentions of all his people and for those here present.

Intentions
1. May our world be healed of the divisions of hatred and injustice.
2. May our Churches be places of healing of the bitterness and angers that block the loving action of God's Spirit.
3. For all who are in despair, darkness or depression through the neglect of others.
4. For children who are neglected by parents and for these parents: that the Lord's grace may bring healing of the spirit.
5. For all whom we have hurt, living and dead: may they forgive us.

Concluding Prayer
Lord God, we pray our hopes to you because they are important to us and because we trust you. Be present to us, we ask you, and to all those for whom we pray. Through Jesus Christ our Lord.

THIRD WEEK OF LENT: TUESDAY

Introduction
Let us ask, my friends, that God may bless all for whom we pray at this Mass.

Intentions
1. That the gospel of love and justice may bring hope to those whose lives are miserable through the greed and selfishness of others.
2. That our Church may more and more be seen to practise the justice the gospel proclaims.
3. For all who have hurt any of us here, in mind or spirit, that we may forgive as we are forgiven.
4. For all whose lives are touched by the weakness and illness of others, whether of body or spirit.
5. That the Lord may call many to be priests and religious in the service of his people.

Concluding Prayer
Lord God, we pray our hopes to you because they are important to us and because we trust you. Be present to us, we ask you, and to all those for whom we pray. Through Christ our Lord.

THIRD WEEK OF LENT: WEDNESDAY

Introduction
Let us pray, my friends, in deep hope and confidence to God our Father.

Intentions
1. For all whom we meet today, in school, home or workplace: may your blessing enrich their lives.
2. For those who are unemployed: we pray they may soon get jobs.
3. For those we know who are ill, depressed, alone: may we help them in their need.
4. For our young people: that we may pass over to them the best things of our faith.
5. For all who are engaged in teaching young people: that God may give them help in their work.

Concluding Prayer
Lord God, we pray our hopes to you because they are important to us and because we trust you. Be present to us, we ask you, and to all those for whom we pray. Through Christ our Lord.

THIRD WEEK OF LENT: THURSDAY

Introduction
Let us pray, my brothers and sisters, that God may hear the prayers we make this day in union with the sacrifice of Jesus.

Intentions
1. May our world grow everywhere in the knowledge of Jesus Christ and his gospel.

2. We pray that your Churches in all their structures may hear God's word this day to be singleminded in your service.
3. For all who have dedicated their lives to the spread of justice in our world: may God's love always encourage them.
4. For young people: that they may be sincerely helped to respond to the call of total service in the gospel.
5. For all who teach the message of the Lord in difficulty or in loneliness.

Concluding Prayer
Lord God, we pray our hopes to you because they are important to us and because we trust you. Be present to us, we ask you, and to all those for whom we pray. We ask this through Christ our Lord.

THIRD WEEK OF LENT: FRIDAY

Introduction
Let us pray, my friends, in deep faith, hope and love to God our Father through Jesus our Brother.

Intentions
1. May our world understand love as the central force of progress and development, and so work everywhere for justice.
2. We pray that our Churches may see their love of God shining forth in structures of love of people.
3. May we be truly grateful for all who love us and show us a glimpse of God's love.
4. For our children and young people: that from us they may experience plenty of love.
5. May our lives be centred on Jesus who loved his people in the midst of great suffering.

Concluding Prayer
Lord God, we pray our hopes to you because they are important to us and because we trust you. Be present to us, we ask you, and to all those for whom we pray. Through Jesus Christ our Lord.

THIRD WEEK OF LENT: SATURDAY

Introduction
Let us pray that God may hear the intentions we make to him through Jesus our Lord.

Intentions
1. Lord, be merciful to us, sinners.
2. Help all your people, Lord, to be truly grateful in humility for all you give us.
3. May all of us use our talents, gifts and wealth in your service.
4. For those in our world who are poor or whose dignity is unrecognised through the greed of others.
5. That we may know you as the source of all we are and have.

Concluding Prayer
Lord God, we pray our hopes to you because they are important to us and because we trust you. Be present to us, we ask you, and to all those for whom we pray. Through Christ our Lord.

LENT: WEEK 4

WEEKDAYS OF THE FOURTH WEEK IN LENT: ALTERNATE READINGS

Introduction
The Lord is our light and our help. We turn to him now confidently in prayer.

Intentions
1. Let us pray for the blind: that they may lead us to rediscover the presence of God in the sound of creation and the touch of friendship.
2. Let us pray for those who are to be enlightened at the Easter Vigil, that they may become beacons of the light of Christ.
3. Let us pray for those in the darkness of despair, that through our example they may receive the light of hope.

Concluding Prayer
God our Father, you know all our needs even before we make
our requests to you. Listen to our prayers and grant all we
ask you through your Son, Jesus Christ the Lord.

FOURTH WEEK OF LENT: MONDAY

Introduction
God's anger lasts but a moment; his favour through life. We
call trustfully upon him now.

Intentions
1. For that true joy which surpasses all we can ever hope for:
we pray to the Lord.
2. For the grace to recognize that God is greater and more
generous than we can ever imagine: we pray to the Lord.
3. For those who minister to the sick and particularly those
who tend sick children: we pray to the Lord.
4. For the Church, that it may be a prophet of Christ both
in and out of season: we pray to the Lord.

Concluding Prayer
God our Father, you know all our needs even before we make
our requests to you. Listen to our prayers and grant all we
ask you through your Son, Jesus Christ the Lord.

FOURTH WEEK OF LENT: TUESDAY

Introduction
Our God is a helper close at hand, a refuge in time of need.
We ask him now to hear our prayers.

Intentions
1. We pray for mercy before sabbath: that we may never put
law before the good of people.
2. We pray that Christ, our Temple, may always be at the
centre of our lives and actions.
3. We pray for those without water of any kind: for those
who thirst, for those denied affection, opportunity or
freedom.

4. We pray for our own spiritual paralysis: that we may experience the healing power of Jesus.

Concluding Prayer
God our Father, you know all our needs even before we make our requests to you. Listen to our prayers and grant all we ask you through your Son, Jesus Christ the Lord.

FOURTH WEEK OF LENT: WEDNESDAY

Introduction
The Lord cares for us as a mother tends the child at her breast. As his sons and daughters we stand before him.

Intentions
1. Let us pray for those children who are mistreated or abandoned by their parents.
2. Let us pray for the gift of prayer, that we may learn to praise God from our hearts and turn to him in our needs.
3. Let us pray for judges, that in their decisions they may show forth fairness and justice, and may promote the dignity of the human person.
4. Let us pray for the deeper knowledge that without God we can accomplish nothing of value.

Concluding Prayer
God our Father, you know all our needs even before we make our requests to you. Listen to our prayers and grant all we ask you through your Son, Jesus Christ the Lord.

FOURTH WEEK OF LENT: THURSDAY

Introduction
Even if we stray from God, he never abandons us, but constantly recalls us to his presence. In humility, then, we present our petitions.

Intentions
1. Let us pray for the grace to persevere in the Lenten

penance which we undertook on Ash Wednesday.
2. Let us pray that no structure, possession or status will ever become a molten calf which keeps us from God.
3. Let us pray that we may not be seduced by human approval, nor worship at the pagan altar of other people's opinions of ourselves.
4. Let us pray that the Church may always bear witness to God's active search for the wanderer.

Concluding Prayer
God our Father, you know all our needs even before we make our requests to you. Listen to our prayers and grant all we ask you through your Son, Jesus Christ the Lord.

FOURTH WEEK OF LENT: FRIDAY

Introduction
The Lord is close to the broken-hearted and hears the prayers of those in need. We stand before him and pray.

Intentions
1. We pray for those who suffer violence or oppression, and for those who die for their human rights.
2. We pray for those who, because of their beliefs, are passed over for promotion in their work.
3. We pray for missionries who travel to preach God's kingdom in the remotest parts of the globe.
4. We pray for ourselves, that we may be active in promoting justice and peace in our local areas.

Concluding Prayer
God our Father, you know all our needs even before we make our requests to you. Listen to our prayers and grant all we ask you through your Son, Jesus Christ the Lord.

FOURTH WEEK OF LENT: SATURDAY

Introduction
God is the shield who protects us, who saves the upright of

heart. We call upon him and ask him to hear our prayer.

Intentions
1. For an increased spirit of self-sacrifice in our own lives: we pray to the Lord.
2. For those brought to public trial and unjustly accused: we pray to the Lord.
3. For the faith to trust when trust seems pointless: we pray to the Lord.
4. For our country, that it may respect and welcome foreigners: we pray to the Lord.

Concluding Prayer
God our Father, you know all our needs even before we make our requests to you. Listen to our prayers and grant all we ask you through your Son, Jesus Christ the Lord.

LENT: WEEK 5

FIFTH WEEK OF LENT: MONDAY

Introduction
The Lord is our shepherd; there is nothing we shall lack. Let us place before him our own needs and those of our world.

Intentions
1. Let us pray for those ensnared by a life of crime from which they cannot escape.
2. Let us pray for those whose lives are ruined by unfavourable publicity or notoriety.
3. Let us pray that we may be slow to criticise others and never hasty in our judgements.
4. Let us pray that in our valley of darkness we will feel the presence of God.

Concluding Prayer
Father, be with us as we prepare for the Easter festival. Listen to our prayers, those spoken out loud, those in the silence of our hearts and grant all we ask through Christ our Lord. Amen.

FIFTH WEEK OF LENT: TUESDAY

Introduction
The Lord listens to our prayer, and hears our cry for help. In faith we call upon him.

Intentions
1. We pray for ourselves: that we may become alive and responsive to Christ's call.
2. We pray that through our Lenten penance we may die not in sin but to sin.
3. We pray for those who have no bread or water, who lack education or medicinal care.
4. We pray for preachers: that their teaching may not be transient but anchored in the truth of Christ.

Concluding Prayer
Father, be with us as we prepare for the Easter festival. Listen to our prayers, those spoken out loud, those in the silence of our hearts and grant all we ask through Christ our Lord.

FIFTH WEEK OF LENT: WEDNESDAY

Introduction
We cannot live on bread alone, but on every word that comes from the mouth of God. Having heard God's word, we now turn to him in prayer.

Intentions
1. Let us ask for the eyes to behold the glory of God in all his works.
2. Let us ask for the spirit of fidelity for those who are not free to gather together for Christian worship.
3. Let us ask God that through the example of our lives others will come to know him.
4. Let us ask for the spirit of creativity for artists, musicians, and all who beautify our worship.

Concluding Prayer
Father, be with us as we prepare for the Easter festival. Listen to our prayers, those spoken out loud, those in the silence of our hearts and grant all we ask through Christ our Lord.

FIFTH WEEK OF LENT: THURSDAY

Introduction
God remembers his covenant for ever. Let us approach him now, and place all our needs before him.

Intentions
1. For the gift of grateful memories for all that God has done for us: we pray to the Lord.
2. For the Jewish people, that they may attain to the promises made to them by God: we pray to the Lord.
3. For those who long for descendants, but are unable to have children: we pray to the Lord.
4. For those parts of the world at war as a result of territorial disputes: we pray to the Lord.

Concluding Prayer
Father, be with us as we prepare for the Easter festival. Listen to our prayers, those spoken out loud, those in the silence of our hearts and grant all we ask through Christ our Lord.

FIFTH WEEK OF LENT: FRIDAY

Introduction
The Lord is a rock and a stronghold. From heaven he hears the voice of those who call upon his name.

Intentions
1. We remember in prayer those who do not know God, or whose God is too small.
2. We remember in prayer those who champion the rights of the poor, the needy, and the oppressed.

3. We remember in prayer those who take refuge not in God but in alcohol or drugs.

4. We remember in prayer those of our community in need: the sick, the dying, the lonely, the unemployed and those in any kind of trouble.

Concluding Prayer
Father, be with us as we prepare for the Easter festival. Listen to our prayers, those spoken out loud, those in the silence of our hearts and grant all we ask through Christ our Lord.

FIFTH WEEK OF LENT: SATURDAY

Introduction
The Lord guards us as a shepherd guards his flock. We pray to him, trusting that what we ask in faith, we receive from his goodness.

Intentions
1. Let us pray for those who govern our nation: that they may be motivated by the common good, with no thought of self-interest.

2. Let us pray for the Christian Church: that we may share Christ's gifts of unity and peace.

3. Let us pray that the richer nations of our world may share their wealth and resources with the poorer nations.

4. Let us pray that the journey we make next week with Christ may lead us from death to life, from sorrow to joy.

Concluding Prayer
Father, be with us as we prepare for the Easter festival. Listen to our prayers, those spoken out loud, those in the silence of our hearts and grant all we ask through Christ our Lord.

HOLY WEEK

HOLY WEEK: MONDAY

Introduction
My dear friends, we stand between two great days, Palm Sunday and Easter Sunday. Relying on the grace of Holy Week, therefore, let us pray with special devotion for the needs of God's people.

Intentions
1. For Christian communities all over the world: that they may sense their unity in the cross of our Redeemer.
2. For those who govern us in our civic life: that they may honour humankind's God and Saviour, in the keeping of his law and the doing of his will.
3. For all those who have sinned or grown lukewarm: that they may turn again to God during this season of reconciliation.
4. For those who experience opposition and conflict in the case of truth and right: that God may give them light, hope and strength.
5. That we may learn to link our pain, sorrows and disappointments with our Lord's victorious death, and our successes and joys with his resurrection.
6. For a spirit of prayer and devotion, for attentive hearts, to participate fruitfully in this week's liturgy.

Concluding Prayer
O God, through his cross and passion, your Son brought us your redeeming love. And so, in this blessed season mercifully hear all our petitions. Through the same Christ our Lord.

HOLY WEEK: TUESDAY

Introduction
Mindful of what the incarnate Son of God did for the world, and knowing he lives on to make intercession for us, let us pray for his Church and for all humankind.

Intentions
1. For the members of Christ's Body enduring affliction, interference, derision or persecution: that they may find new strength in the Lord's passion and resurrection.
2. For the men and women who serve in projects of justice and peace and who work to instil new hope into other people's lives.
3. For all the sick and housebound, for those who cannot come to the church for the solemn liturgies: that they be with us in spirit and obtain the blessings of this great week.
4. For the healing of our soul's infirmities and the ailments of mind and body: may we view them as part of our penitential pilgrimage, a sharing in the passion.
5. For the dead, particularly those who died in loneliness and agony: that they may enjoy for ever the light of the living through the merits of Christ's dying and rising.

Concluding Prayer
Lord, give ear to the petitions of a people consecrated to you in belief and worship. and lead us all into the joy of your kingdom. Through our loving Saviour, Christ the Lord.

HOLY WEEK: WEDNESDAY

Introduction
We are a people redeemed by the mystery of the Lord's Passover. This has brought us within the very family of God as his children. We can trustfully intercede, then, for the world around us and for our own intentions.
  OR:
My dear people, the word of God is alive and active, and gives us the confidence we need for prayer. Let us make our petitions in union with Christ, who prayed to the Father and went to the cross, making light of its shame.

Intentions
1. That the Gospels and all the Scriptures may profoundly influence the lives of the faithful in this holy time, and bear fruit in acts of kindness, forgiveness and love.
2. Let us prepare our souls for the gift of peace at Easter, by

ridding ourselves of old resentments and selfish pursuits.
3. That we may concern ourselves with victims of tyrannical rule; with all who endure the crucifixion of poverty, misery, anguish and disease: may they know that the Father never abandons those who cling to him.
4. So that Christians never come to betray their Lord — in thinking, in speech, in conduct — let us pray for faithfulness and perseverance.
5. May those (of us) who make profession of chastity, poverty and obedience associate them(our)selves more prayerfully with the Redeeming Christ, so as to attract others to the Gospel path and bear constant witness to the reign of God and its demands.
6. As we come to re-enact the mysteries of our redemption sacramentally, may our charity and goodness henceforth know no bounds.

Concluding Prayer
God and Father, meet us at our point of need. With faith and trust your people approaches you in prayer, remembering that saving love which comes to us through Jesus Christ our Lord.

EASTERTIDE

Introduction
In the hope of Easter, and in the light of our baptismal faith, let us pray to the Father who loves us.

Intentions
1. For the pilgrim People of God: that they may journey in faith, in hope and in love towards the glory of resurrection.
2. For our world: that it may soon experience the peace of the risen Christ.
3. That all in secure employment may examine their attitude towards work very carefully, keeping in mind those who have become redundant and the many who have never been given the opportunity to work.
4. For the sick and dying: that through their weakness they may experience the power of their risen Saviour.
5. For this parish community, priests and people: that we may continually grow in faith, in caring and in service.
6. That our dead may share to the full the glory of the risen Jesus.

Concluding Prayer
Father, in prayer we place our needs before you. Increase our faith, and make us ever more aware of your loving presence. Through Christ our Lord.

OCTAVE OF EASTER: TUESDAY

Introduction
In Baptism we are brought into the new life of the resurrection. In a spirit of joyful gratitude, we pray.

Intentions
1. For all priests: that they may be men of prayer, always spending themselves in the service of their people.
2. For world leaders: that they may hear the voice of the Lord

in the cries of the poor and needy, and do all in their power
to raise them up.
3. For those who spread violence and pain in our country:
that, through the special graces of this Easter, they may fully
understand the sorrow they cause.
4. For the sick and dying: that they may enjoy the peace of
the risen Christ.
5. For our parish community: that our love for each other
may show forth more clearly God's love present in the world.
6. That those who have gone before us in faith may now
enjoy the crown of victory.

Concluding Prayer
Father, in prayer we place our needs before you. Increase our
faith, and make us ever more aware of your loving presence.
Through Christ our Lord.

OCTAVE OF EASTER: WEDNESDAY

Introduction
In faith, let us place our petitions before our heavenly
Father.

Intentions
1. For religious leaders: that they may continue to bring
Christ, the light of the world, to all whom they serve.
2. That we as a nation may respect the sacredness of human
life at every stage of its existence and never endanger it
through any action of ours.
3. That those baptized into the faith may really believe God's
message of salvation and allow it to grow through prayer and
service.
4. For all children, particularly those here present: that their
friendship with Jesus may keep them close to him always.
5. For a spirit of prayer in our parish community: that our
lives may be examples to others of our belief in the power of
the Spirit to renew and transform.
6. For our loved ones who have passed through suffering to
death: that the glory of resurrection may be their lasting joy.

Concluding Prayer
Father, in prayer we place our needs before you. Increase our faith, and make us ever more aware of your loving presence. Through Christ our Lord.

OCTAVE OF EASTER: THURSDAY

Introduction
With confidence in his love and mercy, let us place our needs before God, our Father.

Intentions
1. For the Church: that the Spirit of God may be poured forth in all its fulness on those who protect and guide us on our pilgrim way.
2. For peace: that the risen Jesus, Prince of Peace, may be our inspiration and guide us as we strive for true peace in our country, in our homes, and for peace within our own hearts.
3. For the unemployed, the homeless and all those in need: that we may help improve their way of life and give them a greater awareness of their dignity and value.
4. For those who are called to the single way of life: that they may be generous with their time and talents, and that their dedication and service may be appreciated in our community.
5. For our deceased relatives and friends: that they and all who sleep in Christ may enjoy forever light, happiness and peace.

Concluding Prayer
Father, in prayer we place our needs before you. Increase our faith, and make us ever more aware of your loving presence. Through Christ our Lord.

OCTAVE OF EASTER: FRIDAY

Introduction
Let us pray that we may be attentive to the will of God in our lives.

Intentions
1. For the pope, for bishops, priests and religious: that Jesus

may be the cornerstone of their lives and work.

2. For a world living in doubt and despair: that the confidence and joy we share this Eastertime may point to the way God wants us to live.

3. For those suffering in mind or body: that they may be consoled or healed.

4. For priests who hear confessions: that they may radiate at all times the love and compassion of Jesus.

5. For vocations: that many of our young people may be moved through the grace of this Eucharist to dedicate their lives to the service of the Church in the priesthood or religious life.

6. For ourselves: that during these days of spring, when new life comes forth all around us, we may become more aware of God's presence in all creation and in our lives.

Concluding Prayer
Father, in prayer we place our needs before you. Increase our faith, and make us ever more aware of your loving presence. Through Christ our Lord.

OCTAVE OF EASTER: SATURDAY

Introduction
God our Father loves us. Let us bring our needs before him, trusing in his fatherly care for each of us.

Intentions
1. For the whole Church: that during these days it may prepare itself for the outpouring of the Holy Spirit of Pentecost.

2. For those who differ from us in faith or worship: that all who believe in the resurrection of Christ may soon be united in the fulness of faith.

3. For women: that they may use their special gifts and talents to uplift and restore the world to Christ.

4. For those who are afraid of death: that the triumph of Jesus over the grave may inspire in them a living hope and great confidence.

5. For each of here present: that we may continue to grow

spiritually during this Easter season.
6. For our dead, and particularly those who have died because of violence: that they may enjoy everlasting peace.

Concluding Prayer
Father, in prayer we place our needs before you. Increase our faith, and make us ever more aware of your loving presence. Through Christ our Lord.

EASTERTIDE: WEEK 2

SECOND WEEK OF EASTER: MONDAY

Introduction
Let us lift up our hearts to the throne of God, where Jesus his Son is living and praying for us.

Intentions
1. Speak to your Church, Lord, during this Eastertide; lead us once again into the mystery of Christ, your Son.
2. We thank you for our baptism and we pray for all who will be baptized at this season.
3. Protect your Church in the midst of trouble; give her the peace which the world cannot give.
4. Direct our ways; watch over our lives with the power and wisdom of your Spirit.
5. Let all our dead see your face, through Christ your Son, in your Holy Spirit.

Concluding Prayer
In your love, Lord, answer our humble prayer. Give us your grace to see what we have to do and the strength to do it. We ask this through Christ our Lord.

SECOND WEEK OF EASTER: TUESDAY

Introduction
Let us pray to the Father, the all-powerful God, who raised Jesus our Saviour from death.

Intentions

1. Lead all nations into the light of Christ; may they acknowledge him as their Lord and Saviour.
2. Help us to put aside our selfish interests, and enrich us with the mind of Christ.
3. Let justice and peace flourish in our country; show those who are in need that your providence is caring for them.
4. Father of the poor and lowly, we pray for those whom the world forgets.
5. Grant life and glory to our dead, whom Christ redeemed by his precious blood.

Concluding Prayer

In your love, Lord, answer our humble prayer. Give us your grace to see what we have to do and the strength to do it. We ask this through Christ our Lord.

SECOND WEEK OF EASTER: WEDNESDAY

Introduction

Let us pray to the Father, whose Son rose from the dead to be our Saviour.

Intentions

1. Father, we believe that Jesus, your Son, will come to judge the living and the dead; teach us to listen now to his saving words of peace.
2. May your Holy Spirit teach the entire Church to share the joy and hope, the grief and anguish of the people of our time.
3. Open the hearts and minds of the unbaptized to listen to the Gospel, so that they may turn freely to Jesus, the way the truth and the life.
4. For courage and perseverance in our Christian faith and hope.
5. When you summon the dead to raise from their graves, may your people be gathered as one into your joy.

Concluding Prayer

In your love, Lord, answer our humble prayer. Give us your grace to see what we have to do and the strength to do it. We ask this through Christ our Lord.

SECOND WEEK OF EASTER: THURSDAY

Introduction
In union with the whole Church on earth, in peace let us pray
to the Lord.

Intentions
1. Unite all Christians in the fullness of faith in the blessed
Trinity, in whose name they were baptized.
2. Let the world recognize that all authority has been given
to Jesus your Son.
3. Give us the grace of truly inward repentance and a Christian death.
4. For our deliverance from every sorrow and enmity, from
every danger and necessity.
5. For travellers, and those who are suffering, for the sick
and for those in prison.

Concluding Prayer
In your love, Lord, answer our humble prayer. Give us your
grace to see what we have to do and the strength to do it. We
ask this through Christ our Lord.

SECOND WEEK OF EASTER: FRIDAY

Introduction
Let us pray to God our Father for all humankind, for the
whole Church and for all here present.

Intentions
1. We pray for the Jewish people who wait for a Messiah; lead
them to Christ their Brother.
2. Teach your Church to love her risen Saviour.
3. Let the secret power of your divine grace grow and thrive
in our hearts.
4. Father, speak words of life to your Church on earth,
through the mystery of the blessed Eucharist.
5. Strengthen the dying with Christian hope.

Concluding Prayer

In your love, Lord, answer our humble prayer. Give us your grace to see what we have to do and the strength to do it. We ask this through Christ our Lord.

SECOND WEEK OF EASTER: SATURDAY

Introduction

In union with our Lady, with the apostles and all the saints, in peace let us pray to the Lord.

Intentions

1. We entrust ourselves and each other, and the Church throughout the world to Christ, your Son, who is our King to come.
2. Give your Church that peace of Christ, which the world cannot give.
3. Teach us the lesson of silence, of prayer and of quiet.
4. Let the healing hand of Christ, your Son, cure us of our sins.
5. Help us to believe that our future resurrection is in the hands of Jesus.

Concluding Prayer

In your love, Lord, answer our humble prayer. Give us your grace to see what we have to do and the strength to do it. We ask this through Christ our Lord.

EASTERTIDE: WEEK 3

THIRD WEEK OF EASTER: MONDAY

Introduction

Let us lift up our hearts to the throne of God, where Jesus his Son is living and praying for us.

Intentions

1. Help your people throughout the world to celebrate this Eastertide with faith, love and joy.

2. Have mercy on all who refuse to accept Jesus or have forgotten him.
3. Help those who are searching for an unknown God; through your Holy Spirit let them discover the face of Jesus Christ, true God and true man.
4. Teach us the lesson of the Gospel miracles, so that we may truly honour Jesus in our lives.
5. That this whole day may be perfect, holy, peaceful and sinless.

Concluding Prayer
Lord God, teach us at all times to fear and love your holy name, for you never withdraw your guiding hand from those you establish in your love. We ask this through Christ our Lord.

THIRD WEEK OF EASTER: TUESDAY

Introduction
Let us pray to the Father, the all powerful God, who raised Jesus our Saviour from death.

Intentions
1. For all first communicants, for all young people this Easter; let your Holy Spirit guide them to you.
2. Deepen the faith of your Church in the blessed Eucharist.
3. Lord, your word is full of power; let it take root in our hearts this day.
4. We thank you, Father, for the season of spring, which is renewing our countryside; let Easter renew our Christian life.
5. Bring all the dead into the light that no darkness can quench; may we all meet in joy with you.

Concluding Prayer
Lord God, teach us at all times to fear and love your holy name, for you never withdraw your guiding hand from those you establish in your love. We ask this through Christ our Lord.

THIRD WEEK OF EASTER: WEDNESDAY

Introduction
Let us pray to God our Father whose Son rose from the dead
to be our Saviour.

Intentions
1. Bring peace to our life, Lord, and have mercy on your
world.
2. Father, give your Church all that she asks of you in the
name of Jesus.
3. Let your Holy Spirit lead all who teach and all who learn
into the full truth as promised by Jesus.
4. By the cross and burial of Christ bring us to the glory of
his resurrection.
5. Teach your Church all over the world to love what you
command and to desire what you promise.

Concluding Prayer
Lord God, teach us at all times to fear and love your holy
name, for you never withdraw your guiding hand from those
you establish in your love. We ask this through Christ our
Lord.

THIRD WEEK OF EASTER: THURSDAY

Introduction
In union with the whole Church on earth, in peace let us pray
to the Lord.

Intentions
1. Let the whole human race become one People of God,
form one Body of Christ and be built up into one temple of
the Holy Spirit.
2. Give the young Churches in former mission lands, the
wisdom to discern things new and old, for the good of their
Christian members and of all their fellow-countrymen and
women.
3. Gather your people around Christ's altar; end the conflicts

which divide our country.
4. Let Christ be among us as Emmanual, full of grace and truth, by his continued presence in our churches.
5. Comfort the dying, who this day will receive the Body and Blood of Christ as food on their journey to you.

Concluding Prayer
Lord God, teach us at all times to fear and love your holy name, for you never withdraw your guiding hand from those you establish in your love. We ask this through Christ our Lord.

THIRD WEEK OF EASTER: FRIDAY

Introduction
Let us pray to God our Father for all humankind, for the whole Church, and for all here present.

Intentions
1. For your Church passing through this world since the resurrecton of Christ: bring it to its true home in heaven.
2. That we may work out our salvation with fear and trembling.
3. From blindness of the understanding, deliver us, Lord.
4. For a Christian end to our life, painless, blameless and peaceful, and for a good defence at the judgement seat of Christ.
5. That we may ever have the bread of life.

Concluding Prayer
Lord God, teach us at all times to fear and love your holy name, for you never withdraw your guiding hand from those you establish in your love. We ask this through Christ our Lord.

THIRD WEEK OF EASTER: SATURDAY

Introduction
In union with our Lady, with the apostles and all the saints, in peace let us pray to the Lord.

Intentions
1. Draw us to yourself and to one another by our sharing in Holy Communion.
2. Help all widows in their bereavement, and in their daily worries.
3. Help your Church to believe the Gospel of mercy which your Son preached while on earth.
4. Look on those who live without hope, and do not know you: let them believe in the resurrection and in the life of the world to come.
5. At the intercession of our blessed Lady, Queen of the Apostles: make every Christian home a place of peace and prayer.

Concluding Prayer
Lord God, teach us at all times to fear and love your holy name, for you never withdraw your guiding hand from those you establish in your love. We ask this through Christ our Lord.

EASTERTIDE: WEEK 4

FOURTH WEEK OF EASTER: MONDAY

Introduction
In a spirit of faith and in union with Christ Jesus let us offer prayers to God our Father.

Intentions
1. May our bishops and priests become more like Christ the Good Shepherd: may they have wisdom to teach, courage to lead, compassion for the weak.
2. We pray for those who govern our country: may they enact just laws, respect individual rights, and work towards a more equitable distribution of the nation's wealth.
3. In this time of Easter let us not forget the sick and infirm, the old and disabled: may they be strengthened and comforted by the Holy Spirit, and know that Christ the Good Shepherd is caring for them.

4. Let us pray for our brothers and sisters who feel hurt or rejected by the Church: through the understanding and love of other Christians may they be reconciled to the community.
5. Christ our Shepherd calls each one of us by name: may we always listen to that voice and follow wherever it leads us.

Concluding Prayer
Father in heaven, you are the source of life, and you have sent your Son into the world that we may have that life in abundance. Help us so to live that we may come to the fullness of that life in heaven. We ask this through Christ our Lord.

FOURTH WEEK OF EASTER: TUESDAY

Introduction
We believe that Jesus and the Father are truly one. In that faith let us now pray with confidence to the Father.

Intentions
1. Father, your will is that all humankind should be saved: make the Church a faithful and effective instrument of your designs.
2. Help us to appreciate the spiritual patrimony we share with the Jewish people: may we overcome the fear and prejudice which keeps us apart.
3. Disclose to us the riches of our Baptism: may we experience it as the sacrament of new birth and of our incorporation into Christ your Son.
4. At Antioch the disciples were first called Christians: make us proud of that name and help us bear witness to it before the world.
5. Comfort those who suffer bereavement in this season of joy. Strengthen in them the virtue of faith, fill them with the hope of being re-united with their loved ones in your everlasting kingdom.

Concluding Prayer
Father in heaven, you are the source of life, and you have sent your Son into the world that we may have that life in

abundance. Help us so to live that we may come to the fullness of that life in heaven. We ask this through Christ our Lord.

FOURTH WEEK OF EASTER: WEDNESDAY

Introduction
In fervent and united prayer let us present our petitions to God in the name of Jesus his Son.

Intentions
1. We pray for priests, for religious men and women, for lay volunteers, whom the Holy Spirit has set apart for the service of the Gospel: may they be strengthened to endure, and may they carry out their ministry with love.
2. We pray that all nations may come to know God's saving work and may recognise Jesus as the Saviour of the world.
3. Let us pray for fellow Christians who suffer persecution because of the faith they profess. May Christ strengthen them in their resolve.
4. For children preparing for First Communion at this time: may they be drawn to an abiding love of the Eucharist.
5. For ourselves: that we may realize that the Christian vocation implies a commitment to the Church's apostolate, and that we may be generous in fulfilling our role.

Concluding Prayer
Father in heaven, you are the source of life, and you have sent your Son into the world that we may have that life in abundance. Help us so to live that we may come to the fullness of that life in heaven. We ask this through Christ our Lord.

FOURTH WEEK OF EASTER: THURSDAY

Introduction
Let us pray to the Father who has raised up his Son Jesus to be our Saviour.

Intentions
1. Make your Church and its ministers fearless witnesses of the Gospel of your Son.
2. Direct the policies and actions of those who govern in the ways of justice and peace.
3. Fill us with concern for all who hunger and lack the necessities of life. Open our hearts to all who are in need.
4. The servant cannot be greater than the master. Make us like your Son in his humility and service of others.
5. We welcome you, Father, in your Son. Help us to welcome all who come to us in Christ's name.

Concluding Prayer
Father in heaven, you are the source of life, and you have sent your Son into the world that we may have that life in abundance. Help us so to live that we may come to the fullness of that life in heaven. We ask this through Christ our Lord.

FOURTH WEEK OF EASTER: FRIDAY

Introduction
Lord Jesus, you are indeed the way, the truth and the life. In the assurance of our faith we now turn to you in prayer.

Intentions
1. Make the Church, purchased by your blood, more truly one, holy, catholic and apostolic.
2. Be the support of those who suffer for their loyalty to you. Strengthen and console them by your Holy Spirit.
3. Lighten the burden of those weighed down with personal cares, problems and sufferings. May they come to know how close you are to the broken-hearted.
4. Make us long for that home, that kingdom, where you have promised we shall be with you always.
5. Help us to nurture in our heart the life you have implanted in us through Baptism. Make us living members of your body.

Concluding Prayer
Father in heaven, you are the source of life, and you have

sent your Son into the world that we may have that life in
abundance. Help us so to live that we may come to the
fullness of that life in heaven. We ask this through Christ our
Lord.

FOURTH WEEK OF EASTER: SATURDAY

Introduction
We have heard Christ's words: "Whatever you ask for in
my name I will do it." Encouragd by this assurance let us
express our needs in a spirit of faith and trust.

Intentions
1. Let us pray that the spirit of Pentecost may be alive in the
Church of our day, and that the good news of salvation may
reach all peoples.
2. That the peacemakers of this world may not be discouraged by opposition and failure, but may continue to
work resolutely for justice, reconciliation and peace.
3. Let us pray for those who witness to Christ's universal love
by caring for the most deprived and neglected members of
our community.
4. The first disciples of the Lord were filled "with joy and the
Holy Spirit." As his followers may we too experience and
manifest to others that joy which is Christ's Easter gift to
mankind.
5. Jesus reveals to us the mysteries of his life with the Father
and the Holy Spirit. May we give to these mysteries the firm
assent of our faith.

Concluding Prayer
Father in heaven, you are the source of life, and you have
sent your Son into the world that we may have that life in
abundance. Help us so to live that we may come to the
fullness of that life in heaven. We ask this through Christ our
Lord.

EASTERTIDE: WEEK 5

FIFTH WEEK OF EASTER: MONDAY

Introduction
Before we address our prayers to God our Father, from whom all good things come, let us first, with thankful hearts, acknowledge all that he has bestowed on us.

Intentions
1. Let us pray for the Church, the assembly of God's people, in this parish and community: May it grow in love and mutual service to be a living sign of God's presence among us.
2. Let us pray for the world in which we live: may people turn from their idols of power, wealth and sensual pleasure to worship the one true God.
3. Let us pray for men and women of science. As they advance in knowledge of the universe, may they recognise God's handiwork in all created things.
4. For ourselves too we pray: may we heed the words of Christ in today's Gospel calling on us to express our love for him and for the Father by always obeying his commandments.
5. May God the Holy Spirit lead us all to a deeper understanding of the person and words of Jesus.

Concluding Prayer
Father, you have made Jesus our Saviour and High Priest. In union with his unceasing prayer for us we offer you these petitions. In your mercy grant us all that we ask for with faith and devotion. Through Christ our Lord. Amen.

FIFTH WEEK OF EASTER: TUESDAY

Introduction.
Thankful for that peace which Christ alone can give, let us pray for one another and for all people.

Intentions
1. Let us pray for all who endure great hardship in the service of Christ and his Gospel: through their sufferings may they lead many into the kingdom of God.
2. Through his preaching St Paul opened the door of faith to the pagans. In an unbelieving world may Christ through his Church open doors to people's hearts.
3. There are many who are weighed down by cares and sorrow. May they be consoled by Christ's words: "Do not let your hearts be troubled".
4. In this Easter season we celebrate the victory of love over the forces of evil. Through Christ's victory may we overcome all enmity in our own hearts.
5. May our sharing in the Eucharist free us from all attachment to sin and enable us to live our lives for God in union with Christ Jesus.

Concluding Prayer
Father, you have made Jesus our Saviour and High Priest. In union with his unceasing prayer for us we offer you these petitions. In your mercy grant us all that we ask for with faith and devotion. Through Christ our Lord. Amen.

FIFTH WEEK OF EASTER: WEDNESDAY

Introduction
Christ has promised that if we remain united to him by faith and love we may ask what we will and we shall get it. Reassured by that promise, let us now pray.

Intentions
1. Christ, our true Vine, unite the Church more closely to yourself. May it draw life from you and grow in holiness and in numbers.
2. Restore to unity with your Church all severed branches. May the prayer and charity of your faithful people win back their brothers and sisters who have gone astray.
3. Bless all married couples and make tham a living sign of your Church. As they grow older together, may they also grow in mutual understanding and love.

4. Teach us the value of suffering. As branches of the vine, let us accept pruning from your Father's hands so that we may bear more fruit for his glory.
5. Make us truly your disciples by listening to your words and faithfully carrying out all that you ask us to do.

Concluding Prayer
Father, you have made Jesus our Saviour and High Priest. In union with his unceasing prayer for us we offer you these petitions. In your mercy grant us all that we ask for with faith and devotion. Through Christ our Lord. Amen.

FIFTH WEEK OF EASTER: THURSDAY

Introduction
Let us pray to the Father who by raising his Son Jesus Christ from the dead has filled the world with his joy.

Intentions
1. We pray that God may raise up in the Church of our day men and women outstanding in holiness, so that the hearts of unbelievers may be turned to faith.
2. We thank God for the manifestations of his Spirit in the Church. May that same Holy Spirit lead us further along the way of prayer and renewal of Christian life.
3. We pray for priests and religious, that they may be faithful to their calling; and for those who have left the ministry or returned to secular life, that they may continue to seek God's will and that they may find understanding and support from their fellow-Christians.
4. For ourselves too we pray. May we who have been saved by the grace of our Lord Jesus Christ always proclaim the wonders of his love.
5. May we, by faithfully observing all that Jesus commands us, remain in his love, just as he, through his obedience, always remains in his Father's love.

Concluding Prayer
Father, you have made Jesus our Saviour and High Priest. In union with his unceasing prayer for us we offer you these

petitions. In your mercy grant us all that we ask for with faith and devotion. Through Christ our Lord. Amen.

FIFTH WEEK OF EASTER: FRIDAY

Introduction
Let us pray to the Father in the name of Jesus, for he has promised that whatever we ask the Father in his name will be granted to us.

Intentions
1. Holy Father, bestow your Holy Spirit on the leaders of your Church. Give them wise judgement; help them to read the signs of the times: make them courageous in action.
2. On this day we remember your Son's passion. May the world come to know the love whereby Christ laid down his life for all mankind.
3. Bless all those who exercise a ministry for counselling in the Church. Give them a spirit of discernment, deep faith, wisdom, compassion, sensitivity.
4. Jesus has called us his friends. Make us worthy of that friendship by our readiness to bear his cross. Deepen our union with him through prayer.
5. Help us to love one another, as Christ commands, sharing one another's burdens, bearing patiently one another's faults.

Concluding Prayer
Father, you have made Jesus our Saviour and High Priest. In union with his unceasing prayer for us we offer you these petitions. In your mercy grant us all that we ask for with faith and devotion. Through Christ our Lord. Amen.

FIFTH WEEK OF EASTER: SATURDAY

Introduction
May the Holy Spirit, who comes to help us in our weakness, help us to pray according to the mind of God.

Intentions
1. We pray that the Church may be eager to spread the good news of Christ, going wherever the Spirit of Jesus leads it.
2. Jesus warned us of the hatred of the world, but taught us to love our enemies. So let us pray for the conversion of those who persecute the Church. May they be overcome not by violence, but by love.
3. That the Christian churches may grow together towards unity of faith and courageous witness to the Gospel. In their service of mankind may they always take the side of the poor and oppressed.
4. Christ has chosen men and women out of the world to serve him as priests, religious and dedicated lay apostles. May his love support them so that they may never falter in his service.
5. The servant is not greater than the master. May we be given the strength not only to believe in Christ but to suffer for him as well.

Concluding Prayer
Father, you have made Jesus our Saviour and High Priest. In union with his unceasing prayer for us we offer you these petitions. In your mercy grant us all that we ask for with faith and devotion. Through Christ our Lord. Amen.

EASTERTIDE: WEEK 6

SIXTH WEEK OF EASTER: MONDAY

Introduction
We open our hearts to our loving Father and his holy word. May we pray with attention and devotion, trusting in God's love for us and knowing that we have an Advocate in heaven who pleads for us unceasingly.

Intentions
1. That all women who have dedicated their lives to God may open their hearts to the truth of your word.
2. That we may sincerely invite the risen Christ to come among us.

3. That we truly believe that the Lord looks with delight on his people and loves them.
4. That we may be generous enough to accept the gifts of the Spirit, who will make us true witnesses of Christ.
5. That those who are persecuted for the faith may be comforted, strengthened and consoled.

Concluding Prayer
Father, may we realise that you are our heart's desire and that in having you we have all things else besides. May we seek your kingdom first and your justice, knowing that all things else may be added through your loving care. We ask this through Christ our Lord.

SIXTH WEEK OF EASTER: TUESDAY

Introduction
We know that God the Father is the source of all good and in him we live and move and have our being. May he help us to be poor in spirit to realise that we need him who is our rock, our fortress and our source of refuge.

Intentions
1. May we, through experiencing the passion and cross of Christ in our lives be brought to the glory of his resurrection.
2. May the depressed and those without hope find strength and consolation in the words of Jesus, "be not afraid".
3. May the resurrection of Christ teach us that the Father is faithful beyond all knowing.
4. May those in exile endure their pain with hope and trust that one day they will enter their Father's house in heaven.
5. May the example of our lives in Christ be condemnation of all that is contrary to the Gospel in our society.

Concluding Prayer
Father, may we realise that you are our heart's desire and that in having you we have all things else besides. May we seek your kingdom first and your justice, knowing that all things else may be added through your loving care. We ask this through Christ our Lord.

SIXTH WEEK OF EASTER: WEDNESDAY

Introduction
We believe that it is God the Father who gives everything, including life and breath, to all. May he help us not to take his goodness for granted, so that we, his children, may be truly grateful.

Intentions
1. We pray for an understanding of the wisdom of God which has been revealed to us through the death of his Son on the cross.
2. We pray for the courage to stand for the truth even when that is embarrassing and inconvenient.
3. We pray for an awareness of the goodness of God as revealed in all his creatures.
4. We pray for theologians and authors, that they may respect the word of God, the source of all truth.
5. We pray that we may understand that Jesus reveals the Father fully to us.

Concluding Prayer
Father, may we realise that you are our heart's desire and that in having you we have all things else besides. May we seek your kingdom first and your justice, knowing that all things else may be added through your loving care. We ask this through Christ our Lord.

SIXTH WEEK OF EASTER: FRIDAY

Introduction
The Father is always faithful and comes to the help of those who trust in him. He is the source of all our joy. May he make us joyful in his presence today and grant us all we need.

Intentions
1. For the Holy Father and for the bishops and priests: that they may teach fearlessly, we pray to the Lord.
2. For our rulers, our judges and our police: that they may dispense the law justly and with compassion.

3. For those who have been recently bereaved, for the depressed and the lonely.

4. For those who try to bring joy and hope to others through their lives and their dedication to the risen Christ.

5. For those who long to be reconciled and to look once again on the faces of those who have deserted them.

Concluding Prayer
Father, may we realise that you are our heart's desire and that in having you we have all things else besides. May we seek your kingdom first and your justice, knowing that all things else may be added through your loving care. We ask this through Christ our Lord.

SIXTH WEEK OF EASTER: SATURDAY

Introduction
We know that we are always welcome when we come to ask the Father's aid. May he help us as we ask for our needs in Jesus' name. May we believe that Jesus has come from him and that he has returned again to make intercession for us.

Intentions
1. We pray for those who preach and those who teach: that they may come to know Jesus the Word of God.
2. We pray for parents and all those who must teach young people that Jesus is the way to the Father.
3. We pray for those who have implored God's aid and are disappointed because they seem not to have been answered.
4. We pray for those who have no realisation that God is a loving and compassionate Father.
5. We pray for those who have gone before us: that they may come this day to their Father's house.

Concluding Prayer
Father, may we realise that you are our heart's desire and that in having you we have all things else besides. May we seek your kingdom first and your justice, knowing that all things else may be added through your loving care. We ask this through Christ our Lord.

EASTERTIDE: WEEK 7

SEVENTH WEEK OF EASTER: MONDAY

Introduction
We pray to the Father in trust and confidence, knowing that he is our loving Father who cares for us in all our comings and goings. May he make us always truly grateful for his gifts.

Intentions
1. That those who celebrate the sacrament of reconciliation may realise that it is the Holy Spirit who comes among us for the forgiveness of sin.
2. That those preparing for Confirmation and Ordination may invite the Spirit of God to come into their lives.
3. That we may understand that Jesus in the Eucharist is God's gift of himself to us in the world.
4. That those who are experiencing difficulties in their marriage may realise that they are not alone, because the Father is always with them.
5. That we may always trust in the power of God's Spirit to raise up a fallen world.

Concluding Prayer
Loving Father, we know that you always hear our prayers. We trust that you will give what we need rather than what we want and we ask you to help us to accept your gift of life through the workings of the Holy Spirit. We ask this through Christ our Lord.

SEVENTH WEEK OF EASTER: TUESDAY

Introduction
We place all our trust in the Father. May he help us in our necessities so that we may help those who are in need. May we be living signs of his care and love for the world.

Intentions
1. We pray that we may never hesitate to help those who are in need.

2. We pray that all our good intentions of helping others may be turned into action.
3. We pray that we may believe that Jesus is Lord, with the power given him over mankind.
4. We pray that the Spirit may help us to believe and accept all that Jesus taught us.
5. We pray that we may understand that God loves the world, because he sent his only Son to save it.

Concluding Prayer
Loving Father, we know that you always hear our prayers. We trust that you will give what we need rather than what we want and we ask you to help us to accept your gift of life through the workings of the Holy Spirit. We ask this through Christ our Lord.

SEVENTH WEEK OF EASTER: WEDNESDAY

Introduction
Holy Father, you are the source of light and joy and peace. Help us to bring love where there is hatred, light where there is darkness, and joy where there is sadness. Make us instruments of your peace.

Intentions
1. Let us ask the Father to help those who are being led away from the true Father by false teachers.
2. Let us ask the Father to help priests, nuns and brothes not to be anxious about money and their own material welfare.
3. Let us ask the Father to help those who live in religious communities to be one in mind and heart.
4. Let us ask the Father to help those who are bigoted, intolerant and full of hate.
5. Let us ask the Father to help all Christian Churches to search with courage for the truth, which is Christ.

Concluding Prayer
Loving Father, we know that you always hear our prayers. We trust that you will give what we need rather than what we want and we ask you to help us to accept your gift of life

through the workings of the Holy Spirit. We ask this through
Christ our Lord.

SEVENTH WEEK OF EASTER: THURSDAY

Introduction
Loving Father, in our need we turn to you for love, joy,
peace and patience. Send us the Spirit of Jesus with his gifts
that we may always enjoy your consolation in our lives.

Intentions
1. For those who are troubled by doubts, fears, anxieties and
tensions: that they may know the peace given by the Spirit of
God.
2. For those who need the strength to face the realities of life:
that they may have the courage given by the Spirit of God.
3. For those who do not understand that unity and peace can
only come through the love that is poured into our hearts by
the Spirit of God.
4. For those who have no belief: that they may come to know
Jesus by the light of the Holy Spirit.
5. For those who devote themselves to lives of prayer: that
they may allow God's spirit to pray in them.

Concluding Prayer
Loving Father, we know that you always hear our prayers.
We trust that you will give what we need rather than what we
want and we ask you to help us to accept your gift of life
through the workings of the Holy Spirit. We ask this through
Christ our Lord.

SEVENTH WEEK OF EASTER: FRIDAY

Introduction
Father, you alone are holy. May we become like Christ your
Son in all things. Help us never to refuse your grace and may
we understand that we are called to be perfect as you are
perfect.

Intentions
1. That those who accuse the Church of being sectarian, self-complacent, and indifferent to the real problems of life may have no grounds for their complaints.
2. That we may all believe that Jesus is truly risen and living among us.
3. That we may see the sacrament of Penance as a declaration of our choice of Christ above all things.
4. That we may have the courage and the strength to abandon ourselves to the will of God in our regard.
5. That we may follow Christ to the point of living out in our lives the mystery of his death and resurrection.

Concluding Prayer
Loving Father, we know that you always hear our prayers. We trust that you will give what we need rather than what we want and we ask you to help us to accept your gift of life through the workings of the Holy Spirit. We ask this through Christ our Lord.

SEVENTH WEEK OF EASTER: SATURDAY

Introduction
Father, you are the giver of all life human and divine. Free us from imprisonment in ourselves. Help us to live like Jesus, and may we allow him to live in us, for he is the way the truth and the life.

Intentions
1. We pray that we may all be released from our slavery to sin and that we may rejoice in the freedom of God's Spirit.
2. We pray that Christians everywhere may be free to teach the truth about our Lord Jesus Christ.
3. We pray that we may always put others before ourselves, and that we may seek the lowest place.
4. We pray that we may see death as a passing into that eternal life where Jesus awaits us in the home of our Father.
5. We pray that the Holy Spirit may guide us in the way of truth by our reading of the Scriptures.

Concluding Prayer

Loving Father, we know that you always hear our prayers. We trust that you will give what we need rather than what we want and we ask you to help us to accept your gift of life through the workings of the Holy Spirit. We ask this through Christ our Lord.

ORDINARY TIME

FIRST WEEK OF THE YEAR: MONDAY

Introduction
My dear friends, let us pray that the Lord who bids us to follow him may be at our side on life's journey.

Intentions
1. May we ever follow the Lord in joy and simplicity of heart.
2. May our following of Christ be sincere, may we encounter him in the events of life and in the persons we meet each day.
3. May our hearts be always open to the needs of those around us, especially of those who are too shy to make their real needs known and who suffer in silence.
4. May we leave behind us the nets of self-sufficiency, may this Eucharist open our eyes to our own self-seeking.
5. May the Lord of life send his Spirit into our hearts so that we might lead all life back to him.

Concluding Prayer
Lord our God, may our prayers rise like incense before you. May the lifting up of our hands be an oblation in your sight, for you are Lord forever and ever. Amen.

FIRST WEEK OF THE YEAR: TUESDAY

Introduction
The Lord is close to those who call upon his name. With confidence we lift our hearts in prayer and supplication.

Intentions
1. For all whose lives are made miserable by the spirit of evil: that the Lord may aid them in their distress.
2. For young people whose lives are being corrupted by evil, especially in our cities: that the Lord may command the spirit of evil to depart from them and fill them with his peace.
3. For all those who dabble in the occult: that they may not be overpowered by the spirit of evil.

4. For those who are called upon to pray over those who are afflicted with the spirit of evil: and especially for those who exorcise evil spirits: that they may not be overcome by fear.
5. *Year 1:* That we may penetrate the truth of the incarnation of him who was made lower than the angels and is now crowned with glory and splendour.
5. *Year 2:* For all women who are childless: that they may have the faith of Hannah and her deep spirit of prayer.

Concluding Prayer
Lord our God, may our prayers rise like incense before you. May the lifting up of our hands be an oblation in your sight, for you are Lord forever and ever.

FIRST WEEK OF THE YEAR: WEDNESDAY

Introduction
We have listened to the Gospel which presents us with a day in the life of Christ. With confidence let us pray that his grace may fill all our days.

Intentions
1. "He went up to her, took her by the hand and helped her up". May his Church raise up men and women of great compassion.
2. The healing miracle of Jesus points to the resurrection. Let us pray that the Lord may raise us out of our weakness and enable us to have the new life of the risen Christ.
3. Let us pray for all who exercise ministry in the Church, that they may be ever mindful that compassion is at the heart of all ministry.
4. Let us pray for all who are bedridden, especially the elderly, that they may not be forgotten in their loneliness. May Christ the loving Saviour of us all be their strength and hope.
5. Let us pray for those who are beset by evil: that good may triumph in their lives, and that they may be delivered from their sin.

Concluding Prayer
Lord our God, may our prayers rise like incense before you.
May the lifting up of our hands be an oblation in your sight,
for you are Lord forever and ever.

FIRST WEEK OF THE YEAR: THURSDAY

Introduction
We pray to the Lord who brings us into his healing presence
in the liturgy that he may be our deliverer and our hope.

Intentions
1. "If you want to, you can cure me". May the Church
inspire in her children an expectant faith in the Lord who
heals.
2. "If you want to, you can cure me". We bring the suffering
and trials of all people everywhere to the feet of him whose
healing touch can bring back life and hope.
3. 'If you want to, you can cure me". We pray for those who
care for the sick: that they may remember that he who can
cure and restore, is working in them and through them.
4. "If you want to, you can cure me". For those stricken
with the disease of leprosy, and for those whose mission it is
to serve them: that they strengthen each other's faith.
5. "If you want to, you can cure me". May the God of all
mercy rid us of pessimism, of lack of self-esteem and of feelings of hurt and inadequacy. May he strengthen our con-
victions and confirm us in Christian hope.

Concluding Prayer
Lord our God, may our prayers rise like incense before you.
May the lifting up of our hands be an oblation in your sight,
for you are Lord forever and ever.

FIRST WEEK OF THE YEAR: FRIDAY

Introduction
Let us be confident in approaching the throne of grace, that
we shall have mercy from him and find grace when we are in
need of help.

Intentions

1. *Year 1:* For all of us present at this Eucharist: that we may reach the place of rest and find delight in the Lord.

2. *Year 2:* That the Spirit may give us political maturity: that we may cease from unreal expectations of political leaders and governments.

2. "Who can forgive sins but God?" May the Lord help us to see our need for forgiveness and his readiness to pardon us in the sacrament of reconciliation.

3. For young parents bringing up a family: that they may never cease from encourging, guiding, understanding and forgiving their children.

4. For men and women who are trying to follow Christ in the religious life: that they may establish communities of healing and forgiveness.

5. For those who are ministers of the sacrament of reconciliation: that they may be truly ministers of the Lord's compassion.

6. For all those who are afflicted in body, who have not got full use of their limbs: that they may find happiness and harmony in their lives.

Concluding Prayer
Lord our God, may our prayers rise like incense before you. May the lifting up of our hands be an oblation in your sight, for you are Lord forever and ever.

FIRST WEEK OF THE YEAR: SATURDAY

Introduction
Let us be confident, then, in approaching the throne of grace, that we shall have mercy from him and find grace when we are in need of help.

Intentions
1. "I did not come to call the virtuous but sinners". Let us pray today for those who dearly want to respond to his call

but lack the courage to do so.

2. Let us pray that our family meals may remind us of the times Jesus sat down to eat with sinners and tax collectors. May we bring love and understanding to all who break bread with us.

3. Let us pray for the deaf and the blind: that they may grow in an even closer union with the God who lives in them.

4. Let us pray for all who have an unpleasant job to do. We pray especially for the police force in our country, for night workers and for those whose job it is to exact payment.

5. Through the intercession of Mary, may our response to God's call be as willing and as total as was her response. May he give us the strength not to count the cost.

Concluding Prayer
Lord our God, may our prayers rise like incense before you. May the lifting up of our hands be an oblation in your sight, for you are Lord forever and ever.

WEEK 2

SECOND WEEK OF THE YEAR: MONDAY

Introduction
'He submitted so humbly that his prayer was heard'. Through our great High Priest we present our prayers on high.

Intentions
1. May this Eucharist bestow upon us that newness of life which Christ came to bring.

2. May our lives be full of the new wine of God's love. May his Spirit give us vitality and hope.

3. May we have the courage to fast as we await the coming of the bridegroom. May we avoid the temptation to grow soft and to miss the pain of life which brings growth.

4. May we avoid patching over the shrunken cloth of our lives with insincere repentance and half-fulfilled promises.

5. May our deceased relatives and friends find rest in the

company of the bridegroom. May we look forward to our
new life together with them in Christ.

6. *Year 1:* 'In the days of his flesh he offered love's cries and
tears'. May we never be ashamed to express our true feelings
to him who can save us from death.

6. *Year 2:* 'Obedience is better than sacrifice'. May we do his
will in all things.

Concluding Prayer
Almighty God and Father, we offer you our prayers for all
who are in need. May your love come upon them. May they
experience your saving help. We make this prayer through
Christ our Lord.

SECOND WEEK OF THE YEAR: TUESDAY

Introduction
The Lord keeps his covenant ever in mind. In the strength of
that covenant let us approach him with joy.

Intentions
1. Let us pray for those in authority: that they may always
be guided by the demands of justice and peace.
2. 'The Sabbath was made for man, not man for the Sabbath'. May the Lord of the Sabbath preserve us from un-
fairly judging the motives and actions of others.
3. May we learn to enter into his Sabbath rest and into the
immensity of his eternity as we contemplate the deep things
of our faith.
4. May the Lord preserve us from all narrowmindedness,
from harsh application of the law especially towards those
for whom the law is difficult to fulfil in the circumstances of
poverty and deprivation.

5. *Year 1:* Our great High Priest, Jesus Christ, has entered
before us into the heavenly city: may he be for us an anchor
of hope.

5. *Year 2:* 'Man looks at the appearance but the Lord looks at the heart'. May we refrain from judging others by appearances only.

Concluding Prayer
Almighty God and Father, we offer you our prayers for all who are in need. May your love come upon them. May they experience your saving help. We make this prayer through Christ our Lord.

SECOND WEEK OF THE YEAR: WEDNESDAY

Introduction
We stretch out our hands and we lift up our hearts and minds to him who can save us in all our distress.

Intentions
1. 'Stretch out your hand.' May we stretch out our hands as needy beggers to him who can alleviate all our wants.
2. 'Stretch out your hand'. May we stretch out the hand of Christ to all with whom we come in contact this day.
3. 'Stretch out your hand.' May we lift our hands in prayer as we make intercession for all men and women. May we ever remind ourselves of our priestly privilege to intercede.
4. 'Stretch out your hand.' May we grasp the hand of him who healed the man with the withered hand. May we be instruments of his healing.
5. 'Stretch out your hand.' We pray for all those, especially the victims of war and violence, who no longer have the courage to stretch out their hands.

Concluding Prayer
Almighty God and Father, we offer you our prayers for all who are in need. May your love come upon them. May they experience your saving help. We make this prayer through Christ our Lord.

SECOND WEEK OF THE YEAR: THURSDAY

Introduction
Let us pray to him whose mercy is without limit: that he may
come to our assistance in the needs of each day.

Intentions
1. 'All who were afflicted in any way were crowding forward
to touch him'. May the Lord rid humanity of all its sickness,
and may he give us the faith to come to him.
2. May we experience the touch of Christ in the sacraments.
May we have faith in his power to heal, to forgive and to give
new life.
3. The crowds followed Jesus: may all ministers in God's
Church present such a true and attractive image of Christ
that people will be moved to follow and give their loyalty to
him.
4. May the Lord banish the unclean spirits from our society,
especially the unclean spirits of possessiveness, addiction and
hatred.

5. *Year 1:* May our High Priest Jesus Christ, who has ascend-
ed to the right of the throne of the Majesty in the heavens,
enable us to offer gifts and sacrifices worthy of his name.

5. *Year 2:* May the Lord grant us the delicate touch and the
gift of tact; like Jonathan may we bring reconciliation where
there is jealousy and retaliation.

Concluding Prayer
Almighty God and Father, we offer you our prayers for all
who are in need. May your love come upon them. May they
experience your saving help. We make this prayer through
Christ our Lord.

SECOND WEEK OF THE YEAR: FRIDAY

Introduction
Through the Good News God has called us to share the glory

of Jesus Christ. May his love be upon us as we make our intercession for the needs of humanity.

Intentions
1. Jesus summoned those he wanted. The Lord has summoned us through faith and baptism, may we be ever mindful of his call.
2. And he appointed twelve. For the successors of the twelve, for our Holy Father the Pope, and for all the bishops of God's Church: that, like the twelve, they may be tireless in preaching and healing.
3. They were to be his companions and were sent out to preach. May all who engage in the preaching mission, preach from intimacy with him who is the word of life.
4. They had power to cast out devils. May the devils of greed, of hatred and of recrimination be cast out of our society: may we experience the peace that comes from making Christ the measure of our lives.
5. And so he appointed the twelve. May his people grasp even more fully the significance of the twelve who were called to represent him. May we share their mission in whatever way is open to us in the Church and in society.

Concluding Prayer
Almighty God and Father, we offer you our prayers for all who are in need. May your spirit of love come upon them. May they experience your saving help. We make this prayer through Christ our Lord.

SECOND WEEK OF THE YEAR: SATURDAY

Introduction
In the light of today's Gospel we call to mind all those on whom, like Jesus, great demands are made.

Intentions
1. We pray for all leaders in public life whose lives are not their own.
2. We pray for priests who are overworked, especially in areas of mass population.

3. We pray for overburdened parents, especially for mothers who have to hold down a job and care for a family.
4. We pray for all teachers who find the going hard, especially in underprivileged areas.
5. We pray for all those who work on the land, especially for farmers who are struggling for an existence.
6. We pray for all those in public services, for the civil servants, hospital personnel, police, the armed forces, night workers, and especially for those who perform difficult and menial tasks.

Concluding Prayer
Almighty God and Father, we offer you our prayers for all who are in need. May your love come upon them. May they experience your saving help. We make this prayer through Christ our Lord. Amen.

<h1 style="text-align:center">WEEK 3</h1>

THIRD WEEK OF THE YEAR: MONDAY

Introduction
Jesus Christ our light has come into our world to break away the darkness of sin. He has brought salvation to all the nations and to each of us. In him we will find the strength to overcome our sinfulness and the sins of the world.

Intentions
1. That the Church may be a sign of God's presence in our world and a reminder of his forgiveness and support in our lives.
2. That people everywhere may realise that God is calling them to lives of truth, love and forgiveness.
3. That those who experience no forgiveness or mercy in their lives may be strengthened by the example of Jesus and the witness of his followers.
4. That the members of this community, gladdened by the knowledge of the salvation that awaits them in the next life, may joyfully serve God in each other in this present time.
5. That those who are suffering through ill-health, misunder-

standing and human failure may draw strength and encouragement from the suffering of Christ our Lord.

Concluding Prayer
God our Father, mindful of your goodness, we place our prayers before you. Grant us all that we need today to live our lives in the shadow of your presence. We make our prayer through Christ our Lord.

THIRD WEEK OF THE YEAR: TUESDAY

Introduction
The sacrifice of Christ on Calvary has taken away our sins and the sin of the world. Every time we gather to break bread in memory of the passion, death and resurrection of Christ, we share the fruits of that sacrifice. And one of the fruits of that sacrifice is the call to do God's will in our lives.
  Jesus tells us: "Anyone who does the will of God, that person is my brother and sister and mother".

Intentions
1. Let us pray that the Church may be a sign to the world of the sacrifice of Calvary that is at the heart of the Christian message.
2. Let us pray that as a result of the gathering of this community around the Lord's table, we may be united more closely with each other in faith, hope and love.
3. Let us pray for our country: that our leaders may recognise the will and work of God in our struggle for peace in the world.
4. Let us pray for our families: that the closeness of Christ may be reflected in our closeness to each other.
5. Let us pray for those oppressed by hunger and want: that those of us who share the bread of the Lord may also share our bread with our brothers and sisters.

Concluding Prayer
God our Father, mindful of your goodness we place our prayers before you. Grant us all we need today to live our

lives in the shadow of your presence. We make this prayer through Christ our Lord.

THIRD WEEK OF THE YEAR: WEDNESDAY

Introduction
God offers his word to all people. The seed of his love finds a varied soil in the imperfect conditions of humankind. Our inconsistent response underlines how complete and total is God's gift to us.

Intentions
1. For the Church: that we may help our people prepare the soil of their lives for the word of God and that they may yield a rich harvest.
2. For bishops and priests and all who are leaders of our Church: that they may dedicate themselves to God as David did in sincerity and truth.
3. For our young people: that despite the stresses and worries of life they may hear and accept God's word.
4. For those in our community who have drifted away from God: that they may rediscover in their lives his seed of faith, hope and love.
5. For those who interpret God's word: that they may come to a knowledge of his truth.

Concluding Prayer
God our Father, mindful of your goodness we place our prayers before you. Grant us all we need today to live our lives in the shadow of your presence. We make this prayer through Christ our Lord.

THIRD WEEK OF THE YEAR: THURSDAY

Introduction
To be followers of Jesus Christ we see ourselves not as individuals but as members of his community. To be his follower is to work for a unity of heart, a unity of mind, a unity of spirit.

Intentions
1. We pray for the Church: that the light of God's faithfulness to his people may find a response in our love and concern for one another.
2. We pray for families and communities burdened with divisions: that they may see the unifying light of God's message.
3. We pray for those who bear burdens of guilt or fear or hopelessness: that they may have their burdens lightened through Christ's message of eternal life.
4. We pray that the light of Christ may overcome our blindness to the needs of others.
5. We pray for a sincerity of heart, a firmness of hope, a purity of intention in our lives and the life of the world.

Concluding Prayer
God our Father, mindful of your goodness we place our prayers before you. Grant us all we need today to live our lives in the shadow of your presence. We make this prayer through Christ our Lord.

THIRD WEEK OF THE YEAR: FRIDAY

Introduction
We are all sinners. We all need forgiveness. We need to know that God is our stronghold, that our refuge is in him and that he will cleanse us from our sins. And we know too that the effort to do his will and to grow towards him needs a lot of patience, perseverence, endurance, like the growth of a huge tree from a tiny seed.

Intentions
1. That the Church all over the world may grow into a true communion of all God's people, accepting mistakes and failures, and looking forward with faith and confidence to the future.
2. For the congregation present here today: that despite the sins and sinfulness of our lives, we may persevere in our journey of faith towards God.
3. For our political and civil leaders: that they may not abuse

their position of trust for personal or politicl gain.
4. For those crushed by an overwhelming sense of their own sinfulness: that they may experience in their lives the loving mercy of our Saviour.
5. For those who experience physical or mental suffering at this time: that their pain may unite them with the suffering Christ on Calvary.

Concluding Prayer
God our Father, mindful of your goodness we place our prayers before you. Grant us all we need today to live our lives in the shadow of your presence. We make this prayer through Christ our Lord.

THIRD WEEK OF THE YEAR: SATURDAY

Introduction
Life has been compared to a journey, a journey made in faith. A pilgrimage too, often made in hope. There is the occasional gale, the storms of life that frighten us and make us want to give up, to turn back. We need the still centre of a strong faith in God to help us on the way.

Intentions
1. Let us pray that in these difficult days of wars and rumours of wars the Church may give strong witness to faith in God and hope in the future.
2. Let us pray that those to whom God reveals himself in this day may inspire the doubting and the doubtful to a life of faith, hope and love.
3. Let us pray that in all we do and say, this day and always, we may support and not weaken the faith of those around us.
4. Let us pray that God may forgive those of us who by our lives make it difficult for others to believe in his love, mercy and forgiveness.
5. Let us pray that the young people of this community may find a joyful faith in their families and an encouragement to faith in their community.

Concluding Prayer
God our Father, mindful of your goodness we place our prayers before you. Grant us all we need today to live our lives in the shadow of your presence. We make this prayer through Christ our Lord.

WEEK 4

FOURTH WEEK OF THE YEAR: MONDAY

Introduction
In a world of conflict, violence and war, we need to trust in the providence of God. And even though our faith may be mocked, such insult and injury should not shake our confidence in God and our faith in his power over evil.

Intentions
1. That the Church may be a faithful sign of God's goodness in the struggle against the forces of darkness in our world.
2. That those who experience mockery and ridicule for living a good life may be encouraged and strengthened by the faith of their community.
3. That those who minister to the sick and lessen the pain and suffering of the infirm may be rewarded for their goodness.
4. That the leaders of the great nations may recognise the need for peace in our world and work with the determination to achieve it.
5. That we may be able to control our tempers, accept correction, and be patient particularly in the face of insults and injury.

Concluding Prayer
God, you are our Father. You have given us everything we have and everything we are. Help us to use wisely and generously the gifts you have given us to carry out your work in the world. We make our prayer through Christ our Lord.

FOURTH WEEK OF THE YEAR: TUESDAY

Introduction
God is close to us in our suffering. He supports us in our pain. He is with us in all the conflicts and griefs of life, with the sick and the dying, the injured and the maimed, the results of man's failure to live in peace with his fellow-man.

Intentions
1. We pray that the Church may witness to the pointlessness of violence and war in our world and the pressing need for peace.
2. We pray that we may persevere in the effort to live a good life, to avoid sin, and to accept the inevitable difficulties and frustrations of life.
3. We pray for parents who have lost a child: that the pain of their grief may not overcome their faith in the goodness and love of God.
4. We pray that those who are oppressed by serious and prolonged injury or ill-health may be aware of God's goodness and the support of their families and friends.
5. We pray for families broken by the strain of ill-health or conflict.

Concluding Prayer
God, you are our Father. You have given us everything we have and everything we are. Help us to use wisely and generously the gifts you have given us to carry out your work in the world. We make our prayer through Christ our Lord.

FOURTH WEEK OF THE YEAR: WEDNESDAY

Introduction
We place our trust in human wisdom and human expertise. We forget so easily that God is working in our world through his Spirit and the prophets who speak in his name.

Intentions
1. That we may recognise the need to persevere in the struggle

for justice and truth in the Church and in the world.
2. For the community in which we live: that we may never
allow bitterness or prejudice to divide us from one another.
3. That we may be aware of the occasions when our own
pride blinds us to the needs of our fellow man.
4. That our concern for other people may never be measured
by considerations of intelligence, influence or physical
beauty.
5. That the curable diseases that still ravage nations and
peoples throughout the world may be eliminated by the com-
bined efforts of the international community.

Concluding Prayer
God, you are our Father. You have given us everything we
have and everything we are. Help us to use wisely and
generously the gifts you have given us to carry out your work
in the world. We make our prayer through Christ our Lord.

FOURTH WEEK OF THE YEAR: THURSDAY

Introduction
God gave his authority to his Church to preach his gospel to
the world, to give liberty to captives, new sight to the blind
and good news to the poor.

Intentions
1. Let us pray for the leaders of our Church: that they may
guide God's people in bringing Christ's saving mission to the
world.
2. Let us pray that the Christian community may interpret
the concepts of authority and obedience in the light of our
gospel faith.
3. Let us pray that, as members of God's family, we may
witness in our lives the virtue of poverty.
4. Let us pray for all missionaries: that they may be encouraged by the gospel they preach, and supported by their home
Church.
5. Let us pray for the members of other Christian Churches
and all those who proclaim the gospel of Jesus: that we may
all be united in worship of the one true God.

Concluding Prayer
God, you are our Father. You have given us everything we have and everything we are. Help us to use wisely and generously the gifts you have given us to carry out your work in the world. We make our prayer through Christ our Lord. Amen.

FOURTH WEEK OF THE YEAR: FRIDAY

Introduction
The Lord is our light and our help. In a world of changing values Jesus Christ and the quality of life he stands for is an unchanging anchor. We need courage and strength to remain steadfast to the wisdom of his gospel.

Intentions
1. For the Church: that God may bless us with prophets like John the Baptist who will witness to the truth and inspire us to hold firm to Christian values.
2. Let us pray for a deeper appreciation in our society for that quality of life that Jesus challenges us to live.
3. That those who are imprisoned by anxiety, loneliness and their own selfishness may receive the freeing power of Christ's love and the friendship of his followers.
4. That strangers may be welcome and experience among us an unselfish love and concern that is the mark of a true disciple of Jesus.
5. That married couples in this community may be faithful to each other and united in love.

Concluding Prayer
God, you are our Father. You have given us everything we have and everything we are. Help us to use wisely and generously the gifts you have given us to carry out your work in the world. We make our prayer through Christ our Lord. Amen.

FOURTH WEEK OF THE YEAR: SATURDAY

Introduction
God is the shepherd, we are the flock. He cares for us, comforts us and guides us along the right path. May we come to dwell in his house forever.

Intentions
1. We pray for Pope N, and our bishop, N: that they may guide our Church with wisdom and care in the way of faith, hope and love.
2. We pray that all those in positions of authority and political leadership may receive the virtue of wisdom as Solomon did.
3. We pray that we may be aware of the need for periods of silence and prayer in our lives.
4. We pray for parents and teachers and all who bring God's word to the young: that they may know something of God's compassion and care for his people.
5. We pray that the God of peace may make us ready to do his will in any kind of good action.

Concluding Prayer
God, you are our Father. You have given us everything we have and everything we are. Help us to use wisely and generously the gifts you have given us to carry out your work in the world. We make our prayer through Christ our Lord.

WEEK 5

FIFTH WEEK OF THE YEAR: MONDAY

Introduction

Year 1: With thanksgiving to God for his gifts of light and life, let us offer him our prayers.

Year 2: Recalling the Lord's presence in Solomon's temple, let us give him thanks and praise for this holy place in which we are gathered, and offer him our prayers.

Intentions
1. For the Church's ministry to the sick through prayer and sacrament.
2. For the work of doctors and nurses in hospitals.
3. For all sick people: that they may seek strength from the Lord and find peace and healing.
4. For the friends and relatives of the sick: that they may be a support to those in need.

Concluding Prayer
Lord Jesus Christ, we give thanks that you yourself are the bread of life. Lord, evermore give us this bread of eternal life that, coming to you, we may never hunger.

FIFTH WEEK OF THE YEAR: TUESDAY

Introduction

Year 1: With thanksgiving to our heavenly Father for creating us in his likeness, let us offer our prayers.

Year 2: As Solomon prayed that the Lord would hear the prayers that were offered up in the temple, we have faith that the Lord will hear the prayers we offer now.

Intentions
1. That your Church may offer the pure sacrifice of praise continually.
2. That your people throughout the world may understand what you expect of them.
3. That family life may be strengthened and enriched by true love.
4. That we may gladly accept our responsibilities for one another.

Concluding Prayer
Lord Jesus Christ, we give thanks that you yourself are the bread of life. Lord, evermore give us this bread of eternal life that, coming to you, we may never hunger.

FIFTH WEEK OF THE YEAR: WEDNESDAY

Introduction

Year 1: The Lord put man in the garden of Eden to cultivate and take care of it. Let us now pray for God's world and its needs.

Year 2: Recalling the wisdom of Solomon which was God's gift to him, let us pray for a wise use of our lives.

Intentions
1. That we may listen attentively to our Lord's teaching.
2. That the Holy Spirit will give us the right understanding of it.
3. That we may put away evil thoughts and intentions before they turn into actions which hurt us and other people.
4. That our local communities may live according to God's will.

Concluding Prayer
Lord Jesus Christ, we give thanks that you yourself are the bread of life. Lord, evermore give us this bread of eternal life that, coming to you, we may never hunger.

FIFTH WEEK OF THE YEAR: THURSDAY

Introduction

Year 1: In the word of the Lord we learn that in marriage a man and a woman are one flesh. Let us pray today for all married people.

Year 2: In the word of the Lord we learn that God's servant Solomon made many mistakes in married life. Let us offer our prayers to God for all married people.

Intentions
1. That all married couples have a better understanding of this sacrament, and that the love of a husband and wife may continually grow

2. That those whose marriage is in trouble may use every means to overcome their problems.
3. That as our Lord Jesus Christ heard the cry of a stranger, so may all look to him for mercy, that we may learn from the faith and humility of others.

Concluding Prayer
Lord Jesus Christ, we give thanks that you yourself are the bread of life. Lord, evermore give us this bread of eternal life that, coming to you, we may never hunger.

FIFTH WEEK OF THE YEAR: FRIDAY

Introduction
In the word of the Lord we learn of the results of giving in to temptation. We pray today for grace to be faithful to our Christian calling.

Intentions
1. In disobedience and sin we feel the pain of being separated from God. We give thanks and praise for forgiveness through the saving work of our Lord Jesus Christ and ask for mercy.
2. We live in a world that has turned its back on God. For this world we ask for mercy.
3. The Lord healed the deaf man. May he open our ears to the gospel and enable us to sing his praises.
4. The Lord has done all things well. Let his gospel be proclaimed in all the world.

Concluding Prayer
Lord Jesus Christ, we give thanks that you yourself are the bread of life. Lord, evermore give us this bread of eternal life that, coming to you, we may never hunger.

FIFTH WEEK OF THE YEAR: SATURDAY

Introduction
In the word of the Lord we hear that life is harder when we

move away from him. Let us pray that we may find our home
in God.

Intentions
1. In the Lord's feeding of the hungry people we see a sign
of the Eucharist. Lord Jesus Christ, in your mercy give us a
hunger for the bread of life.
2. As we share this holy sacrament with all your faithful
people, Lord, satisfy our longing.
3. Let us see that in your bounty you will give more than
enough for the needs of all.

Concluding Prayer
Lord Jesus Christ, we give thanks that you yourself are the
bread of life. Lord, evermore give us this bread of eternal life
that, coming to you, we may never hunger.

WEEK 6

SIXTH WEEK OF THE YEAR: MONDAY

Introduction
Let us pray for all men and women according to what they
need.

Intentions
1. For the Church throughout the world: that in faith we
search for no other sign than the resurrection of Jesus Christ.
2. That the people of the world may learn to accept responsibility for each other as members of one family.
3. For all who offer their lives in the service of others: that
what they do may be a sign of their faith in Christ.
4. For those who have no family or friends to care for them:
that in the fellowship of their parish they may find support
and love.
5. For ourselves, for the courage and endurance to practise
the faith we profess.

Concluding Prayer
God, grant to the living grace; to the departed, rest; to the

Church, the nation and all mankind, peace and concord; and to us and all his servants life everlasting.

SIXTH WEEK OF THE YEAR: TUESDAY

Introduction
Let us pray to the Lord of creation.

Intentions
1. That the Church, like an ark of salvation, may carry us safely through the storms of temptation and the perils of persecution.
2. For peace among the nations: that we may use what the earth yields as God wills, and for the good of all mankind.
3. That we may open our eyes to the good things God has given us, and to the opportunities for sharing with others the blessings we enjoy.
4. For those who are suffering from hunger and poverty: that they may be encouraged and assisted by our efforts to help them.
5. For the realisation of a new heaven and a new earth, and a share in the heavenly banquet promised to those who love and serve the Lord.

Concluding Prayer
God, grant to the living grace; to the departed, rest; to the Church, the nation and all mankind, peace and concord; and to us and all his servants life everlasting.

SIXTH WEEK OF THE YEAR: WEDNESDAY

Introduction
Let us pray for the whole Church of God in Christ Jesus and for all men and women who need our prayers.

Intentions
1. *Year 1:* For the Church: that it may be a vessel of new life when hope has perished.
1. *Year 2:* For the Church: that we may accept and submit

ourselves to the word of God, which has been planted in us.
2. For the leaders of the nations: that they speak with
restraint and be ready to listen to one another.
3. For the blind: that they may discover doors of perception
opening out of their darkness.
4. For the widows and orphans and single parents: that our
love may surround and sustain them.
5. For the departed who no longer see darkly, but face to
face.

Concluding Prayer
God, grant to the living grace; to the departed, rest; to the
Church, the nation and all mankind, peace and concord; and
to us and all his servants life everlasting.

SIXTH WEEK OF THE YEAR: THURSDAY

Introduction
In the power of the Spirit and in union with Christ, let us
pray to the Father.

Intentions
1. *Year 1:* For the Church bound by the new covenant in
Christ's blood: that we may become agents of reconciliation
between man and God.
1. *Year 2:* For the Church: that by our faith we break down
barriers between different classes of people.
2. For the rich nations of the world: that they may use their
resources to the benefit of the developing nations.
3. For boldness to preach the Gospel to all the world, and like
Peter to proclaim that Jesus is God's chosen one.
4. For prisoners of conscience, and for those persecuted
because of their Christian conviction: that they may have
courage and hope in their sufferings.
5. For all who in our time have died a martyr's death: that
the stand they take may inspire and encourage us.

Concluding Prayer
God, grant to the living grace; to the departed, rest; to the
Church, the nation and all mankind, peace and concord; and
to us and all his servants life everlasting.

SIXTH WEEK OF THE YEAR: FRIDAY

Introduction
Let us pray with Christ, in the Spirit, to the Father who loves us.

Intentions
1. For the Church scattered throughout the world: that it may grow in unity, and bring all men to faith in God.
2. For people who have the advantage of urban technology: that they may remain humble in their achievements, and not ashamed to confess the faith of Christ crucified.
3. That the people of God have grace to understand God's word and to act upon it.
4. For all who administer the law: that they may uphold justice and maintain truth.
5. That our hearts may love and fear God and his word.

Concluding Prayer
God, grant to the living grace; to the departed, rest; to the Church, the nation and all mankind, peace and concord; and to us and all his servants life everlasting.

SIXTH WEEK OF THE YEAR: SATURDAY

Introduction
Let us pray to the Lord, in faith, for transformation through his Spirit.

Intentions
1. *Year 1:* That we remember with humility the faith of those who have gone before us.
1. *Year 2:* For the renewal of the Church, that we may all be transformed by the power of the risen Christ.
2. For the transformation of society through the lives and example of Christian people.
3. For writers and broadcasters: that they use words wisely to communicate with honesty and openness.
4. For this parish: that we may hear Christ speaking and find

our lives transformed by his presence.
5. For our families, our friends and all our neighbours: that we may see Christ in one another, and love as he loves us.

Concluding Prayer
God, grant to the living grace; to the departed, rest; to the Church, the nation and all mankind, peace and concord; and to us and all his servants life everlasting.

WEEK 7

SEVENTH WEEK OF THE YEAR: MONDAY

Introduction
With confidence in God's infinite wisdom and fatherly love let us pray with expectant faith.

Intentions
1. That all engaged in apostolic work may be united more closely to Christ the source of their power.
2. *Year 2:* For God's holy Church: that the Lord may inspire the pope and all the bishops with the wisdom which comes from above.
3. *Year 1:* Let us pray that the Lord and Creator may direct by his wisdom the efforts of man to subdue the earth.
4. For our country: that the Lord may preserve our leaders from selfish ambition, our people from apathy towards their civil duties.
5. Let us remember handicapped children and their parents: that through our Christ-like concern for them they may experience the Lord's healing presence in their lives.
6. For the deaf: that pastors and Christian communities everywhere may help them to become actively engaged in the life of their parishes.

Concluding Prayer
Father, we acknowledge our dependence on you. In your love give your people the gifts which your word had prompted us to ask for in the name of Jesus the Lord.

SEVENTH WEEK OF THE YEAR: TUESDAY

Introduction
God our Father helps those who wait for his mercy. In humility of heart and with steadfast hope let us entrust our cares to him.

Intentions
1. Let us pray that the Church may be seen to express Christ's care for the lowly and the disadvantaged.
2. That we and all members of the Church may express our dignity as a kindly people by our readiness to render humble service.
3. For all who hold public office: that they may strive to foster good community relations in society.
4. *Year 1:* Let us remember with compassion people experiencing trials in their particular states of life: that through the power of the Eucharist they may be delivered from anxiety and confirmed in their vocations.
4. *Year 2:* For those who feel overwhelmed by temptations: that the suffering Saviour and glorified Lord may support them.

Concluding Prayer
Father, we acknowledge our dependence on you. In your love give your people the gifts which your word had prompted us to ask for in the name of Jesus the Lord.

SEVENTH WEEK OF THE YEAR: WEDNESDAY

Introduction
People of God, let us pray to the Father for the welfare of the Church and the salvation of the world.

Intentions
1. We pray for missionaries: that they may bring growth and increase to the Church through sincere and patient dialogue with non-Christians.
2. That all members of the Church may promote Christian

unity by gratefully acknowledging the presence of Christ in the lives and good works of our separated brethern.

3. For the peace and prosperity of all peoples, let us pray to the Lord.

4. That the nations of the world may co-operate to ensure a fairer distributon of the world's resources.

5. That all who are oppressed by the power of evil may experience deliverance and healing.

6. *Year 1:* We pray that the Lord may guide to himself all who with a sincere heart are groping to find him.

Concluding Prayer
Father, we acknowledge our dependence on you. In your love give your people the gifts which your word had prompted us to ask for in the name of Jesus the Lord.

SEVENTH WEEK OF THE YEAR: THURSDAY

Introduction
Gathered as a priestly people in the peace of Christ, let us pray together to the Father who wishes to fill his creatures with every blessing.

Intentions
1. That the Lord Jesus may preserve his Church from attachment to worldly wealth.

2. For all the baptised, that they may be strengthened to eliminate from our lives anything that would endanger the gift of faith which we have received.

3. We pray for all who work to cultivate international understanding and brotherhood, that the Lord may bless their efforts.

4. *Year 2:* Let us pray for those who are deputed to administer justice, that they may in fact be impartial dispensers of true justice to all.

5. *Year 1:* Let us remember with Christ-like concern all who have put their eternal salvation at risk by presumption, that they may not delay to be reconciled to the Father of mercies.

6. *Year 2:* For the workers who are being treated unjustly, that their dignity may be respected and that their rights may be recognised.

Concluding Prayer
Father, we acknowledge our dependence on you. In your love give your people the gifts which your word had prompted us to ask for in the name of Jesus the Lord.

SEVENTH WEEK OF THE YEAR: FRIDAY

Introduction
As we gather to be nourished by word and sacrament, let us pray that the sacrifice we offer may fill us with every blessing and advance the peace and salvation of all the world.

Intentions
1. That Jesus the Teacher may guide his Church to impart his truth to all men.
2. For all who serve the people of God on marriage tribunals: that they may discern the law of God and apply it according to the mind of Christ.
3. That the governments of the world may always respect the institution of marriage and the rights of the family.
4. *Year 1:* We pray for people who have been betrayed by false friends, humiliated through imprudent relationships: that the Lord of steadfast love and mercy may relieve their loneliness and pain.
4. *Year 2:* Let us remember those who are perplexed by God's strange ways: that they may stand firm in times of trial and inherit everlasting life.

Concluding Prayer
Father, we acknowledge our dependence on you. In your love give your people the gifts which your word had prompted us to ask for in the name of Jesus the Lord.

SEVENTH WEEK OF THE YEAR: SATURDAY

Introduction
God is our loving Father. Conscious of his care for all that he has made, we turn to him with childlike trust.

Intentions
1. That through the intercession of Mary, mother and model of catechists, the Lord may enrich his Church with teachers who will impart a simple and true image of Jesus to the children under their care.
2. *Year 2:* For the Church: that by more fruitful celebration of the sacrament of Penance we may be moulded into a reconciling community.
3. *Year 1:* That people everywhere may use their God-given talents to make our world a better place to live in.
4. *Year 2:* For our country: that our public representatives may allocate sufficient resources to provide an adequate public health service for all our people.
5. For the children and young people who are being abused or exploited in any way, that the Lord Jesus may rescue them.
6. *Year 2:* Let us remember those who are seriously ill and all who are notably weakened by old age: that they may be supported by the sacrament of the sick and by the love of their local Christian communities.

Concluding Prayer
Father, we acknowledge our dependence on you. In your love give your people the gifts which your word had prompted us to ask for in the name of Jesus the Lord.

WEEK 8

EIGHTH WEEK OF THE YEAR: MONDAY

Introduction
Let us pray in the presence of God, the source of every good, that the peace of Christ may live in our hearts and come to the world.

Intentions
1. *Year 1:* For all the baptized: that we may courageously face the challenge of being converted anew each day.
2. *Year 2:* That the pope and all pastors may zealously cultivate in the people of God a deep love of Jesus.

3. Let us ask the Lord to bless the earth and the sea with an abundant harvest of food for the peoples of the world.
4. We pray that the cry of the poor may meet with a generous response from all who profess to follow Christ.
5. *Year 1:* Let us remember those whose sins have separated them from God: that they may soon experience the joy of the Father's forgiveness.

Concluding Prayer
God our Father, you alone are good. Guide the course of world events. Hear our petitions made in faith and hope. Grant them in the name of Jesus the Lord.

EIGHTH WEEK OF THE YEAR: TUESDAY

Introduction
God has called us to his presence. Let us trust that he who has called us may hear our prayers for ourselves, the Church, and for all mankind.

Intentions
1. Let us ask the Lord to bless with abundant fruit the apostolic work of many laymen and laywomen who have left the security of family and possessions for the sake of the gospel.
2. That the Lord may endow the religious orders, contemplative and active, with a renewal of zeal and a growth in vocations.
3. *Year 1:* We pray that those whom God had blessed with material wealth may make a realistic contribution towards the support of the Church.
4. That public authorities may recognise and respect the right of all citizens to religious freedom.
5. For all who have sustained material loss on account of their fidelity to the gospel: that their sharing in Christ's self-emptying may be rewarded in this life and in the life to come.
6. *Year 2:* We remember our fellow Christians who are living in a hostile environment: that through our solidarity with them in this Eucharist, they may be heralds of Christian hope.

Concluding Prayer
God our Father, you alone are good. Guide the course of world events. Hear our petitions made in faith and hope. Grant them in the name of Jesus the Lord.

EIGHTH WEEK OF THE YEAR: WEDNESDAY

Introduction
We know and believe in God's love for us. Let us pray that the Lord may touch the whole of creation and the hearts of all men with his love.

Intentions
1. That the Lord Jesus may preserve his Church from all divisiveness of factions and the influence of power struggles.
2. For all who hold authority in the Church: that they may exercise it in a spirit of service.
3. Let us pray for our country: that political parties may place the common good above party interests.
4. For governments everywhere: that the Lord may inspire them to abandon any ambition to dominate other nations.
5. Let us remember with compassion all who have been degraded and victimised by the selfish ambitions of their fellow man: that their rights may be vindicated.
6. We pray for all who have died in religious persecutions: that, having shared in the cup of the Lord's suffering, they may reign with him forever.

Concluding Prayer
God our Father, you alone are good. Guide the course of world events. Hear our petitions made in faith and hope. Grant them in the name of Jesus the Lord.

EIGHTH WEEK OF THE YEAR: THURSDAY

Introduction
Gathered to celebrate the mystery of Christ's love and acknowledge that our help is in the name of the Lord, we present our petitions to the giver of all good things.

Intentions
1. We pray for all the ministers of the Church: that Christ the healer may enable them to discern and meet the real needs of the sick and the handicapped whom they serve.
2. *Year 1:* Let us pray that all peoples may come to acknowledge the Creator of the wonders revealed by the natural sciences.
2. *Year 2:* For the laity: that all pastors may willingly strive to make the faithful aware of their common priesthood and encourage them to exercise it.
3. *Year 2:* That Christians everywhere may give good example and promote the improvements of civil society by conscientiously fulfilling their civic responsibility.
4. Let us pray for the blind and for those whose sight is impaired: that they may receive consideration from public authorities, understanding from their friends, and courtesy from all.

Concluding Prayer
God our Father, you alone are good. Guide the course of world events. Hear our petitions made in faith and hope. Grant them in the name of Jesus the Lord.

EIGHTH WEEK OF THE YEAR: FRIDAY

Introduction
Our Father has called us to worship him in this holy place. With reverence in the presence of God and following the teaching of Jesus, we express our needs with that confidence which is born of faith.

Intentions
1. For the up-building of the Church: that all Christians may listen to the word of God and allow it to form them in the likeness of Jesus.
2. Let us pray that the Lord may cleanse his Church of all that is unworthy of the Bride of Christ.
3. For the peace and well-being of the world: that all nations may honour lawful international agreements which they have freely accepted.

4. That God may guide the efforts of the United Nations Organisation to strengthen the fragile peace in our world; that he may preserve its peace-keeping personnel from danger.

5. Let us remember all travellers especially migrants, refugees and stateless persons: that the Lord may keep them in his care and lead them to shelter and security.

6. *Year 1:* We include in our prayer all who are afflicted with physical or mental illnesses: that, having shared in Christ's suffering, they may also rejoice and be glad when his glory is revealed.

Concluding Prayer
God our Father, you alone are good. Guide the course of world events. Hear our petitions made in faith and hope. Grant them in the name of Jesus the Lord.

EIGHTH WEEK OF THE YEAR: SATURDAY

Introduction
In union with the whole Church and uniting our prayers with those of Mary and all the saints, we pray that God may give us and all mankind his constant help and protection.

Intentions
1. That in his love for his Mystical Body the Lord Jesus may enable each member to see ever more clearly the source of authority in the Church.

2. *Year 2:* Let us pray that the pastoral practice of the Church may prolong Christ's concern for the return of those who have strayed.

3. For the welfare of the world: that the Lord may preserve us from the horrors of nuclear war.

4. Let us pray earnestly that public authorities may take effective measures to protect the young from corrupting· influences.

5. We remember the Jewish people who seek the truth with sincere hearts, and we pray that he who is truth may enlighten their minds and lead them to himself.

Concluding Prayer
God our Father, you alone are good. Guide the course of
world events. Hear our petitions made in faith and hope.
Grant them in the name of Jesus the Lord.

WEEK 9

NINTH WEEK OF THE YEAR: MONDAY

Introduction
The Son of God came to his own and his own rejected him.
They left him alone and went away.

Intentions
1. Let us pray for all suffering people especially for the poorer
nations who have been oppressed by powerful neighbours.
2. Let us remember in love the physically and mentally handicapped who may feel rejected by others.
3. For those who experience rejection by a society which is
itself troubled by recession, unemployment and poverty.
4. That instead of judging and rejecting others, we may
encourage and build them up.
5. That instead of leaving those in need to walk away alone,
we may strive to put new heart into them.

Concluding Prayer
Lord our God, may you bless us in all that we do and say.
May you hearken to our voices as we offer you our prayers
and supplications through Christ our Lord.

NINTH WEEK OF THE YEAR: TUESDAY

Introduction
Jesus invites us to live well in both worlds, to commit
ourselves to the upbuilding of our country, and at the same
time to remember that we have not here a lasting city but seek
one that is to come.

Intentions
1. Let us pray for our country, for its rulers and all its people.
2. That our leaders may provide a just and fairly distributed system of taxation, so that the strong may help to carry the weak.
3. That those who hold authority may be men and women of honesty and integrity seeking only the common good.
4. That in all our dealings as a people we may seek the glory of God, and that Jesus Christ may be acknowledged as Lord of every situation.

Concluding Prayer
Lord our God, may you bless us in all that we do and say. May you hearken to our voices as we offer you our prayers and supplications through Christ our Lord.

NINTH WEEK OF THE YEAR: WEDNESDAY

Introduction
Our God reigns: he reigns over all generations, past, present and to come. The whole world of here and hereafter is in is hands.

Intentions
1. Let us pray for a greater faith and hope in the mystery of life after death.
2. Let us pray for all our beloved dead: that they may share in the glory of Christ's own resurrection.
3. "I am the resurrection and the life," said Jesus. "He who believes in me shall never die." May we, who have shared "the fellowship of his sufferings," come to know "the power of his resurrection."
4. That after this our exile we may, through the intercession of Mary and of all our patron saints, be joined to our families and friends in the kingdom of heaven.

Concluding Prayer
Lord our God, may you bless us in all that we do and say. May you hearken to our voices as we offer you our prayers and supplications through Christ our Lord.

NINTH WEEK OF THE YEAR: THURSDAY

Introduction
In the light of the first reading let us remember that the heart
of the Good News is that Jesus is risen from the dead; and
that where he is, we are to be.

Intentions
1. Let us pray for missioners who bring the good news of the
Gospel to those who sit in darkness and in the shadow of
death.
2. For the Church of silence, where men and women are "in
chains" today for preaching the good news.
3. "Ignorance of the Scriptures is ignorance of Christ,"
remarked St Jerome: Let us pray for all scholars who provide
the sacred texts and for preachers who spread the message of
the Gospel.
4. That Jesus may open to us the Scriptures, and that our
hearts may burn within us, as we come to know the Lord
present in power and speaking to us through his word.

Concluding Prayer
Lord our God, may you bless us in all that we do and say.
May you hearken to our voices as we offer you our prayers
and supplications through Christ our Lord.

NINTH WEEK OF THE YEAR: FRIDAY

Introduction
Jesus Christ is Lord of lords and King of kings. But if if he
is not Lord of all, he is not Lord at all.

Intentions
1. That every power in heaven and on earth may acknowledge Jesus as Lord; and that we have no strange gods
before him.
2. That we may be a people of praise and thanksgiving,
realizing that honest praise is a due debt and must be paid.
3. That, knowing how to praise and seek first the kingdom

of God and his glory, we may only then stretch forth our hands to beg our daily bread.
4. That by the grace and enlightenment of God we may dispel all darkness that would prevent the light of Christ from shining in our lives.

Concluding Prayer
Lord our God, may you bless us in all that we do and say. May you hearken to our voices as we offer you our prayers and supplications through Christ our Lord.

NINTH WEEK OF THE YEAR: SATURDAY

Introduction
Jesus echoes this day the words of the prophet Micah: "This is what the Lord asks of you, only this, to act justly, to love tenderly and to walk humbly with your God."

Intentions
1. Let us pray for all God's ministers: that they may be humble instruments of the Lord, performing their sacred ministry with reverence for God and respect for his people.
2. That the Church may be a witness to the world of the simplicity and the poverty of Jesus, the Carpenter of Nazareth.
3. That following the example of the poor widow, we may be generous in contributing to the missionary activity of the Church at home and abroad.
4. That we may see Jesus in the poor, the down-trodden and the rejected, remembering that on this will we be judged: "As long as you did it to one of these, you did it to me."

Concluding Prayer
Lord our God, may you bless us in all that we do and say. May you hearken to our voices as we offer you our prayers and supplications through Christ our Lord.

TENTH WEEK OF THE YEAR: MONDAY

Introduction
Hearing his word is an encouragement to pray and to make intercession for God's people.

Intentions
1. That, becoming aware of our spiritual poverty, we may feel the need of healing forgiveness and the richness of grace.
2. That we may seek to bring about good by gentleness rather than through forceful and violent actions.
3. That in times of mourning and sadness people may look to God for consolation, in a spirit of faith and hope.
4. That, faced with the temptations of materialism and sensuality, Christians may approach all things in purity of mind and heart.

Concluding Prayer
Graciously help us, Lord, in our need and hear our every prayer, that we may devote ourselves to serving you in freedom and in gladness. Through Christ our Lord.

TENTH WEEK OF THE YEAR: TUESDAY

Introduction
Christ's followers, through the way they behave and act, are to be like a light in darkness. Let us pray for this grace, and that all mankind may benefit from its effect.

Intentions
1. That bishops and theologians and all who participate in handing on the faith may continue untiringly with their task.
2. That we may share the light of faith and knowledge, according to our abilities and opportunities, with those who are handicapped by doubts and fears.
3. That we may not hinder others from having a perfect view of Christ and his Church through bad example or the lack of justice and charity in our lives.

4. That those who have recently been enlightened by Christ in baptism may shed that light on all in the household of the faith and bring its health-giving rays wherever they go.

Concluding Prayer
Graciously help us, Lord, in our need and hear our every prayer, that we may devote ourselves to serving you in freedom and in gladness. Through Christ our Lord.

TENTH WEEK OF THE YEAR: WEDNESDAY

Introduction
God has revealed his intentions for us and shown us the path we should take. Let us pray that his will may be done on earth as in heaven.

Intentions
1. Let us recognize the providential hand of God throughout human history and in our own lives, drawing good from evil and leading all things unto good.
2. Let us acknowledge our Lord Jesus Christ as fulfilling the meaning of all events and promises of the past, and bringing them all to completion.
3. Let us search for the will of God, and obey his commands every day.
4. Let the example of our lives and our attitudes teach others to respect the laws of mankind's Creator and Father.
5. Let us pray for the dead: that God may take them into his love for ever.

Concluding Prayer
Graciously help us, Lord, in our need and hear our every prayer, that we may devote ourselves to serving you in freedom and in gladness. Through Christ our Lord.

TENTH WEEK OF THE YEAR: THURSDAY

Introduction
The light of God which shines in the face of Christ Jesus is

meant to shine also in the features of Christians. Let us pray that we may truly live his Gospel.

Intentions
1. That love and kindness may truly govern our actions so that we may strive to treat others with the gentleness of Christ.
2. That while speaking the truth in charity we may work for understanding and reconciliation with all who differ from us.
3. That the seed of God's word may take root in our hearts and the Good News be manifested to all humankind.
4. That each Mass we offer may bring us closer in charity to those whose lives we touch.

Concluding Prayer
Graciously help us, Lord, in our need and hear our every prayer, that we may devote ourselves to serving you in freedom and in gladness. Through Christ our Lord.

TENTH WEEK OF THE YEAR: FRIDAY

Introduction
God saves us in his Son through the Gospel. Let us make intercessory prayer that all may recognize the dignity of the human calling.

Intentions
1. That the virtues of purity and chastity may be respected and upheld in our society.
2. That people preparing for marriage may give the fullest attention to their Christian responsibilities in this life-long commitment.
3. That those who instruct others in the way of Christian love and marriage, and who help unhappy couples and families, may do so untiringly and meet with success.
4. That lives strengthened by the Gospels, and nourished by Sacraments and prayer may curb the evils of lust and unfaithfulness.
5. That we may not refuse to carry our cross after Christ who suffered that we might recover the dignity of God's children.

Concluding Prayer
Graciously help us, Lord, in our need and hear our every prayer, that we may devote ourselves to serving you in freedom and in gladness. Through Christ our Lord.

TENTH WEEK OF THE YEAR: SATURDAY

Introduction
The Lord is compassion and love, and listens to our prayers. Let us approach him with confidence.

Intentions
1. That we may reverence God's holy name, and lead quiet and holy lives.
2. That all members of the Church may cultivate fidelity and trustworthiness, and edify others by the truth of their lives.
3. That the Church's leaders and teachers and all the faithful pay close attention to the demands of the Gospel, and ever strive to become its true disciples.
4. That we may help our people to be positive and hopeful, and to uphold Christian values by their words and deeds.

Concluding Prayer
Graciously help us, Lord, in our need and hear our every prayer, that we may devote ourselves to serving you in freedom and in gladness. Through Christ our Lord.

WEEK 11

ELEVENTH WEEK OF THE YEAR: MONDAY

Introduction
The Father delights to hear the prayers of his children. Let us now turn to him with utter confidence and present our petitions to him.

Intentions
1. For the whole Church: that she might be a sign to the whole

world that mutual love is the only way to lasting peace.
2. For the leaders of the nations: that they might pursue peaceful solutions to world problems.
3. For those who are persecuted because of their faith in Christ: that they might know his peace in their hearts.
4. For the little ones of this world: that they might know the power of God in their lives.
5. For peace and harmony in our land.

Concluding Prayer
Father of mercies, you always hear your children when they call to you. Grant all the prayers we have made to you if they be according to your will. We ask this through Christ our Lord.

ELEVENTH WEEK OF THE YEAR: TUESDAY

Introduction
We have been commanded to love all men and women, even our enemies, so that they shall become perfect just as our heavenly Father is perfect. Let us now pray to the Lord for our needs and for the needs of mankind.

Intentions
1. Let us pray for the Church throughout the world: that she might be a convincing sign of the power of God's love.
2. Let us pray for all the bishops of the Church: that they might exercise their authority in loving service of their people.
3. Let us pray for those nations which are involved in war: that they might quickly be reconciled with their enemies.
4. Let us pray for those who profit from wars: that the Lord may open their hearts to receive his love.
5. Let us pray for ourselves: that our love may extend to all those we meet today.

Concluding Prayer
Father of mercies, you always hear your children when they call to you. Grant all the prayers we have made to you if they be according to your will. We ask this through Christ our Lord.

ELEVENTH WEEK OF THE YEAR: WEDNESDAY

Introduction
God sees all that we do in secret. Let us open our hearts to him in prayer, and present our petitions before the throne of grace.

Intentions
1. We pray for the Church: that she might act as a leaven in society, raising up all things to the Father through his Son.
2. We pray for all Christians: that their love for one another may be from a pure heart and not be tainted by hypocrisy.
3. We pray for the governments of this world: that their deliberations might be guided by a spirit of truth for the benefit of all mankind.
4. We pray for those who are persecuted because they refuse to compromise with the truth: that the Lord might give them strength in their trials.
4. We pray that we might not live according to the opinions of others but in conformity with the will of God.

Concluding Prayer
Father of mercies, you always hear your children when they call to you. Grant all the prayers we have made to you if they be according to your will. We ask this through Christ our Lord.

ELEVENTH WEEK OF THE YEAR: THURSDAY

Introduction
The Father is merciful to those who are merciful. We now pray to him, asking that he shower his mercy on all mankind.

Intentions
1. For the holy Church of God: that she might always seek to do the will of our Father in heaven.
2. For all Christians: that they might always pray as Jesus taught, glorifying the name of God by the way they live their lives.

3. For all the nations of the world: that their policies might be governed be concern for the weak and the poor.
4. For all those who are hungry: that they might receive their daily bread this day.
5. For ourselves: that we might forgive those who have wronged us, so that we might receive the forgiveness of God.

Concluding Prayer
Father of mercies, you always hear your children when they call to you. Grant all the prayers we have made to you if they be according to your will. We ask this through Christ our Lord.

ELEVENTH WEEK OF THE YEAR: FRIDAY

Introduction
All power comes from the Lord and without him we can do nothing. Let us now present to him our needs and the needs of the Church and the world.

Intentions
1. We pray to the Lord for the whole Church: that she may always seek her treasure not on this earth but in heaven with God.
2. We pray to the Lord for the wealthy nations of the world: that they might share their wealth with their poorer neighbours.
3. We pray to the Lord for those who live in the darkness of sin: that the light of Christ may shine in their hearts.
4. We pray to the Lord that the good things of this world may be appreciated for what they are, and not be made the ultimate value of existence.
5. We pray to the Lord that we might seek him above all things and be distracted by nothing from our final destiny.

Concluding Prayer
Father of mercies, you always hear your children when they call to you. Grant all the prayers we have made to you if they be according to your will. We ask this through Christ our Lord.

ELEVENTH WEEK OF THE YEAR: SATURDAY

Introduction
The Lord cares for his people. Let us now in confidence present our petitions to him.

Intentions
1. Let us pray for the whole community of the Church: that it may always seek to serve the Lord and not its own worldly interest.
2. Let us pray for all Christians: that they might seek the kingdom of God before any reality.
3. Let us pray for those who are rich in this world's goods: that they might understand that in God alone is lasting wealth.
4. Let us pray for those who have very little: that the Lord might provide them with what is necessary for their lives.
5. Let us pray for ourselves: that we might put the Gospel into practice today.

Concluding Prayer
Father of mercies, you always hear your children when they call to you. Grant all the prayers we have made to you if they be according to your will. We ask this through Christ our Lord.

WEEK 12

TWELFTH WEEK OF THE YEAR: MONDAY

Introduction
Jesus taught us to be sincere with God our Father and with one another. Let us now pray to the Father for ourselves and for all mankind in sincerity of heart.

Intentions
1. For the Church: that she might be the leaven of love and forgiveness in the world.
2. For those who have authority in the Church: that they

might sincerely seek to serve all the people under them and not be corrupted by their power.

3. For those who have been entrusted with worldly authority: that they might use it to further peace and harmony in the world.

4. For those who are despised for any reason: that they might come to know God's love for them.

5. For ourselves: that we may experience the forgiveness of God in our lives.

Concluding Prayer
Father, we believe in you. Make us always attentive to the voice of your Spirit in our hearts. Grant all the prayers we have made with faith in the name of Jesus Christ your Son and our Lord.

TWELFTH WEEK OF THE YEAR: TUESDAY

Introduction
God has always taken care of his people in their need. Let us now come before him, trusting in his love and mercy, to present our petition to him.

Intentions
1. We pray to the Lord for all Christians: that they might be filled with the love of God so as to love other people with the same love.

2. We pray to the Lord for the pope and all the bishops of the Church: that they might exercise their function of leadership in a spirit of fraternal charity.

3. We pray to the Lord for the unity of Christians: that we all might enter the one fold and follow the one shepherd.

4. We pray to the Lord for non-Christians: that he might guide them into a deep love and respect for all mankind.

5. We pray to the Lord for ourselves: that our faith and love may make us co-workers with him in establishing his kingdom on earth.

Concluding Prayer
Father, we believe in you. Make us always attentive to the

voice of your Spirit in our hearts. Grant all the prayers we
have made with faith in the name of Jesus Christ your Son
and our Lord.

TWELFTH WEEK OF THE YEAR: WEDNESDAY

Introduction
God has made an everlasting bond of friendship with mankind. Let us now go before him to present our needs and the
needs of all our brothers and sisters.

Intentions
1. We pray for the whole Church: that she might attract men
and women to Christ by the good fruits which she bears.
2. We pray for all who call themselves Christians: that their
lives might be guided by a sincere love of God and of other
people.
3. We pray for those who make laws and those who execute
them: that they might seek justice for all.
4. We pray for young people: that they might not be led
astray by false guides but that they might listen to the voice
of God in their hearts.
5. We pray for the mentally handicapped: that they might
elicit true love and concern from those who live around them.

Concluding Prayer
Father, we believe in you. Make us always attentive to the
voice of your Spirit in our hearts. Grant all the prayers we
have made with faith in the name of Jesus Christ your Son
and our Lord.

TWELFTH WEEK OF THE YEAR: THURSDAY

Introduction
We build our house on the rock which is the word of God and
so we come before the Lord now humbly to present our
petitions to him.

Intentions
1. We pray that the leaders of the Church might always seek to make their decisions based on the will of God for the good of the whole flock.
2. We pray that all the peoples of the world might be allowed to develop in a spirit of freedom and mutual aid.
3. We pray that those who feel lonely and abandoned may find the courage to go out of themselves in love of God and of their neighbour.
4. We pray that those who have been abandoned by society may experience the love of God through the ministry of the Church and of individual Christians.
5. We pray that the sick may know that they are not alone in their sufferings but that they have a share in the passion of Christ.

Concluding Prayer
Father, we believe in you. Make us always attentive to the voice of your Spirit in our hearts. Grant all the prayers we have made with faith in the name of Jesus Christ your Son and our Lord.

TWELFTH WEEK OF THE YEAR: FRIDAY

Introduction
To God all things are possible. Let us now approach him in utter confidence, and present our petitions to him.

Intentions
1. Let us pray that the Church might reach out to all the outcasts of society with the healing love of Christ.
2. Let us pray that those who have political power may use it justly and wisely on behalf of all the people.
3. Let us pray that all people may be valued not for what they have or do but for what they are.
4. Let us pray that doctors and nurses may be motivated always by a true concern for their patients.
5. Let us pray that we may see the face of Christ in all those we meet today.

Concluding Prayer
Father, we believe in you. Make us always attentive to the
voice of your Spirit in our hearts. Grant all the prayers we
have made with faith in the name of Jesus Christ your Son
and our Lord.

TWELFTH WEEK OF THE YEAR: SATURDAY

Introduction
Jesus took upon himself all our infirmities. By his wounds we
are healed. Let us now present our prayers to the Father in
Jesus' name, certain that we will be heard.

Intentions
1. For the universal Church: that it may proclaim the Gospel
to all peoples without fear or self-interest.
2. For vocations to the priesthood and the religious life: that
many young men and women will respond with faith to the
call of God.
3. For the sick who are deprived of care because they lack
money: that the Lord will send someone to alleviate their
distress.
4. For the progress of all peoples towards truly caring
societies.
5. For the dying: that they might know the peace of Christ
in their hearts.

Concluding Prayer
Father, we believe in you. Make us always attentive to the
voice of your Spirit in our hearts. Grant all the prayers we
have made with faith in the name of Jesus Christ your Son
and our Lord.

WEEK 13

THIRTEENTH WEEK OF THE YEAR: MONDAY

Introduction
The Lord is a merciful judge who always hears our prayers.

In that spirit, let us pray.

Intentions
1. That we may remember that, when men look for God's love and mercy, they expect believers to show signs of his presence.
2. Let us remember all those who feel separated from the love of God and feel that life has no meaning.
3. Let us pray for all those held in prison awaiting trial: that they may know the mercy of God in their lives.
4. Let us pray for all those who are asked to execute justice in our society: that they may always be aware that our heavenly Father is the source of all justice.

Concluding Prayer
Father in heaven, the light of Jesus has scattered the darkness of hatred and sin. Called to that light, we ask for your guidance. Form our lives in your truth, our hearts in your love. This we ask through Christ our Lord.

THIRTEENTH WEEK OF THE YEAR: TUESDAY

Introduction
The Lord God, Creator of heaven and earth, is also our Father who cherishes and protects us amid the pressures and problems of life.

Intentions
1. Let us pray for the Church: that it will, in its members, always be a true beacon of salvation.
2. May we always realize that our true happiness lies in valuing those around us as gifts from God.
3. Let us pray and work to overcome those ways of life that enslave man or lessen his dignity.
4. May men and women always respect each other and through the guidance of the Spirit may narrow sexist attitudes become a thing of the past.
5. Let us pray for those who have died recently as victims of exploitation.

Concluding Prayer
Father in heaven, the light of Jesus has scattered the darkness of hatred and sin. Called to that light, we ask for your guidance. Form our lives in your truth, our hearts in your love. This we ask through Christ our Lord.

THIRTEENTH WEEK OF THE YEAR: WEDNESDAY

Introduction
We must serve the Lord with an undivided heart, and our prayer must give meaning to our life. In that spirit we turn to God, and pray.

Intentions
1. That our community may always live the Gospel with all its heart, mind and strength.
2. That our faith will always be shown in loving care for those in need.
3. That we will always have the courage to challenge injustice.
4. That we will always seek reconciliation before we come to the altar.
5. That we may always realize that our worship must come from a sincere heart.

Concluding Prayer
Father in heaven, the light of Jesus has scattered the darkness of hatred and sin. Called to that light, we ask for your guidance. Form our lives in your truth, our hearts in your love. This we ask through Christ our Lord.

THIRTEENTH WEEK OF THE YEAR: THURSDAY

Introduction
The Lord often asks us to walk in ways that can seem to demand too much of us.

Intentions
1. Let us pray that we may be surprised by his power and strength.

2. Let us pray for those who feel bewildered by the pressures of our society.

3. Let us pray for parents who find they can no longer make contact with their growing children.

4. Let us pray for parents whose children feel the call to serve God as priests and religious: that they may all come to understand what is being asked of them.

5. Let us pray for the Church: that it may grow in effectiveness in building up God's kingdom in the hearts of mankind.

Concluding Prayer
Father in heaven, the light of Jesus has scattered the darkness of hatred and sin. Called to that light, we ask for your guidance. Form our lives in your truth, our hearts in your love. This we ask through Christ our Lord.

THIRTEENTH WEEK OF THE YEAR: FRIDAY

Introduction
God's word challenges us to change our society. As we listen to this word, let us know that with God's grace all things are possible.

Intentions
1. Let us pray that our leaders, inspired by the gospel, will work for a just world order.

2. That those who are oppressors will be healed.

3. That people living on the margin of life will be given hope by the actions of those who hear God's word and act on it.

4. That those who have turned to violence out of frustration will leave aside the gun.

5. That we will not rest until we have brought the peace of Christ to our neighbours.

Concluding Prayer
Father in heaven, the light of Jesus has scattered the darkness of hatred and sin. Called to that light, we ask for your guidance. Form our lives in your truth, our hearts in your love. This we ask through Christ our Lord.

THIRTEENTH WEEK OF THE YEAR: SATURDAY

Introduction
As human beings we make our plans and projections, but let us be surprised by God's power of renewing all things.

Intentions
1. That we may commend to the Lord whatever projects of our own we hold dear.
2. That we ask the Lord to be the inspiration of our country.
3. That scientists may realize that their discoveries are the revealing of God's marvellous creative plan.
4. That we accept in our inmost being that our life finds its full meaning in the resurrection.
5. That we trust that the departed find in the Lord their total fulfilment.

Concluding Prayer
Father in heaven, the light of Jesus has scattered the darkness of hatred and sin. Called to that light, we ask for your guidance. Form our lives in your truth, our hearts in your love. This we ask through Christ our Lord.

WEEK 14

FOURTEENTH WEEK OF THE YEAR: MONDAY

Introduction
The Lord calls us to the closest possible loving friendship. Because we are so intimate we can share our needs and hopes with him.

Intentions
1. That we may see time for prayer as a priority.
2. That, because we know we are loved by God, we may be more open with our friends.
3. That we may freely and joyfully proclaim to others the goodness of God.

4. That we ask the Lord to receive into his love those who have died recently, especially friends and family.

Concluding Prayer
Father, make us one with you always, so that our joy may be holy, and our love may give life. Through Christ our Lord.

FOURTEENTH WEEK OF THE YEAR: TUESDAY

Introduction
We often want to turn God into something less than he is. Let us accept his power and know it is best expressed in merciful love.

Intentions
1. We pray that we may never reduce God's message to some human wisdom.
2. We pray that mankind may open its eyes to its need for God's presence in our world.
3. We pray for those wrestling with doubts: that they may find peace.
4. We pray that, from among us, men and women may answer God's call to be his ministers.

Concluding Prayer
Father, make us one with you always, so that our joy may be holy, and our love may give life. Through Christ our Lord.

FOURTEENTH WEEK OF THE YEAR: WEDNESDAY

Introduction
Where our treasure is so will be our heart. Let us pray that we can use the good things around us to give us freedom in working for the kingdom.

Intentions
1. That our possessions do not become a hindrance to good relations with God and our neighbour.
2. That we realize that we must give not just of our goods but

of our very selves.
3. That our local Church be not inward looking or complacent.
4. That we have the courage to make radical changes in our lives.
5. That our lives may always be a showing of God's loving kindness.

Concluding Prayer
Father, make us one with you always, so that our joy may be holy, and our love may give life. Through Christ our Lord.

FOURTEENTH WEEK OF THE YEAR: THURSDAY

Introduction
The power of forgiving is the sign of God's presence among men. Jesus, the fulfilment of all the Old Testament figures, lived healing and forgiveness; and in that spirit let us pray.

Intentions
1. That nations may learn to walk away from fear into ways of understanding.
2. That our local communities may overcome the sickness of prejudice.
3. That Christians may acknowledge past failings and all work together to build the kingdom.
4. That families may be healed of tensions and misunderstanding.
5. That the sick and dying may be shown how much Christ loves them.

Concluding Prayer
Father, make us one with you always, so that our joy may be holy, and our love may give life. Through Christ our Lord.

FOURTEENTH WEEK OF THE YEAR: FRIDAY

Introduction
The Lord is patient with us as we go our own way and often

forget him; but let us now pray that we may stay in his way and his love.

Intentions
1. Let us pray for those who have never had the Gospel proclaimed to them.
2. Let us pray for our brothers and sisters who feel cut off from the Christian community.
3. Let us pray for those who are so caught up in life's business that they have forgotten about their loving Father.
4. Let us pray for those who have been enslaved by ideologies.

Concluding Prayer
Father, make us one with you always, so that our joy may be holy, and our love may give life. Through Christ our Lord.

FOURTEENTH WEEK OF THE YEAR: SATURDAY

Introduction
God is light and truth. Let us pray that we may continue Christ's work of bringing light and truth to our world.

Intentions
1. Let us pray that the light of God's goodness may overcome the sins of our society.
2. That we may know that God will empower us to proclaim his message.
3. That we may be served by ministers who, knowing God's word, proclaim it faithfully to the people.
4. That Christians in the media use their gifts to glorify God among men.
5. That we may never disown the Lord in the presence of men.

Concluding Prayer
Father, make us one with you always, so that our joy may be holy, and our love may give life. Through Christ our Lord.

WEEK 15

FIFTEENTH WEEK OF THE YEAR: MONDAY

Introduction
Jesus did not promise an easy life to his followers, and so we pray.

Intentions
1. For the holy Church of God: that it may be fearless and courageous in preaching the Gospel.
2. For our civil leaders: that they may always fight for social justice even at the risk of losing popularity.
3. For those who suffer rejection because of their belief in Jesus Christ.
4. For families who are divided for any reason: that they may seek the way of reconciliation.
5. For all who have died: that they may enjoy the peace that only God can give.

Concluding Prayer
God, our Father, we ask you to listen to these and all our prayers which we make with confidence through Christ our Lord.

FIFTEENTH WEEK OF THE YEAR: TUESDAY

Introduction
Remembering how Jesus reproached those who refuse to repent, let us pray.

Intentions
1. For Christians everywhere: that they may constantly remember the need for repentance and forgiveness.
2. For countries at war: that they may discover repentance as the pathway to peace.
3. For those who have rejected the Gospel message: that they may come to discover the unsearchable riches of Jesus Christ.

4. For those who are weighed down by feelings of guilt: that they may be refreshed by the Sacrament of Reconciliation.
5. For all who have died, especially our own relatives and friends: that God may grant them forgiveness for their sins.

Concluding Prayer
God, our Father, we ask you to listen to these and all our prayers which we make with confidence through Christ our Lord.

FIFTEENTH WEEK OF THE YEAR: WEDNESDAY

Introduction
Jesus rejoiced that children could understand his message, and so we pray.

Intentions
1. That the Church may always strive to hand on the light of faith to the young.
2. That those in government may make every effort to cherish all the children of our country.
3. That children who are suffering from hunger and disease may know our care and God's love.
4. That we may share the hope of the Gospel with our young people who are discouraged by unemployment.
5. That our children who have died prematurely may enjoy the eternal springtime of heaven.

Concluding Prayer
God, our Father, we ask you to listen to these and all our prayers which we make with confidence through Christ our Lord.

FIFTEENTH WEEK OF THE YEAR: THURSDAY

Introduction
Jesus offers rest to all who labour and are overburdened, and so we pray.

Intentions
1. For those who hold office in the Church: that they may experience God's support and our loyalty.
2. For those in civil authority: that their labour may bear abundant fruit.
3. For those overburdened by the demands of everyday life: that we may help them to cope.
4. Fro those crushed by sin: that they may know the joy of God's forgiveness.
5. For those whose work is difficult: that they may know our appreciation and understanding.

Concluding Prayer
God, our Father, we ask you to listen to these and all our prayers which we make with confidence through Christ our Lord.

FIFTEENTH WEEK OF THE YEAR: FRIDAY

Introduction
Jesus recognised that kindness is more important than the ritual observance of the law, and so we pray.

Intentions
1. That the Church may always have compassion for those in need.
2. That our courts may be places of justice and mercy.
3. That those unjustly oppressed by law may experience liberation.
4. That we may never forget our obligations towards the hungry.
5. That we may be slow to judge and condemn other people.
6. That our discipleship of Jesus may never be confined to external ritual.

Concluding Prayer
God, our Father, we ask you to listen to these and all our prayers which we make in confidence through Christ our Lord.

FIFTEENTH WEEK OF THE YEAR: SATURDAY

Introduction
Jesus did not break the crushed reed nor put out the
smouldering wick and so we pray.

Intentions
1. That the Church may encourage and help all those whose
faith is weak.
2. That the weak and defenceless members of our society may
receive the assistance and support they need from the state.
3. That we may seek out and cherish those in our neigh-
bourhood who are lonely and depressed.
4. That the sick. and the old may be treated with gentleness
and compasson.
5. That God may welcome into his kingdom all who have suffered in the name of Jesus Christ.

Concluding Prayer
God, our Father, we ask you to listen to these and all our
prayers which we make in confidence through Christ our
Lord.

WEEK 16

SIXTEENTH WEEK OF THE YEAR: MONDAY

Introduction
Jesus reminded his listeners that God was to be seen in the
ordinary things of every day, and so we pray.

Intentions
1. For the Church: that it may spread the Gospel by doing
ordinary things extraordinarily well.
2. For the salvation of the world: that people everywhere may
discover the divinity of Christ by knowing his humanity.
3. For those who do not believe in God: that the beauty of
creation may help them to find him.
4. For those who are sick and dying: that they may find

meaning in their suffering.
5. For all who have died, especially those we love: that they may share in the resurrection of Jesus.

Concluding Prayer
God, our Father, we believe that no prayer goes unanswered, and so we ask you to listen to these our prayers which we make through Christ our Lord.

SIXTEENTH WEEK OF THE YEAR: TUESDAY

Introduction
Jesus assures us that all who do the will of his Father in heaven are his sisters and brothers, and so we pray.

Intentions
1. That Christians everywhere may grow in fellowship as they strive to discern and carry out God's will.
2. For all who hold public office: that they may be attentive to God's will and the needs of people.
3. For those who are blind to God's will through prejudice or ignorance: that the light of the Gospel may help them to see more clearly.
4. For those who have disobeyed God's will: that they may recognize their sin, and seek forgiveness.
5. For our deceased relatives and friends: that they may be at peace in the family of heaven.

Concluding Prayer
God, our Father, we believe that no prayer goes unanswered, and so we ask you to listen to these our prayers which we make through Christ our Lord.

SIXTEENTH WEEK OF THE YEAR: WEDNESDAY

Introduction
Jesus compared the preaching of the Gospel with the sower going out to sow the seed, and so we pray.

1. That disciples of Jesus everywhere may be attentive to the word of God in the Scriptures.
2. That the marginalised in our society may hear and be comforted by the good news of the Gospel.
3. That those whose hearts are closed to God may discover the joy of knowing Jesus Christ.
4. That those who are preoccupied with possessions and pleasure may find true happiness in their discipleship of Jesus.
5. That those who have tried to live their lives in accordance with the Gospel may be rewarded a hundredfold.

Concluding Prayer
God, our Father, we believe that no prayer goes unanswered, and so we ask you to listen to these our prayers which we make through Christ our Lord.

SIXTEENTH WEEK OF THE YEAR: THURSDAY

Introduction
Jesus told his listeners that they were fortunate to have seen and heard him, and so we pray.

Intentions
1. That the Church may constantly give thanks to God for the gift of Jesus Christ by worthily celebrating the liturgy.
2. For those in our society who are deprived and disadvantaged: that we may never forget our obligations towards them.
3. For people who are blinded by sinfulness and selfishness: that they may have their eyes opened to see themselves as they really are.
4. For those who turn a deaf ear to the Gospel: that they may come to hear the word of God.
5. For people who have not heard of Jesus Christ: that through the Church's missionary activity they may come to know him.

Concluding Prayer
God, our Father, we believe that no prayer goes unanswered, and so we ask you to listen to these our prayers which we make through Christ our Lord.

SIXTEENTH WEEK OF THE YEAR: FRIDAY

Introduction
Jesus spoke of the importance of the word of God, and so we pray.

Intentions
1. For the Church: that it may faithfully preach and teach the word of God.
2. For those who devote their lives to the study of Scripture: that their labours may bear fruit.
3. For those who preach the Gospel to people who do not want to hear it: that they may not lose heart.
4. For missionaries, especially those who are persecuted: that they may draw inspiration and courage from the word of God.
5. For all who have died having lived their lives in fidelity to the Gospel: that their efforts may be rewarded in eternity.

Concluding Prayer
God, our Father, we believe that no prayer goes unanswered, and so we ask you to listen to these our prayers which we make through Christ our Lord.

SIXTEENTH WEEK OF THE YEAR: SATURDAY

Introduction
Jesus taught us to love our enemies, and to be patient with them even when they injure us, and so we pray.

Intentions
1. That the Church may treat its enemies with gentleness and compassion.
2. That countries who are at war with each other may seek the way of peace together.
3. That divided communities may seek to replace bitterness and prejudice with forgiveness and reconciliation.
4. For those who suffer because they have offended God: that they may be comforted by making their peace with him.

5. For all who have died: that they may experience God's mercy and forgiveness.

Concluding Prayer
God, our Father, we believe that no prayer goes unanswered, and so we ask you to listen to these our prayers which we make through Christ our Lord.

WEEK 17

SEVENTEENTH WEEK OF THE YEAR: MONDAY

Introduction
In its final stages the reign of God will be like a mighty tree. We are part of this growth, and so we pray.

Intentions
1. For the insignificant beginnings of faith invisible to the human eye, from which God builds his mighty kingdom.
2. For all God's people: that we will be able to welcome newcomers to the Church and make them feel at home.
3. For those who listen to the word of God: that they may understand the things which have been hidden since the foundation of the world.
4. For the tiny seeds of our new enterprises in the parish: that by God's power they may grow to greatness.
5. *Year 1:* For God's weak and headstrong people especially when we waste our time with idols that we have made with our own hands.
5. *Year 2:* For those who wish to cling to the Lord: that their determination may not be spoiled.

Concluding Prayer
All powerful Father, giver of breath and bread, lead us to seek the pearl of great price the everlasting treasure of Christ, your Son, who lives and reigns forever and ever.

SEVENTEENTH WEEK OF THE YEAR: TUESDAY

Introduction
At the end of the world, the good will be rewarded and the
bad will be punished. We pray that we may persevere in a life
of integrity.

Intentions
1. The field of our lives is sown with good and evil desires;
may God give us patience in our daily struggle with wrong-
doing.
2. Our time is short and eternity is long; may we live by the
Gospel that we may not be punished at the end.
3. Good and evil grow side by side, for God is patient; may
we not judge our brothers and sisters rashly, but pray that
they will turn their hearts to him.
4. Our ears have been opened by God's word; may we be
faithful to what we have heard so as to shine like the sun in
the kingdom of the Father.
5. *Year 1:* The Lord spoke to Moses face to face as a man
speaks with his friend; may we enjoy the same privilege in
our daily prayer.
5. *Year 2:* In many places peoples' lives are being smashed by
war; in their devastation may they turn to the Lord, who is
their only hope.

Concluding Prayer
All powerful Father, giver of breath and bread, lead us to
seek the pearl of great price the everlasting treasure of Christ,
your Son, who lives and reigns forever and ever.

SEVENTEENTH WEEK OF THE YEAR: WEDNESDAY

Introduction
To know the Lord Jesus is to have riches beyond the price of
pearls. With joy we pray.

Intentions
1. That we will set our hearts on finding real treasure in loving and serving the Lord.

2. That we will find the pearl of great price and be filled with joy and gladness.
3. That the hardships we endure will be worth the great joy of discovering what is of lasting value.
4. That those men and women who have been called to sell all they have and give it to the poor, will be a sign for us that the real treasure is found only in the kingdom of God.
5. *Year 1:* That, as we search for God, we will become aware that he protects and saves us.
5. *Year 2:* That, like the prophet Jeremiah, we will delight in hearing God's word.

Concluding Prayer
All powerful Father, giver of breath and bread, lead us to seek the pearl of great price the everlasting treasure of Christ, your Son, who lives and reigns forever and ever.

SEVENTEENTH WEEK OF THE YEAR: THURSDAY

Introduction
We are all little fishes in God's net; may he sustain whatever is good in us.

Intentions
1. God's net drags in a great variety of people; may we be sensitive to those of different culture and background.
2. When the time comes for sorting out good from bad, may the Lord show us his mercy and loving kindness.
3. We are God's people, a Church of sinners; may we turn again and follow the way of the Lord.
4. Like the Christian scribes may we preserve what is good from our tradition and seek fresh ways of dealing with new problems.
5. *Year 1:* Like the people of Israel in the desert, may we recognise that the glorious Lord shares our journey.
5. *Year 2:* The Lord is the potter, we are the clay. May we recognise his strong and capable hands in the shaping of our lives.

Concluding Prayer
All powerful Father, giver of breath and bread, lead us to

seek the pearl of great price the everlasting treasure of Christ, your Son, who lives and reigns forever and ever.

SEVENTEENTH WEEK OF THE YEAR: FRIDAY

Introduction
We are brothers and sisters of the Lord, members of his family. We pray to the Father.

Intentions
1. That we will not be blinded by unbelief and be guilty of rejecting the Lord Jesus.
2. That we will not be rash in our judgement of our fellow Christians, simply because we think we know all about them.
3. That we will avoid talking scandal because our Church is human.
4. That we will encourage and affirm each other in whatever we attempt to do.
5. *Year 1:* That each time we celebrate the Eucharist, we will bring our thanks to God for his goodness.
5. *Year 2:* That we will be open and humble even when it comes to unpleasant truths we would rather not hear.

Concluding Prayer
All powerful Father, giver of breath and bread, lead us to seek the pearl of great price the everlasting treasure of Christ, your Son, who lives and reigns forever and ever.

SEVENTEENTH WEEK OF THE YEAR: SATURDAY

Introduction
John the Baptist was the herald of the new covenant. We honour this great man and pray with him to our Father.

Intentions
1. John the Baptist was outspoken for God. We pray that we will be brave enough to speak the truth, even when it is dangerous for us to do so.
2. We thank God for all men and women who have witnessed

to Christ by their death. Even today may their blood be the seed of the Church.
3. John was put into prison because he spoke the truth. We pray for all prisoners of conscience who have lost their freedom because of what they believe.
4. Just as John the Baptist pointed the way to Jesus, may our lives give a glimpse of the Lord to those who do not believe.
5. *Year 1:* We ask that we will be given strength never to wrong our neighbour.
5. *Year 2:* May we have the courage to act with integrity even if we risk the displeasure of those in power.

Concluding Prayer
All powerful Father, giver of breath and bread, lead us to seek the pearl of great price the everlasting treasure of Christ, your Son, who lives and reigns forever and ever.

WEEK 18

EIGHTEENTH WEEK OF THE YEAR: MONDAY

Introduction
Like the people in the gospel, we also gather round the Lord and are hungry. Knowing his kindness we pray.

Intentions
1. That we will be happy to come together and be fed by the Lord himself.
2. That the priests, who are told to feed the crowd themselves, will be able to break the bread of the word for the people as well as the Eucharist.
3. That the sick and the suffering will attract the pity of the Lord so that he will heal us.
4. That artists, writers and musicians will help us by their creative work to catch sight of the hand of God.
5. *Year 1:* That the anger of God will not flare out against us even though we are greedy, stubborn and ungrateful.
5. *Year 2:* That those among us who speak for God will tell us what he is saying, rather than the easy speeches we want to hear.

Concluding Prayer
In your love, Father, you have given us bread and work. You are the giver of all things. We trust you will know our deepest needs and hear our prayer. Through Christ our Lord.

EIGHTEENTH WEEK OF THE YEAR: TUESDAY

Introduction
The risen Lord comes to take away our fear and build up our faith.

Intentions
1. In the early morning Jesus went into the hills by himself to pray. May we take time to share the day with God.
2. Peter was the leader of the apostles. He needed strong faith to cope with his special responsibility. For the same reason, we pray for Pope N . . ., and our Bishop N . . .
3. The disciples thought that they were seeing a ghost, yet Jesus calmed their fears as well as the sea.
4. In his day the people would touch the hem of the Lord's cloak. We pray that we may be the healing consoling loving, generous body of Christ in the world today.
5. *Year 1:* Sometimes we are full of pride and self-importance. May the Lord have mercy and not deal with us as our sins deserve.
5. *Year 2:* Our sins have made us weak and bowed down. Only God finds us lovable now. We ask him to bring us close to him and heal us.

Concluding Prayer
In your love, Father, you have given us bread and work. You are the giver of all things. We trust you will know our deepest needs and hear our prayer. Through Christ our Lord.

EIGHTEENTH WEEK OF THE YEAR: WEDNESDAY

Introduction
There is something very attractive in the Canaanite woman's persistence, even when she is discouraged. Following her, we pray.

Intentions

1. The persistent woman would not take No for an answer. Even when we are discouraged, may we never give up praying.
2. Her faith and wit made the Lord grant her request. We pray for all parents who worry over sick children.
3. The apostles preached to gentiles as well as Jews. We pray for all men and women far from home who bring the good news to others.
4. Wherever he found it, Jesus did not refuse faith. May he give us great faith and hear our prayers.
5. *Year 1:* People do not change. We too are grumblers. We pray for patience when our plans go wrong and we meet opposition.
5. *Year 2:* In the midst of destruction and war, there is hope because God loves us. We pray that we will be his people in all that we say and do.

Concluding Prayer

In your love, Father, you have given us bread and work. You are the giver of all things. We trust you will know our deepest needs and hear our prayer. Through Christ our Lord.

EIGHTEENTH WEEK OF THE YEAR: THURSDAY

Introduction

The Father says "I have loved you with an everlasting love. I am constant in my affection for you". We make our prayers with confidence.

Intentions

1. The Holy Spirit has shown us Jesus and given growth to our faith. We pray that we will be seen to be happy in our belief.
2. The faith of Peter and the apostles is the bedrock of the Church. We pray for the leaders and pastors, that their faith may not fail and that they may encourage their brothers and sisters.
3. The power of the keys means leadership and service. We

pray for the bishops of our country, especially N . . . in his diocese.

4. Peter believed Jesus to be the Messiah, but could not accept that he must suffer. When we question the Lord may we realise that the way we are thinking is not God's way, but man's.

5. *Year 1:* Like the Israelites. we often think that we know better than God. May he take away our pride and show us his holiness.

5. *Year 2:* The law of love is written on our hearts, not written in a book. May the Lord forgive us when we spoil love.

Concluding Prayer
In your love, Father, you have given us bread and work. You are the giver of all things. We trust you will know our deepest needs and hear our prayer. Through Christ our Lord.

EIGHTEENTH WEEK OF THE YEAR: FRIDAY

Introduction
The lesson in today's Gospel is hard and will take a lifetime to learn. We ask for strength.

Intentions
1. God our Father gives us value; in ourselves we are empty. May we follow him faithfully today.
2. We pray for men and women who, for whatever reason, are obliged to take the strain of bringing up children on their own.
3. A soft and easy life is an illusion; we live only when we know God. Grant that we do not reach out for the whole world and let go life itself.
4. Like athletes in training, may we practise in small things so as to be able to take up the heavy cross when it comes.
5. God is the only Lord, he and no other. May we keep his commandments and so prosper and live.
6. We pray for the little countries where the great powers fight their wars, that they may no longer hear the sound of

gunfire and explosions and sobbing, but may be restored with peace.

Concluding Prayer
In your love, Father, you have given us bread and work. You are the giver of all things. We trust you will know our deepest needs and hear our prayer. Through Christ our Lord.

EIGHTEENTH WEEK OF THE YEAR: SATURDAY

Introduction
In the name of the Lord our God we come together and offer him our common prayer.

Intentions
1. Even if we have a tiny grain of faith, we can achieve great results. May we allow the power of Jesus to work through us.
2. Jesus healed the epileptic boy in answer to his father's prayer. We pray for all who suffer from mental illness and those who love them.
3. We pray for doctors and nurses, specialists and surgeons that they may treat their patients with courtesy and understanding.
4. The disciples ask our Lord about their lack of success with the epileptic boy. May we also realise that we are inadequate and need his help.
5. *Year 1:* Everything good in us, everything we possess, is a gift from God. May we love him with all our heart and soul and strength.
5. *Year 2:* Sometimes we know our prayer is good and feel God is slow. May we wait and have patience. The Father is not deaf. He will hear us.

Concluding Prayer
In your love, Father, you have given us bread and work. You are the giver of all things. We trust you will know our deepest needs and hear our prayer. Through Christ our Lord.

WEEK 19

NINETEENTH WEEK OF THE YEAR: MONDAY

Introduction
Knowing that the Lord God wishes nothing for us but our true good, we turn to him in prayer.

Intentions
1. We pray for the Church: that it may not be saddened by persecution and opposition, but rather rejoice and be glad in the death and resurrection of the Son of Man.
2. We pray that together with all citizens we may recognize and fulfil our legitimate duties to the state.
3. We pray for a deeper realisation of the fact that we are children of God and can therefore count on his love.
4. We pray for the sick and the dying: that their sufferings may be alleviated by the hope of the resurrection.
5. *Year 1:* We pray that all obstinacy be rooted out of our hearts and that we may obey the commandments of God joyfully and lovingly.
5. *Year 2:* We pray for people in despair: that they may glimpse the glory of God and so find hope.

Concluding Prayer
Father, we do not know how to pray as we ought. Our hopes, our fears, our needs and our desires are limited by our sinfulness. Send your Spirit into our hearts that our weaknesses may become his strength and our feeble words find acceptance before you. This we ask through Christ our Lord.

NINETEENTH WEEK OF THE YEAR: TUESDAY

Introduction
As children in need of the help of our loving Father let us place all our needs before him.

Intentions
1. For all ministers in the Church: that they may be strong

and confident in the leadership of God's people.
2. For the gift of child-like innocence without malice and guile
so that we may give ourselves over totally to the will of God.
3. For the sick and the handicapped: that they may feel the
power of God in their weakness.
4. For all children, especially the ones we know and love: that
they may never lose their sense of trust and wonder.
5. For the down-and-outs, the tramps and others whom
society often ignores: that they be treated by us as persons of
dignity and worth whom God loves with a special love.
6. For all pastors in the Church: that they have the strength
and resolution to seek out and save those who have gone
astray.

Concluding Prayer
Father, we do not know how to pray as we ought. Our hopes,
our fears, our needs and our desires are limited by our sinfulness. Send your Spirit into our hearts that our weaknesses
may become his strength and our feeble words find acceptance before you. This we ask through Christ our Lord.

NINETEENTH WEEK OF THE YEAR: WEDNESDAY

Introduction
Conscious of our sinfulness and our need of God's mercy we
turn to him with open hearts.

Intentions
1. Let us pray that the Church may be a sign of that peace
and reconciliation which Christ won for all peoples.
2. Let us pray that more and more people may discover the
love and compassion of God in the sacrament of reconciliation.
3. Let us pray for the true sorrow for our sins and the hope
of God's forgiveness.
4. Let us pray that we may always reach out promptly to
those separated from us by anger and discord.
5. Let us pray for an end to all wars so that nations may live
together in the peace of Christ.

6. Let us pray for those religious communities whose vocation is to intercede for us and the whole Church.

Concluding Prayer
Father, we do not know how to pray as we ought. Our hopes, our fears, our needs and our desires are limited by our sinfulness. Send your Holy Spirit into our hearts that our weaknesses may become his strength and our feeble words find acceptance before you. This we ask through Christ our Lord.

NINETEENTH WEEK OF THE YEAR: THURSDAY

Introduction
In response to the word of God which has been proclaimed to us in the Scriptures we pray to him for ourselves and the needs of all the world.

Intentions
1. For the pope and those who assist him in the government of the Church: that they be generous and sympathetic to those who fail in faith and allegiance.
2. For judges and magistrates: that their decision be never ruled by vindictiveness but by justice and mercy.
3. For those persecuted or imprisoned for matters of conscience.
4. For ourselves when we fall into disagreement with friends or neighbour: that we do not give way to spite.
5. For the gift of forgiving others as readily as we have been forgiven in Christ.

Concluding Prayer
Father, we do not know how to pray as we ought. Our hopes, our fears, our needs and our desires are limited by our sinfulness. Send your Holy Spirit into our hearts that our weaknesses may become his strength and our feeble words find acceptance before you. This we ask through Christ our Lord.

NINETEENTH WEEK OF THE YEAR: FRIDAY

Introduction
The Lord God is always eager to hear the needs of his children. Let us make them known to him now in confidence and love.

Intentions
1. Let us pray that the Church's teaching on marriage may be heard and understood by all peoples of the world.
2. Let us pray that lawgivers around the world have a reverence for the sanctity of married life.
3. Let us pray for all married couples: that they remain loving and faithful to each other in good times and in bad.
4. Let us pray for those whose marriage had failed and for any children involved.
5. Let us pray for priests and religious who have forgone the chance of marriage that they be generous in their renunciation.

Concluding Prayer
Father, we do not know how to pray as we ought. Our hopes, our fears, our needs and our desires are limited by our sinfulness. Send your Holy Spirit into our hearts that our weaknesses may become his strength and our feeble words find acceptance before you. This we ask through Christ our Lord.

NINETEENTH WEEK OF THE YEAR: SATURDAY

Introduction
No one who approaches the Lord in humble faith will be turned away. Therefore we have the courage to offer him our prayers.

Intentions
1. We pray for the Catholic Church throughout the world, in our diocese and in our parish: that it put into practice the justice and equality it preaches.

2. We pray for all those organisations dedicated to bringing about racial harmony.

3. We pray that each one of us may have the courage to recognise in himself any bias on the grounds of race, colour, creed or position in society, and have the grace to treat all people as equal in the eyes of God.

4. We pray for the children in our community: that they may grow in the love of God and lose nothing of their joy in living.

5. We pray for those people who think they cannot get near to God: that they will realise that God is with them at all times.

Concluding Prayer
Father, we do not know how to pray as we ought. Our hopes, our fears, our needs and our desires are limited by our sinfulness. Send your Holy Spirit into our hearts that our weaknesses may become his strength and our feeble words find acceptance before you. This we ask through Christ our Lord.

WEEK 20

TWENTIETH WEEK OF THE YEAR: MONDAY

Introduction
Let us call upon the Lord who heeds us in all our needs.

Intentions
1. We pray for the entire Catholic Church, pope, bishops, religious, priests, laity: that it may always seek to know and carry out God's will.

2. We pray that the gap between the rich and the poor will be bridged so that poverty, hunger and homelessness become things of the past.

3. We pray that each of us will cast out the worship of the false gods of money and possessions.

4. We pray for those who are considering giving up everything for the service of God. May they have the courage to do his will.

5. We pray for young people, especially those we know: that they keep Christ as their leader and follow him in all things.

Concluding Prayer
Father, you love us with a love which is beyond all we could ever hope for or imagine. You are attentive to every need before ever we know them ourselves. Look upon us, your children, and look kindly upon us as we call upon you in the name of Christ our Lord.

TWENTIETH WEEK OF THE YEAR: TUESDAY

Introduction
Let us call on God in our need, for he is ever anxious to hear our prayer.

Intentions
1. For the Church of God: that it shed all semblance of worldliness and be ever prepared to do his will.
2. For the rich, industrialists, landowners and all people of power: that they use their gifts for the good of all mankind.
3. For ourselves: that we may not be dazzled by the attraction of possessions and power but always keep our hearts with God.
4. For religious and priests: that they do not count the cost but give themselves wholeheartedly to the service of God.
5. For the lonely and forsaken: that they do not give way to despair but put their trust in him who is the treasure of all.

Concluding Prayer
Father, you love us with a love which is beyond all we could ever hope for or imagine. You are attentive to every need before ever we know them ourselves. Look upon us, your children, and look kindly upon us as we call upon you in the name of Christ our Lord.

TWENTIETH WEEK OF THE YEAR: WEDNESDAY

Introduction
The Lord is calling us to the work of prayer and desires to open our hearts to him.

Intentions
1. We pray that more young men and women will heed the voice of God and offer themselves for work in his vineyard.
2. We pray for the grace not to be envious of others but to rejoice in the gifts God gives them.
3. We pray that those who do voluntary Church work in this parish may do so selflessly and with generosity of spirit.
4. We pray that in doing God's will we do not count the cost but be happy simply to be his instruments.
5. *Year 1:* We pray that our lives may not be governed by pride and ambition.
5. *Year 2:* We pray for all pastors of the Church: that they care for the flock entrusted to them in the spirit of the Good Shepherd.

Concluding Prayer
Father, you love us with a love which is beyond all we could ever hope for or imagine. You are attentive to every need before ever we know them ourselves. Look upon us, your children, and look kindly upon us as we call upon you in the name of Christ our Lord.

TWENTIETH WEEK OF THE YEAR: THURSDAY

Introduction
As the Lord calls us to the banquet of the Eucharist let us speak to him in prayer.

Intentions
1. For the Church: that it may so speak and act through us that the world will respond to God's call.
2. For the government and other secular authorities: that the

concerns of this world may not blind them to the concerns of God.

3. For the vision to understand that, no matter how important worldly affairs may appear, all that really matters is to be one with God in the heavenly banquet.

4. For the gift of charity which is the true wedding garment.

5. For the conversion of our stony hearts that they be ready to love and do God's will.

Concluding Prayer
Father, you love us with a love which is beyond all we could ever hope for or imagine. You are attentive to every need before ever we know them ourselves. Look upon us, your children, and look kindly upon us as we call upon you in the name of Christ our Lord.

TWENTIETH WEEK OF THE YEAR: FRIDAY

Introduction
Let us turn to the Lord in prayer and put before him our weakness and sinfulness, our needs and our hopes.

Intentions
1. Let us pray that the whole Church, through the sacraments and its pastoral care, may shine forth as the dwelling place of the love of God.

2. Let us pray that the worship of God may be carried out by us with hearts filled with the love of God.

3. Let us pray that we may rid ourselves of our petty prejudices and selfish concerns and so love our neighbour as ourselves.

4. Let us pray that all members of society will more readily come to the aid of those in any kind of need.

5. Let us pray that we never allow adherence to the law to become an excuse for refusing to love our neighbour.

Concluding Prayer
Father, you love us with a love which is beyond all we could ever hope for or imagine. You are attentive to every need

before we know them ourselves. Look upon us, your children, and look kindly upon us as we call upon you in the name of Christ our Lord.

TWENTIETH WEEK OF THE YEAR: SATURDAY

Introduction
Knowing that all we have is from God and that without him we are as nothing, we call upon him in prayer.

Intentions
1. That all members of the Church, especially those in authority, be protected from seeking personal gain for themselves.
2. That those who have the ministry of handing on the word of God be empowered to practise what they preach.
3. That we may never use double standards in judging ourselves and others.
4. That we may speedily come to the aid of those of our brothers whom society condemns or rejects.
5. That we may never puff ourselves up with pride but realise that without God we are nothing.

Concluding Prayer
Father, you love us with a love which is beyond all we could ever hope for or imagine. You are attentive to every need before we know them ourselves. Look upon us, your children, and look kindly upon us as we call upon you in the name of Christ our Lord.

WEEK 21

TWENTY-FIRST WEEK OF THE YEAR: MONDAY

Introduction
We are called to be watchful in prayer at all times. With trust and confidence let us pray to God for all our needs.

Intentions
1. Let us pray for the work of evangelization in the Church: that through it the doors of God's kingdom may be opened to all.
2. Let us pray for a true sense of what is of value in our lives: that we may not place all our trust in material goods that do not last.
3. Let us pray for the right use of the gift of speech: may we be thankful for it, not defile it, but use it for truth and charity.
4. Let us pray for all who have the responsibility of teaching others: that through their own actions and way of life they may authenticate their message.
5. Let us pray for this community: that God may make us worthy of his call, and fulfil by his power our good intentions and honest work, for his greater glory.

Concluding Prayer
Father, we are the people you have chosen as your own and we give thanks. Be our protection and our help at all times. Through the saving merits of Jesus Christ, our Lord.

TWENTY-FIRST WEEK OF THE YEAR: TUESDAY

Introduction
We are called to be watchful in prayer at all times. With trust and confidence let us pray to God for all our needs.

Intentions
1. Let us pray for the Church throughout the world: that all Christians may be an authentic sign of Christ, showing justice and mercy and good faith.
2. Let us pray for deeper faith and love: that our following of Christ may not be a superficial response but be truly a guiding force in all our actions.
3. Let us pray for all who work for justice and peace in our world today: that they may be sustained in their courage, trust and efforts.
4. Let us pray for all who serve in public office: that they may

reject all temptations to corruption, be not respectors of persons, and may always care for the poor and needy.

5. *Year 1:* Let us pray for perseverance in the faith: that we do not give credence to falsehood but hold fast to the traditions we have received.

Concluding Prayer
Father, we are the people you have chosen as your own and we give thanks. Be our protection and our help at all times. Through the saving merits of Jesus Christ, our Lord.

TWENTY-FIRST WEEK OF THE YEAR: WEDNESDAY

Introduction
We are called to be watchful in prayer at all times. With trust and confidence let us pray to God for all our needs.

Intentions
1. Let us pray for the development of ministry in the Church. We remember our pope and bishops, the priests and deacons and all who serve in ministries.
2. Let us pray for all who work for peace. We remember the work of the United Nations, and all the work in security forces for our protection.
3. Let us pray for the safety and wellbeing of all who are on holiday. We remember all who work in the service of tourists and holidaymakers, and those who give hospitality to strangers.
4. Let us pray for the work of food production. We remember all who work on the land and those who assist them, and we ask at this time for suitable weather.

Concluding Prayer
Father, we are the people you have chosen as your own and we give thanks. Be our protection and our help at all times. Through the saving merits of Jesus Christ, our Lord.

TWENTY-FIRST WEEK OF THE YEAR: THURSDAY

Introduction
We are called to be watchful in prayer at all times. With trust and confidence let us pray to God for all our needs.

Intentions
1. Let us pray that we may take to heart the warning to be always watchful for the coming of the day of the Lord.
2. Let us pray for the grace to be faithful servants of the Lord, attentive to our daily duties and working to the best of our abilities.
3. Let us pray for a greater sense of honesty in public life: that we may in no way condone stealing and robbery as acceptable in our society.
4. Let us pray for the gift of temperance: we pray for all who are victims of alcoholism, and for their families and friends; and we pray for all who educate the young to the dangers of drug abuse.

Concluding Prayer
Father, we are the people you have chosen as your own and we give thanks. Be our protection and our help at all times. Through the saving merits of Jesus Christ, our Lord.

TWENTY-FIRST WEEK OF THE YEAR: FRIDAY

Introduction
Through our baptism we are members of Christ's body, the Church. We pray now that we may be worthy of the vocation to which we are called.

Intentions
1. The Church is the bride of Christ eagerly awaiting his coming; may we never be distracted from that watchfulness.
2. Our privilege of taking part in the Eucharist is an anticipation of our entry to the great marriage feast of the kingdom of the Lord; may we always celebrate that Eucharist with faith and joyful hope.

3. The Church, like Christ, is to be a sign of reconciliation to the world; may we work in every way for peace and justice in the place where we live.
4. That Church calls to life and conversion all who hear the words of Christ; may we always receive the poor and needy, the weak and sinful, and all who need hope and comfort.
5. The Church is to be always a sign of hope in the kingdom of God; may we be mindful of those who have gone before us to the place of refreshment, light and peace.

Concluding Prayer
Father, we are the people you have chosen as your own and we give thanks. Be our protection and our help at all times. Through the saving merits of Jesus Christ, our Lord.

TWENTY-FIRST WEEK OF THE YEAR: SATURDAY

Introduction
Th celebration of the Eucharist is an act of praise and thanksgiving; in acknowledging God's goodness in the past we have confidence to ask for his continuing favour.

Intentions
1. Let us praise and thank God for his unexpectedness in calling all sorts and conditions of people to his Church: may we always respond to the grace of his call.
2. Let us praise and thank God for calling us to the service of others and giving us particular gifts to carry out the work: may we always give generously in our vocation.
3. Let us praise and thank God for the variety of services we receive from other people: may we always be grateful, and may we be a help in creating employment for all.
4. Let us praise and thank God for all who work in the care of the sick and aged: may we never abandon the old and infirm ourselves but help them to witness to the power of God in human weakness.

Concluding Prayer
Father, we are the people you have chosen as your own and

we give thanks. Be our protection and our help at all times. Through the saving merits of Jesus Christ, our Lord.

WEEK 22

TWENTY-SECOND WEEK OF THE YEAR: MONDAY

Introduction
We are called by Christ to be a sign of his love for all mankind. Let us pray now for his help and support in all our needs.

Intentions
1. We pray for the whole Church: that, guided by the Spirit of God, it may be an active sign of justice and truth to the world.
2. For those in authority: that they may be filled with the wisdom of God, and may work towards peace and justice for all.
3. We remember those who are suffering at this time from oppression: that they may find support in Christian people everywhere.
4. Let us pray for all those gathered here, for our families and friends, that being accepted by society will not hinder us from building a community based on love.

Concluding Prayer
Father, hear the prayer we make trusting in your loving concern. Help us to become a community of caring love. We make our prayer through Christ our Lord.

TWENTY-SECOND WEEK OF THE YEAR: TUESDAY

Introduction
We are called by Christ to be a sign of his love for all mankind. Let us pray now for his help and support in all our needs.

Intentions
1. We pray for our Church leaders: that they may be true to the authority given to them by Christ.
2. For all those who are actively working for peace and unity: that they may be supported by the prayers and actions of all who live in the name of Christ and bear the name of Christian.
3. Let us pray for those who can see no hope in their situation, no light in their darkness. May they find signs of a loving and faithful God in those around them.
4. We remember especially those in our own community who are lonely and anxious. May the love of God and the encouragement and support of us all be a source of strength to them.

Concluding Prayer
Father, hear the prayer we make trusting in your loving concern. Help us to become a community of caring love. We make our prayer through Christ our Lord.

TWENTY-SECOND WEEK OF THE YEAR: WEDNESDAY

Introduction
We are called by Christ to be a sign of his love for all mankind. Let us pray now for his help and support in all our needs.

Intentions
1. For the Church throughout the world: that, with confidence in the power of God, it may continue to bring a message of the love and peace of God's kingdom to all people.
2. We remember those who have left their homes to preach the word of God, and pray that their faith and their dedication to their call may be a source of encouragement to all Christians.
3. Many people throughout the world are engaged in bringing healing and relief to others. We pray that the power of Christ within them will sustain their mission of love.
4. In today's Gospel we hear of the healing power of Christ.

Trusting in his compassion and love we call on Jesus to lay his hands on those in our parish who are experiencing pain, depression or loneliness. Let their hearts be opened to the touch of his healing love.

Concluding Prayer
Father, hear the prayer we make trusting in your loving concern. Help us to become a community of caring love. We make our prayer through Christ our Lord.

TWENTY-SECOND WEEK OF THE YEAR: THURSDAY

Introduction
We are called by Christ to be a sign of his love for all mankind. Let us pray now for his help and support in all our needs.

Intentions
1. Let us pray for the community of Christ throughout the world: that our faith may be strengthened, and that we continue to bear witness to Christ with humility and love.
2. We pray for our leaders: that they may realise the limitations of their own authority, and that, helped by our prayers, they may come to know the will of God and act as true servants and friends.
3. Jesus invites us all to follow him. Let us pray for the trust and openness to give our hearts and our lives to God, and allow ourselves to be a sign of his hope and love to those in need.
4. For each of us here, our families and our friends: that we respond fully to the call of our baptism, and strive to build a true community of Christ in this parish.

Concluding Prayer
Father, hear the prayer we make trusting in your loving concern. Help us to become a community of caring love. We make our prayer through Christ our Lord.

TWENTY-SECOND WEEK OF THE YEAR: FRIDAY

Introduction
We are called by Christ to be a sign of his love to all
mankind. Let us pray now for his help and support in all our
needs.

Intentions
1. For a strengthening of our Church's faith, so that it may
continue to serve God and to steeer mankind along the path
to salvation.
2. Let us pray for those in authority, who have been called
upon by society to judge others, that they may do so with the
justice of God in their hearts.
3. God will never forget his people. We pray for those who
are the victims of injustice, that their faith may be
strengthened, and with a trustful heart they can commit their
experiences to God who is our refuge in time of need.
4. We pray that our community may be a living sign of God
to all men, and that our faith may be a source of strength and
encouragement to all who call on us.

Concluding Prayer
Father, hear the prayer we make trusting in your loving concern. Help us to become a community of caring love. We
make our prayer through Christ our Lord.

TWENTY-SECOND WEEK OF THE YEAR: SATURDAY

Introduction
We are called by Christ to be a sign of his love to all
mankind. Let us pray now for his help and support in all our
needs.

Intentions
1. We pray for an increase in the faith of our Church: that
it may find encouragement to endure in the hope promised by
the Good News.
2. For our leaders of Church and state: that they may be

guided by the Son of Man, and recognise him alone as master of all.

3. We pray that as a Christian people our faith will stand up to those who call us "fools for the sake of Christ". Let us be a sign of the love of God for all those who need it.

4. The Lord is close to all who ask his help. So with confidence we pray from our hearts for the intentions of all here, and for those who need our prayers, knowing that God will be just and loving in his response.

Concluding Prayer
Father, hear the prayer we make trusting in your loving concern. Help us to become a community of caring love. We make our prayer through Christ our Lord.

WEEK 23

TWENTY-THIRD WEEK OF THE YEAR: MONDAY

Introduction
Our God is a God who saves and who wants to fill us with life. We come in confidence to him with our needs.

Intentions
1. We pray for the whole Church: especially for preachers and catechists, that the word they speak may be a word of life for the many who experience struggle, weariness and emptiness today.

2. We pray for those who have lost hope: that they may experience the enlivening touch of the Spirit of God in their lives.

3. We pray for those who are rejected by society — the travellers, the unemployed, the imprisoned, the handicapped: that they come to new hope and life through the hands of christian brothers and sisters.

4. We pray for the gift of compassion: that in seeing the pain of others we may be moved to help and serve.

5. We pray for the courage to do the good thing for others especially in the face of pressure to do otherwise.

Concluding Prayer
God our Father, these are the prayers of your children who are beloved to you in your Son. We present them to you in full joy and confidence through the same Jesus Christ our Lord.

TWENTY-THIRD WEEK OF THE YEAR: TUESDAY

Introduction
Gathered together in prayer to our Father, with Jesus, in this Mass we gladly bring him our needs and concerns.

Intentions
1. We pray for the apostles of today, expecially the pope, the bishops, priests and missionaries: that they may be reaffirmed in their vocations and strengthened in their ministries.
2. We pray that we may all know and share in the power of Jesus at work in the Church today, healing the illnesses of poverty, injustice, division and materialism which cripple our world.
3. We pray for the sick, the old and the lonely among us: that they may receive comfort and strength from those around them.
4. We pray that we may be people of prayer who find time for God in our busy lives and so hold firm the faith we have received and pass it on to young people of tomorrow.
5. We pray for all those who have been apostles to us, living or dead — our parents, teachers, friends, strangers: may they experience the richness of God's kindness.

Concluding Prayer
God our Father, these are the prayers of your children who are beloved to you in your Son. We present them to you in full joy and confidence through the same Jesus Christ our Lord.

TWENTY-THIRD WEEK OF THE YEAR: WEDNESDAY

Introduction
The Lord is good to all, the great and the small, the just and the unjust alike. Because he has no favourites we can come to him knowing that he hears our prayer.

Intentions
1. For Christians everywhere: that we may become more conscious of the great injustice done to peoples today and may use our resources and talents to answer the cry of the poor.
2. For our political and economic leaders: that they may make a greater effort to share the nation's goods more equitably.
3. For the poor and oppressed: that they may trust God's promise to care for them and that they may experience that care through each of us.
4. For ourselves, whether rich or poor: that we may not be engrossed in material things but be happy to use what we have for the benefit of all.
5. For true community amongst us and an end to class distinctions so that we may be all one body, the people of God who love and serve one another, bringing hope to a distressed world.

Concluding Prayer
God our Father, these are the prayers of your children who are beloved to you in your Son. We present them to you in full joy and confidence through the same Jesus Christ our Lord.

TWENTY-THIRD WEEK OF THE YEAR: THURSDAY

Introduction
The compassionate love of God our Father never fails us even though we are still sinners. This gives us great confidence to pray.

Intentions
1. That we may always be aware of God's forgiving love and care for us, especially in times of trouble and difficulty.
2. That as disciples of Christ we may witness to the special character of Christian love which reaches out and includes those who misjudge us or mistreat us in any way.
3. That those who suffer persecution or who have been seriously wronged by others may experience fellowship with Christ and be able to forgive and pray for those who hurt them.
4. That as Christians we may learn to give without counting the cost and like Christ share ourselves and our resources without always expecting a return.
5. That we may be instruments of peace in a troubled world by learning to understand and forgive rather than to judge and condemn.

Concluding Prayer
God our Father, these are the prayers of your children who are beloved to you in your Son. We present them to you in full joy and confidence through the same Jesus Christ our Lord.

TWENTY-THIRD WEEK OF THE YEAR: FRIDAY

Introduction
We come in humility before our God who sees into our hearts and who knows our needs before we ask for them.

Intentions
1. We pray for the whole people of God that we may have the grace of humility to admit our failure and unfaithfulness in sincerity and truth.
2. We pray for the grace of repentence that we may turn back to God and seek his help to live in love and peace.
3. We pray for the grace to listen to those who challenge our way of living the Gospel: that we may learn to be more authentic as Christians.
4. We pray for the light of the Holy Spirit for Church leaders: that they may see what needs to be renewed so that we may

be true disciples of the Master.

5. We pray for the grace of mutual love and respect between the Christian Churches so that the prayer of Christ for unity may be fulfilled one day.

6. We pray for those who have no voice: that others will speak for them and lead them to the freedom of sharing in the decisions which affect their lives.

Concluding Prayer
God our Father, these are the prayers of your children who are beloved to you in your Son. We present them to you in full joy and confidence through the same Jesus Christ our Lord.

TWENTY-THIRD WEEK OF THE YEAR: SATURDAY

Introduction
Jesus has called us to listen to his word and obey it. Let us come and ask for the strength to be doers of the word and not hearers only.

Intentions
1. Let us pray for strength for the whole Church to live ever more fully the Gospel call to love, peace and shared life.
2. Let us pray for strength for the pope, bishop and ministers of the word: that they may continue to speak the word of Christ and preserve the unity of his body.
3. Let us pray for strength for families, especially those under stress: that they may find the courage to build genuine faith community in their homes.
4. Let us pray for strength for those who are sick, bereaved or tormented by problems: that they may continue to trust God's love for them and may find support in friends.
5. Let us pray for strength for those who have no work: that they may be able to carry the cross of insecurity and find ways of using their time and talents for the good of others.
6. Let us pray for strength for ourselves: that we may be faithful to our commitments at home, at work, and to others.

Concluding Prayer
God our Father, these are the prayers of your children who are beloved to you in your Son. We present them to you in full joy and confidence through the same Jesus Christ our Lord.

WEEK 24

TWENTY-FOURTH WEEK OF THE YEAR: MONDAY

Introduction
As we bring the needs of God's people before him in this Mass let us have the faith of the centurion and trust that God will answer our prayers too.

Intentions
1. We pray for all those in leadership in the Church: that they may have a deep trust in God and lead his people to have a similar trust in him.
2. We pray for all those in leadership in political life: that they may be concerned for the good of all but especially of the most disadvantaged.
3. We pray for ourselves: that our faith may be strong, that it may be a beacon of light and hope to others.
4. We pray for those who do not believe: that they may discover God in the events of their lives and come to know his love for them.
5. We pray for peace among divided Christians: that their common faith in Christ may bring them unity.

Concluding Prayer
Almighty Father and loving God, you are constantly at work in our hearts making us holy. Our intercessions are the work of your Spirit who prays in us and who leads us confidently to commit our needs to you through Christ our Lord

TWENTY-FOURTH WEEK OF THE YEAR: TUESDAY

Introduction
It is characteristic of God that he puts life where there is death. Let us come to him with our need that we may give him the glory of being a people fully alive.

Intentions
1. We pray for the continuing renewal of the Church of God: that she may clearly show forth the face of Christ to all.
2. We pray for the renewal of the priesthood and religious life: that many young people may be led to give their lives completely to the service of God and his people.
3. We pray for the renewal of the laity: that they may actively share in the spiritual mission of the Church, revealing the presence of God in the economic and political spheres of life.
4. We pray for the renewal of charism and gifts among the people of God: that the Church may be equipped to meet the task of bringing the good news to the world today.
5. We pray for the renewal of our own hearts: that with hearts of flesh and not of stone we may reach out to those who are lost or abandoned, those who are searching or confused.

Concluding Prayer
Almighty Father and loving God, you are constantly at work in our hearts making us holy. Our intercessions are the work of your Spirit who prays in us and who leads us confidently to commit our needs to you through Christ our Lord

TWENTY-FOURTH WEEK OF THE YEAR: WEDNESDAY

Introduction
God our Father is patient and kind. In our confusion and pain we confidently come to him with our needs and those of our brothers and sisters.

Intentions
1. For wisdom for our Holy Father Pope N.: that he may

know how to guide the Church today.

2. For wisdom for the bishops of our country: that they may know how to speak to current issues in leading the flock they have been entrusted with.

3. For wisdom for parents and educators: that they may know how to hand on the faith to their children.

4. For wisdom for our political, social and economic planners: that they may know how to plan for a just and healthy society.

5. For wisdom for ourselves: that we may recognise what is good and true in every area of life and respond to it.

Concluding Prayer
Almighty Father and loving God, you are constantly at work in our hearts making us holy. Our intercessions are the work of your Spirit who prays in us and who leads us confidently to commit our needs to you through Christ our Lord

---

TWENTY-FOURTH WEEK OF THE YEAR: THURSDAY

Introduction
In the presence of him whose forgiveness is boundless we pray for the grace of forgiveness in the hearts of all people.

Intentions
1. That nations and peoples may forgive the wrongs of history and look towards former enemies with openness and respect.

2. That countries at war at present may come to acknowledge, and live by, the better way of peace and forgiveness.

3. That families may be freed from traditional feuds by the reconciliation of mutual forgiveness, and begin to work together for good of their local communities.

4. That each of us may forgive the personal wrongs done to us by others and so be healed of the hurts which cripple us and prevent us accepting Christ's love and the love of those around us.

5. That through a greater appreciation of the sacrament of forgiveness we may grow in an attitude of forgiveness.

Concluding Prayer
Almighty Father and loving God, you are constantly at work in our hearts making us holy. Our intercessions are the work of your Spirit who prays in us and who leads us confidently to commit our needs to you through Christ our Lord.

TWENTY-FOURTH WEEK OF THE YEAR: FRIDAY

Introduction
Jesus was tireless in his work of preaching the Father's love. Let us pray that the whole Church will not grow weary of preaching that message today.

Intentions
1. For the peoples of all nations and cultures: that their hearts may be tuned to the presence of God in the world and that they may come to the knowledge of his Son Jesus who loved us and gave himself for us.
2. For those whose special task it is to preach the Gospel: that their own faith may be renewed as they show the way to others and that they may be supported by the whole body of Christ.
3. For those involved in the arts and in scientific and economic development: that their work may serve to disclose the presence of the Creator, God of beauty, power and love.
4. For those whose lives are surrounded by poverty, war, fear and injustice: that they may experience the presence of the risen Christ overcoming all evil and be filled with hope and not despair.
5. For those who are single and who live alone: that they may find companionship and Christian community with others and so live full and fruitful lives.

Concluding Prayer
Almighty Father and loving God, you are constantly at work in our hearts making us holy. Our intercessions are the work of your Spirit who prays in us and who leads us confidently to commit our needs to you through Christ our Lord

TWENTY-FOURTH WEEK OF THE YEAR: SATURDAY

Introduction
At the end of the week and conscious of God's goodness to us every day we come to ask for the grace of perseverance for ourselves and for the whole Church.

Intentions
1. We pray for the Church, the bride of Christ: that she may persevere in faithfulness, in works of charity and in proclaiming the good news of God's faithful love.
2. We pray for our leaders in Church and State: that they may persevere in doing good in spite of opposition.
3. We pray for young people: that they may persevere in hope, trusting in God's faithfulness to them through their own special difficulties.
4. We pray for those fighting addiction to drugs or drink: that they may persevere in depending on God's strength in their own weakness.
5. We pray for those who care for the sick, the old, the handicapped: that they may persevere in this work of love by the power of the Holy Spirit.
6. We pray for those who have persevered unto the end, the dead: that they may receive the reward of their perseverance, the peace and joy of the full presence of God.

Concluding Prayer
Almighty Father and loving God you are constantly at work in our hearts making us holy. Our intercessions are the work of your Holy Spirit who prays in us and who leads us confidently to commit our needs to you, through Christ our Lord.

WEEK 25

TWENTY-FIFTH WEEK OF THE YEAR: MONDAY

Introduction
We who dwell amid the shadows of darkness call upon Christ, our light.

Intentions
1. For the holy Church of God: that her faith in Christ may be a light that shines brightly for all to see.
2. For the leaders of nations: that neither ambition nor power blind them to the needs of their people.
3. For all who seek to know the truth: that their searching may lead them at last to the one true light.
4. For all who suffer from any infirmity: that Christ may be their strength, healing, and tranquility.
5. For those of our parish/congregation who have died: that they may rejoice in the light of the Father's glory.

Concluding Prayer
Lord, we strive to be your faithful followers; we ask you to be faithful to your promises, and grant our requests through Christ our Lord.

TWENTY-FIFTH WEEK OF THE YEAR: TUESDAY

Introduction
We who are called to be the Lord's brothers and sisters call upon him as we present our needs.

Intentions
1. *Year 1:* For the leaders of God's holy Church: that they may help all the faithful to become the living stones from which Christ builds the temple of his glory.
1. *Year 2:* For the leaders of God's holy Church: that they may always guide the faithful along the ways of truth.
2. For all the nations of the world: that each person may see in our common brotherhood the way to peace.
3. For all those who have no family to call their own: that in their loneliness they may experience union with Christ.
4. For the families of our parish/congregation: that we who rejoice in belonging to the Lord may always experience the joy of unity with each other.
5. For all the faithful departed: that they may fully rejoice in unity with Christ.

Concluding Prayer
Lord, we strive to be your faithful followers; we ask you to
be faithful to your promises, and grant our requests through
Christ our Lord.

TWENTY-FIFTH WEEK OF THE YEAR: WEDNESDAY

Introduction
We who have heard the good news of God's love for us, in
loving confidence set forth our petitions.

Intentions
1. For the holy Church: that she may always have as leaders
men and women of faith and charity, wisdom and courage.
2. For those who are eager to hear the word of God: that the
Church may minister to them by sending forth missioners
zealous to answer Christ's call to announce the Father's love.
3. For the destitute nations of the world: that by God's
gracious goodness they may come to share both spiritual and
material abundance.
4. For those of our congregation who suffer from physical or
mental infirmity: that the healing power of Christ may bring
them peace in affliction, light in darknes, confort in pain.
5. For those who feel unjustly rejected: that they may find
friends to stand by them, colleagues in their labour, and
support in time of need.

Concluding Prayer
Lord, we strive to be your faithful followers; we ask you to
be faithful to your promises, and grant our requests through
Christ our Lord.

TWENTY-FIFTH WEEK OF THE YEAR: THURSDAY

Introduction
We turn to the Lord, the Saviour of his people, for he
answers our cry.

Intentions
1. For the holy Catholic Church: that she may everywhere

prosper in faith, increase in hope, grow in love.
2. For those who are persecuted for their faith: that they may
have the courage to give witness to that faith.
3. For the leaders of nations: that they may not misuse the
power with which they have been entrusted.
4. For the victims of injustice: that in their time of suffering
they may experience the consoling presence of Christ who
suffered injustice that we may be saved.
5. For all who labour: that their work — even the most
menial — may redound to God's glory.

Concluding Prayer
Lord, we strive to be your faithful followers; we ask you to
be faithful to your promises, and grant our requests through
Christ our Lord.

TWENTY-FIFTH WEEK OF THE YEAR: FRIDAY

Introduction
We who look forward in hope to the day of the Lord's
coming pray for his deliverance in this our time.

Intentions
1. For the Holy Father, Pope N.: that he may courageously
proclaim the sovereign majesty of Christ.
2. For the bishop of our diocese, N: that he may confirm and
support the faith of his people.
3. For all those who seek refuge from any tribulation: that
they may see Christ as their saviour and strength.
4. For those who do not know the Lord: that the faith of
those assembled here may lead them to Christ.
5. For those among us whose families are forcibly separated
from each other: that they may be assembled together in joy
and harmony.

Concluding Prayer
Lord, we strive to be your faithful followers; we ask you to
be faithful to your promises, and grant our requests through
Christ our Lord.

184

TWENTY-FIFTH WEEK OF THE YEAR: SATURDAY

Introduction
We who know that the Lord is our guard and our refuge present our petitions in faith and in hope.

Intentions
1. For the holy Church of God: that wherever she suffers she may still cling strongly to her faith in the Lord who suffered for her salvation.
2. For the leaders of nations: that in their deliberations and their decisions they may respond to the highest aspirations of their people.
3. For those who are imprisoned or unjustly held against their will: that they may one day walk in the freedom of God's children.
4. For those who suffer in any way: that Christ, the Suffering Servant, may heal their pain, calm their fears, and gently use their afflictions to accomplish his purposes.
5. For those of us whose faith is weak: that Christ may be our strength.

Concluding Prayer
Lord, we strive to be your faithful followers; we ask you to be faithful to your promises, and grant our requests through Christ our Lord.

WEEK 26

TWENTY-SIXTH WEEK OF THE YEAR: MONDAY

Introduction
We who are in need place our petitions before the Lord.

Intentions
1. For the holy Church: that she may recognize that her true glory rests in fellowship with Christ.
2. For the nations of the world: that neither pride nor arrogance deflect them from the paths of peace.

3. For those who suffer unjustly: that even in their persecution they may experience the consolation of the eternal Father's love.

4. For children who have been abandoned, abused, or neglected: that they may find a true haven in the Christian community, a place of welcome in our midst.

5. For all the faithful departed: that they may be welcomed into the eternal kingdom of the loving Father.

Concluding Prayer
Father, with sincerity of heart we labour to be your faithful people, true to the Gospel calling in fellowship with our brothers and sisters; hear the requests which our voices raise, and answer even our unspoken prayers, too strong for words, too deep for tears, through Christ our Lord.

TWENTY-SIXTH WEEK OF THE YEAR: TUESDAY

Introduction
Lord, to hear us is to know we need; to see us is to know we are asking.

Intentions
1. *Year 1:* For the holy Church: that she may always be a sign to all that God is with us.

1. *Year 2:* For the holy Church of God: that there may be in her midst men and women of prayer whose very lives continually intercede for her needs.

2. For the nations of the world: that war, civil strife, violence be abolished, and that the hate which causes these horrors be cut from our hearts.

3. For the Christians of the world: that the discord which separates us, one sect from the other, may dissolve into unity with Christ and each other.

4. For missionaries throughout the world: that rejection by their listeners not deter them from their resolve to preach Christ's message.

5. For those who have died in the service of God's holy people: that Christ may receive them into fellowship with himself.

Concluding Prayer
Father, with sincerity of heart we labour to be your faithful people, true to the Gospel calling in fellowship with our brothers and sisters; hear the requests which our voices raise, and answer even our unspoken prayers, too strong for words, too deep for tears, through Christ our Lord.

TWENTY-SIXTH WEEK OF THE YEAR: WEDNESDAY

Introduction
Lord, we who seek to follow you, place our petitions before you in faith and in hope.

Intentions
1. For those who are persecuted for their faith: that Christ may be their strength and consolation.
2. For priests and religious: that they may be faithful to their vows and loyal to the Church.
3. For those who strive to follow Christ: that the difficulty of the task not deter their efforts.
4. For the poor, the sick, the lonely: that there always be men and women of faith and charity to care for their needs.
5. For the deceased members of our families: that they may find a place of rest and a haven of peace.

Concluding Prayer
Father, with sincerity of heart we labour to be your faithful people, true to the Gospel calling in fellowship with our brothers and sisters; hear the requests which our voices raise, and answer even our unspoken prayers, too strong for words, too deep for tears, through Christ our Lord.

TWENTY-SIXTH WEEK OF THE YEAR: THURSDAY

Introduction
Lord, we your people pray that we be a harvest worthy to be yours.

Intentions
1. For the holy Church: that we her members be gathered, as the harvest is gathered, into one, in unity and in peace — one faith, one calling, one hope.
2. For those who do not know what to do with their lives: that in Christ's call to service they may find spiritual sustenance to fill their emptiness.
3. For peace throughout the world: that those who are peacemakers may prevail over the evils erected by hatred, dissention, intolerance, and religious factionalism.
4. For the hungry of the world: that the rich harvest season be for them a time of refreshment, deliverance, and plenty.
5. For us gathered here: that this assembly be a true foretaste of our final harvest, gathered together with Christ.

Concluding Prayer
Father, with sincerity of heart we labour to be your faithful people, true to the Gospel calling in fellowship with our brothers and sisters; hear the requests which our voices raise, and answer even our unspoken prayers, too strong for words, too deep for tears, through Christ our Lord.

TWENTY-SIXTH WEEK OF THE YEAR: FRIDAY

Introduction
We who work to serve the Lord, pray that we be faithful in service.

Intentions
1. For the holy Church: that her members be attentive to the Gospel of Christ and sincere in following his word.
2. *Year 1:* For the nations of the world: that they be honourable in their conduct with each other, and just in their dealings with their people.
2. *Year 2:* For the peoples of the world: that they may see in the beauty of creation the hand of the loving Creator, and come to believe in God whose wisdom is beyond measure.
3. For those who believe in Christ: that spiritual pride not blind us to his call to continual reform and constant re-

pentance, that we may come to true fellowship with himself.
4. For the unbelivers of the world: that the humility and faith
of true Christians lead them to belief in God.
5. For us assembled here: that pride, arrogance, infidelity be
removed from our hearts so that our every word, action,
thought serve God's glory.

Concluding Prayer
Father, with sincerity of heart we labour to be your faithful
people, true to the Gospel calling in fellowship with our
brothers and sisters; hear the requests which our voices raise,
and answer even our unspoken prayers, too strong for words,
too deep for tears, through Christ our Lord.

TWENTY-SIXTH WEEK OF THE YEAR: SATURDAY

Introduction
As disciples of the Lord, we pray to be worthy of our calling.

Intentions
1. For our Holy Father, Pope N.: that Christ's call to
discipleship with himself may be a source of joy that
intensifies the faith of the Church throughout the world.
2. For our Bishop N.: that his guidance of our diocese
inspires the faithful, gladden the sorrowful and strengthen
the weak.
3. For all men and women throughout the world: that they
may find in Christ their source of contentment, peace, and
security.
4. For the children of the world: that they be delivered from
fear, civil strife, human indifference, hatred, parental
neglect, and spiritual emptiness.
5. For the faithful departed: that we who mourn their passing
may have the faith to recognize that their names are inscribed
in the heavens.

Concluding Prayer
Father, with sincerity of heart we labour to be your faithful
people, true to the Gospel calling in fellowship with our
brothers and sisters; hear the requests which our voices raise,

and answer even our unspoken prayers, too strong for words, too deep for tears, through Christ our Lord.

WEEK 27

TWENTY-SEVENTH WEEK OF THE YEAR: MONDAY

Introduction
Challenged by the Gospel command to love God and neighbour, let us pray that we may live by what we have heard.

Intentions
1. That we may accept the challenge of the Gospel as a way of life with the values of Jesus Christ.
2. That our faith and hope may be strengthened as we worship God who sets no limit to his mercy.
3. That we may recognise the needs of those about us and bring them a comforting word and deed.
4. That those who help to build good neighbourhoods may be blessed in ther endeavours.
5. That those who have died, and especially our departed neighbours, may have eternal rest.

Concluding Prayer
God our Father, we place our needs before you, the needs that we have spoken aloud, the needs that remain unspoken but known to you, and the needs of all your people. Help us now to celebrate this Eucharist through Jesus Christ our Lord.

TWENTY-SEVENTH WEEK OF THE YEAR: TUESDAY

Introduction
We pray that God's people may be a people of hospitality and prayer, like Mary and Martha.

Intentions
1. Like Mary, may we listen to the voice of God. Like Marthy, may we busy ourselves in caring for others.
2. Like Mary, may we give ourselves time to spend with God.
3. Like Martha, may we see our service to one another as done to Jesus.
4. Like the friends of Jesus, may all who have died be brought to eternal peace in heaven.

Concluding Prayer
God our Father, we place our needs before you, the needs that we have spoken aloud, the needs that remain unspoken but known to you, and the needs of all your people. Help us now to celebrate this Eucharist through Jesus Christ our Lord.

TWENTY-SEVENTH WEEK OF THE YEAR: WEDNESDAY

Introduction
Encouraged by the prayer that Jesus has taught us, we now pray to God our Father for our needs.

Intentions
1. May all people acknowledge God and keep his name holy. May we work to build a kingdom of truth, love, peace and unity.
2. May we share our good fortune, even our daily bread, with those in need.
3. May we be a people who offer and accept the gift of forgiveness.
4. May we find encouragement and nourishment in the gift of the Bread of Life.

Concluding Prayer
God our Father, we place our needs before you, the needs that we have spoken aloud, the needs that remain unspoken but known to you, and the needs of all your people. Help us now to celebrate this Eucharist through Jesus Christ our Lord.

TWENTY-SEVENTH WEEK OF THE YEAR: THURSDAY

Introduction
Jesus tells us to ask and it will be given to us. Trusting in his work, we pray.

Intentions
1. We ask God to help us to put our real needs before him so that he can give of his goodness to us.
2. We ask the Lord to direct us in his way and to hear his voice amid all the noice of our world.
3. We pray that we may be gifted with a faith and hope that we can share and pass on to others.
4. We remember those who lose hope, that they may persevere and be persistent in calling on the help of God and other people.,
5. In silence, we place our personal needs before God. We pray that the names of all who have died may be written in the Lord's book of remembrance.

Concluding Prayer
God our Father, we place our needs before you, the needs that we have spoken aloud, the needs that remain unspoken but known to you, and the needs of all your people. Help us now to celebrate this Eucharist through Jesus Christ our Lord.

TWENTY-SEVENTH WEEK OF THE YEAR: FRIDAY

Introduction
Let us, with faith and hope, turn to the Lord, placing the needs of his people before him.

Intentions
1. *Year 1:* The prophet called for prayer and fasting — may we live this day in a spirit of penance.
1. *Year 2:* Abraham was the person of faith — may we be strengthened in faith, relying on God.
2. Jesus said that he who is not with him is against him —

may there be unity and peace among his people.
3. The Gospel warns against division — may we work together to heal the divisions of our country and our world.
4. In our Mass we remember the death of Jesus — May all who have died share the glory of his resurrection.

Concluding Prayer
God our Father, we place our needs before you, the needs that we have spoken aloud, the needs that remain unspoken but known to you, and the needs of all your people. Help us now to celebrate this Eucharist through Jesus Christ our Lord.

TWENTY-SEVENTH WEEK OF THE YEAR: SATURDAY

Introduction
Jesus praised his mother as one who heard God's word and kept it. We pray that, like Mary, we may open our hearts and lives to the same word.

Intentions
1. We ask the Lord to bless his Church — may it always witness to the truth and power of God's word.
2. We pray for readers and preachers of God's word — may they be inspired to live according to what they read and preach.
3. We remember parents and teachers — may they have courage and faith to speak God's word through what they say and do.
4. We pray for those who work in the media of communication — may they use the human word with honesty and responsibility.
5. We remember those who have departed this life — may they be with God in the company of Mary and the saints.

Concluding Prayer
God our Father, we place our needs before you, the needs that we have spoken aloud, the needs that remain unspoken but known to you, and the needs of all your people. Help us now to celebrate this Eucharist through Jesus Christ our Lord.

WEEK 28

TWENTY-EIGHTH WEEK OF THE YEAR: MONDAY

Introduction
We have been given a person greater than Jonah who invites us to follow him and now encourages us to pray in his name.

Intentions
1. That God's people may understand and appreciate the freedom that has come to them through the death and resurrection of Jesus.
2. That the Church may be seen throughout the world as a people of repentance and reconciliation.
3. That we translate repentance into our lives so that we turn from sin to grace.
4. That we promote the work of reconciliation in our own country so that there may be peace and harmony among all people.
5. That those who have died, especially NN., may be brought to eternal peace and rest.

Concluding Prayer
Gracious God, your word challenges and transforms us. Help us to walk in your ways. Your word transforms our gifts of bread and wine so that they become for us the body and blood of Christ. Help us to celebrate his saving mysteries. We ask this through the same Christ our Lord.

TWENTY-EIGHTH WEEK OF THE YEAR: TUESDAY

Introduction
Jesus invites us to this holy meal where we have been challenged by his word.

Intentions
1. That the Church may be a people who live in grace.
2. That those in positions of authority in society may lead us in ways of justice and peace.
3. That those who are sick among us may be comforted.

4. That those who care for the sick and needy may be blessed in their work.
5. That the faithful departed may rest in eternal peace.

Concluding Prayer
Gracious God, your word challenges and transforms us. Help us to walk in your ways. Your word transforms our gifts of bread and wine so that they become for us the body and blood of Christ. Help us to celebrate his saving mysteries. We ask this through the same Christ our Lord.

TWENTY-EIGHTH WEEK OF THE YEAR: WEDNESDAY

Introduction
The Gospel challenges us to live without compromise.

Intentions
1. We pray that we may build a sense of equality and fairness among all people.
2. We pray that prejudices that divide and cause discrimination may be eliminated in our society.
3. We pray that barriers between people, based on class, colour and age, may be broken down among us.
4. We pray that an equality of opportunity may be given to all men and women, in Church and in society.
5. We pray that the Spirit may lead us in ways of love, peace, compassion and self-control.

Concluding Prayer
Gracious God, your word challenges and transforms us. Help us to walk in your ways. Your word transforms our gifts of bread and wine so that they become for us the body and blood of Christ. Help us to celebrate his saving mysteries. We ask this through the same Christ our Lord.

TWENTY-EIGHTH WEEK OF THE YEAR: THURSDAY

Introduction
We pray for the needs of the Church and the world in the name of Jesus Christ.

Intentions
1. That we do not silence the prophets of our time who challenge us in the ways of peace and justice.
2. That we listen to the cries of those who hunger and thirst each day in our world.
3. That the pleas of those who suffer for human rights may be heard and acted upon.
4. That we share our riches and good fortune with those in need.
5. That we accept our responsibilities to the poorer countries and to the poor among us.

Concluding Prayer
Gracious God, your word challenges and transforms us. Help us to walk in your ways. Your word transforms our gifts of bread and wine so that they become for us the body and blood of Christ. Help us to celebrate his saving mysteries. We ask this through the same Christ our Lord.

TWENTY-EIGHTH WEEK OF THE YEAR: FRIDAY

Introduction
Gathered as God's people, we pray in the name of Jesus for the needs of the Church, the world and our own needs.

Intentions
1. That we may be a people of faith.
2. That we may be a people of hope.
3. That we may be a people of love.
4. That we may be a people of trust.
5. That we may be a people of courage.
6. That we may be a people of prayer.

Concluding Prayer
Gracious God, your word challenges and transforms us. Help us to walk in your ways. Your word transforms our gifts of bread and wine so that they become for us the body and blood of Christ. Help us to celebrate his saving mysteries. We ask this through the same Christ our Lord.

TWENTY-EIGHTH WEEK OF THE YEAR: SATURDAY

Introduction
That good news of Jesus empowers us to pray in his name for our needs.

Intentions
1. *Year 1:* We pray for the Church, Abraham's descendants, walking in faith and with hope.
1. *Year 2:* We pray for the Church, the body of Christ, united under Christ as head.
2. We pray for those who hold positions of authority and leadership in our society.
3. We remember those who, declaring themselves for Christ, suffer for their faith.
4. We pray for those who have asked for our prayers and for those who pray for us.
5. We remember the dead, especially those who have died recently.

Concluding Prayer
Gracious God, your word challenges and transforms us. Help us to walk in your ways. Your word transforms our gifts of bread and wine so that they become for us the body and blood of Christ. Help us to celebrate his saving mysteries. We ask this through the same Christ our Lord.

WEEK 29

TWENTY-NINTH WEEK OF THE YEAR: MONDAY

Introduction
From today's Gospel we realize that it is not what we have that makes us secure. Our hearts will only find ultimate rest in our Father, so we pray.

Intentions
1. For those who have an abundance of this world's goods:

may they realise their responsibility to share with those who have little or nothing.
2. That married couples will not become so preoccupied with their own needs as to forget that they are also called to witness to the whole community.
3. For the whole Church: may we have the courage to follow the gospel value of giving in a world that encourages greed.
4. May our leaders not use our serious problems here at home as an excuse for doing only the bare minimum for those worse off in the Third World.
5. For those who are denied the most basic human rights on account of the selfishness of others: may their hunger for justice be satisfied.

Concluding Prayer
Lord our God, we thank you for your constant presence in our changing world. May your presence ever remind us that we are not alone. We make this prayer through Christ our Lord.

TWENTY-NINTH WEEK OF THE YEAR: TUESDAY

Introduction
Our Father in heaven is always calling us to be more than we are at present. We pray with confidence.

Intentions
1. For the sick whose life is often one long time of waiting: May God come to assure them of his presence here and now as they suffer.
2. That those living through the troubled time of adolescence will not get lost in the future and miss the challenge offered them today.
3. For engaged couples: may they use their time of waiting to prepare for their married life together and not just for a wedding day.
4. For those who feel that their life has been wasted — they have waited only to be disappointed. May their distress move us to action.

5. For those who work in official caring agencies: may they put people before rules and systems so that they can effectively help the poor.

Concluding Prayer
Lord our God, we thank you for your constant presence in our changing world. May your presence ever remind us that we are not alone. We make this prayer through Christ our Lord.

TWENTY-NINTH WEEK OF THE YEAR: WEDNESDAY

Introduction
We are God's servants; he has placed great trust in us. Aware of this call we turn to him in prayer.

Intentions
1. For the Church under the guidance of Pope N., and his fellow bishops: let us become more and more a community where people can discover their gifts, and use them.
2. May world leaders be constantly reminded that they are servants called to give to the poor what is theirs by right.
3. For those who feel no need of God: may they come to see his power and beauty in every truly human achievement.
4. For ourselves in this parish (community): may we be renewed by opening our hearts joyfully to each other and to the Lord of all life.
5. May all Christian people, as a matter of urgency, unite to give common witness to a waiting world.

Concluding Prayer
Lord our God, we thank you for your constant presence in our changing world. May your presence ever remind us that we are not alone. We make this prayer through Christ our Lord.

TWENTY-NINTH WEEK OF THE YEAR: THURSDAY

Introduction
May the Lord enkindle in us the fire of his love as we pray.

Intentions
1. May our leaders have the courage to risk calling us to greater things which we can achieve with his power.
2. For those who find it impossible to cope with the stress of life: may they be led to discover the freedom and peace of a simpler life-style.
3. For other members oof the great family of the Church: may they discover, with us, the powerful unity that we do share through one faith and one baptism.
4. For our bishops: may they lead us to tackle the major burning issues of our time. May we never become isolated from the real concerns around us.
5. For all people of goodwill who are dedicated to removing discrimination between people: may they find sympathy, acceptance and support in the fellowship of the Church.

Concluding Prayer
Lord our God, we thank you for your constant presence in our changing world. May your presence ever remind us that we are not alone. We make this prayer through Christ our Lord.

TWENTY-NINTH WEEK OF THE YEAR: FRIDAY

Introduction
The Father, as a sign of his care for us, has given us Jesus; in his name, we pray.

Intentions
1. For the Church: may we be faithful to the mission of Christ by facing up to the really important issues of our day.
2. For those whom God has called to be prophets in our world: as they highlight injustice at home and abroad may they discover that they, with us, are members of the one body.

3. For world leaders: may they invest more and more in the development of people and less in exploiting the natural resources of our world.
4. For prisoners and all who are away from those they love: may they be assured of a welcome when they return.
5. For all who work for human development: may they have the light to see that the Lord's is the earth and its fullness.

Concluding Prayer
Lord our God, we thank you for your constant presence in our changing world. May your presence ever remind us that we are not alone. We make this prayer through Christ our Lord.

TWENTY-NINTH WEEK OF THE YEAR: SATURDAY

Introduction
Aware of the Spirit living in us, we pray.

Intentions
1. For Church leaders: by what they say and do may we be moved always to welcome and never condemn those who have sinned.
2. For those who find no meaning in their suffering lives: may they be prevented from thinking that they are being punished.
3. For priests who are called to minister God's reconciliation: may they always show a spirit of patience and understanding.
4. If today we hear his call to repent, may we open our hearts; may the Lord grant the grace of ever deeper conversion.
5. For the many who, in different ways, share in the one ministry of Christ: may they work together in harmony for the good of the whole Church.

Concluding Prayer
Lord our God, we thank you for your constant presence in our changing world. May your presence ever remind us that we are not alone. We make this prayer through Christ our Lord.

WEEK 30

THIRTIETH WEEK OF THE YEAR: MONDAY

Introduction
The Lord alone is the source of our freedom and joy and so we place our needs before him.

Intentions
1. The Lord's people are bent low under many burdens. May we help to reduce the weight of unemployment, bad housing and inadequate health care.
2. His world is suffering from many oppressions. May we, in his name, do all we can to remove the threat of nuclear power, the tyranny of dictatorships, and other forces that attack the dignity of human life.
3. For those who are weighed down with burdens, at home or at work: may they know once again the joy of his help.
4. The Church brings the message of freedom to a troubled world; may it never limit his power to transform, heal and make new.
5. "The one you love is ill". We think of those who are hurting because of broken relationships, the widow who is lonely, the person who always feels unwelcome, the person without a home. May they come to know the Lord as the one who sets them free.

Concluding Prayer
Father, may Christ your Son, who gathered together his scattered apostles after rising from the dead and nourished them anew in the bread of the Eucharist, bring to all who are estranged or parted from loved ones, something of his nourishment, strength and reassurance. We make this prayer through Christ our Lord.

THIRTIETH WEEK OF THE YEAR: TUESDAY

Introduction
The Lord alone has the message of eternal life. We ask him

to create in each of us a longing for the coming of his kingdom.

Intentions
1. At our baptism the seeds of faith were sown. May the Church, through its leaders, always help these to grow, through example, encouragement and prayer.
2. May his kingdom come. Wherever there is injustice, lack of freedom, or oppression, we pray that the truth of the Gospel may penetrate.
3. That we may not be disheartened by failure but wait patiently for the life he has promised.
4. That husbands and wives may genuinely love and tenderly care for each other. May his kingdom come amongst them and heal them of any bitterness or resentment.
5. That the community called Church may be a place of shelter, warmth and growth.
6. That Christians everywhere will see themselves as a leavening force, seeking a more human way of life and witnessing to the values of the Gospel.

Concluding Prayer
Father, may Christ your Son, who gathered together his scattered apostles after rising from the dead and nourished them anew in the bread of the Eucharist, bring to all who are estranged or parted from loved ones, something of his nourishment, strength and reassurance. We make this prayer through Christ our Lord.

THIRTIETH WEEK OF THE YEAR: WEDNESDAY

Introduction
We pray with confidence to the Father, knowing that his Spirit is praying in us.

Intentions
1. That those who have heard the good news will not become complacent but will always see room for growth in their relationship with God and with each other.
2. That all who are confused by suffering and weakness may

use these times as an opportunity for even greater openness
to God's living Spirit.
3. That parents may genuinely love and respect their children
and never drive them to resentment.
4. May God's Church show an openness and true respect for
the dignity of each person, irrespective of race, social class or
creed.
5. May our work today be satisfying and fulfilling. May we
be generous in serving God and hasten the coming of his
kingdom.
6. May God increase in us daily the desire to receive his many
gifts that we may live lives worthy of his name and calling to
the heavenly feast.

Concluding Prayer
Father, may Christ your Son, who gathered together his scattered apostles after rising from the dead and nourished them
anew in the bread of the Eucharist, bring to all who are
estranged or parted from loved ones, something of his
nourishment, strength and reassurance. We make this prayer
through Christ our Lord.

THIRTIETH WEEK OF THE YEAR: THURSDAY

Introduction
Today we pray that we may always recognise the one who
comes to us in the name of the Lord.

Intentions
1. May our Church leaders readily acknowledge prophets and
be urged to action by their example.
2. That in an age of nuclear threat we may humbly rely only
on God's armour to keep us safe.
3. *Year 1:* May we come to know that nothing can separate
us from the love of God, but that we may conquer in all
dangers through the power of Christ.
4. For those who suffer rejection, imprisonment and even
death in their giving witness to the Gospel: may they know
the power of God's love.
5. Our hearts are hardened by our greed and our craving after

power. May we be open to the call of the prophet to a true repentance.

6. That we here today may recognise the witness of Christian married love as a call to deeper community within the Church.

7. Let us pray for all who have experienced disruption in their lives: for family members living far away; for emigrants and exiles; for victims of broken homes; may we be united in prayer and come at last to our Father's house.

Concluding Prayer
Father, may Christ your Son, who gathered together his scattered apostles after rising from the dead and nourished them anew in the bread of the Eucharist, bring to all who are estranged or parted from loved ones, something of his nourishment, strength and reassurance. We make this prayer through Christ our Lord.

THIRTIETH WEEK OF THE YEAR: FRIDAY

Introduction
The Creator of the universe entrusts to his people the cultivation and care of the earth we inhabit. We ask him to make us more responsive to his call and more conscientious in our creative task.

Intentions
1. The creative Spirit of God awakens our imagination and inventiveness. May we create new possibilities for those whose lives are dulled by boredom and routine, and new openings for the unemployed and the redundant.

2. The productive Spirit of God makes fruitful our daily toil. May the goods we produce enrich the lives of our fellow men and women and bring them renewed strength in body and spirit.

3. The artistic Spirit of God blesses those who enrich our world with artistic skill, architectural design, musical composition and dramatic performance. May he awaken in all men and women those hidden talents which add radiance and joy to human life.

4. The transforming Spirit of God works through those who bring healing and hope to the broken spirit of man. May he bless all those involved in the medical profession and those who care for our sick and elderly.

Concluding Prayer
Father, may Christ your Son, who gathered together his scattered apostles after rising from the dead and nourished them anew in the bread of the Eucharist, bring to all who are estranged or parted from loved ones, something of his nourishment, strength and reassurance. We make this prayer through Christ our Lord.

THIRTIETH WEEK OF THE YEAR: SATURDAY

Introduction
The Father guided his people as they wandered through the desert for forty years. We pray today for all who are far from home, those who have no home to live in, and those forced to live in exile.

Intentions
1. May the Lord of mercy and compassion look upon the prodigal sons and daughters of this world. May he give them the peace which he alone can give.
2. We pray for those who feel rejected, who, time and again, are told that there is no room at the inn. In the depth of their loneliness may they be saved from the bitterness that destroys and may their hearts be open to the gentle touch of love and acceptance.
3. We pray for all foreigners living in our own country: that they may find among us hospitality and supportive friendship.
4. We pray in a special way for the victims of war, particularly those forced to flee for protection or from the aftermath of ruin and destruction: may the Lord bring healing and hope to their broken hearts; may he restore their strength and help them to build a brighter future for themselves and their dear ones.
5. May Christ be with all who travel in exile or alone as he

was with the bewildered disciples on the road to Emmaus.
May he bring their journeyings to a happy and fruitful end.

Concluding Prayer
Father, may Christ your Son, who gathered together his scattered apostles after rising from the dead and nourished them
anew in the bread of the Eucharist, bring to all who are
estranged or parted from loved ones, something of his
nourishment, strength and reassurance. We make this prayer
through Christ our Lord.

WEEK 31

THIRTY-FIRST WEEK OF THE YEAR: MONDAY

Introduction
My brothers and sisters, let us pray through our Lord Jesus
Christ, not only for ourselves but for the many urgent needs
of the human family and particularly of its weakest
members.

Intentions
1. That Christians everywhere throughout the world may reach
out to the needy and readily recognise Jesus in the person of
the most abandoned.
2. That our public authorities may use the standards of the
Gospel in their allocation of the resources of the community.
3. That we may today show concern for the handicapped, the
discouraged, the ignored, the withdrawn and the disadvantaged.
4. That Christ may touch with his love those in the community who are alienated, smarting under rejection or insult.

Concluding Prayer
Father, hear the prayers of your suppliant people. You know
our needs. Grant our requests. Keep us always in your love,
loyal and true in the service of your Son. Bring all Christians
together in unity and mutual respect. We present our prayers
in the name of Jesus the Lord.

THIRTY-FIRST WEEK OF THE YEAR: TUESDAY

Introduction
My brothers and sisters, as we look forward to the heavenly banquet with Jesus and the saints, let us pray that we may constantly prepare ourselves for the final call and be ready to answer the summons when it comes.

Intentions
1. We pray that the face of Christ will be radiated by his faithful Church members throughout the world so that mankind may believe.
2. We pray for the liberation of those whose minds and desires are centred on money, power, revenge or domination.
3. We pray that public representatives may work for the common good unselfishly and generously.
4. We pray that all our neighbours, friends, workmates and family members may become increasingly aware of their Christian calling and the glorious destiny God has appointed for us.

Concluding Prayer
Father, hear the prayers of your suppliant people. You know our needs. Grant our requests. Keep us always in your love, loyal and true in the service of your Son. Bring all Christians together in unity and mutual respect. We present our prayers in the name of Jesus the Lord.

THIRTY-FIRST WEEK OF THE YEAR: WEDNESDAY

Introduction
My brothers and sisters, God wants us all to be diligent workers for the coming of his kingdom. We are his hands and his feet. Let us pray for greater generosity and sincerity in God's service.

Intentions
1. May the Church be transparent to its Lord, freed from the bondage of seeking power or wealth.
2. May those with responsibility for the common good over-

come self-interest and pursue justice, equality and fair play.
3. May we lighten the cross of others by our sympathy, our
readiness to share time, possessions and friendship.
4. May all our leisurely activities be in harmony with our love
of Christ and his teachings.
5. May we constantly test the values by which we live and
make decisions in conformity with the standards Jesus puts
before us in his Gospel.

Concluding Prayer
Father, hear the prayers of your suppliant people. You know
our needs. Grant our requests. Keep us always in your love,
loyal and true in the service of your Son. Bring all Christians
together in unity and mutual respect. We present our prayers
in the name of Jesus the Lord.

THIRTY-FIRST WEEK OF THE YEAR: THURSDAY

Introduction
My brothers and sisters, the God and Father of our Lord
Jesus Christ wills all mankind to be saved. Let us pray for an
all-embracing charity that excludes nobody.

Intentions
1. For the Church of God throughout the world: that it may
reconcile the estranged, eliminate divisions, heal wounds,
advance human solidarity.
2. For an end to war, recrimination, the armaments race and
nationalistic rivalries.
3. For the conversion of sinners, the rehabilitation of drug
addicts, the reform of alcoholics, the redress of injustice.
4. For harmony and mutual forgiveness in families, neighbours, industry and sport.
5. For mutual respect between members of opposed political
parties, for an end to discrimination on the basis of colour,
race or religious conviction.
6. For a more responsible use of tv and the other electronic
media.

Concluding Prayer
Father, hear the prayers of your suppliant people. You know
our needs. Grant our requests. Keep us always in your love,
loyal and true in the service of your Son. Bring all Christians
together in unity and mutual respect. We present our prayers
in the name of Jesus the Lord.

THIRTY-FIRST WEEK OF THE YEAR: FRIDAY

Introduction
Gathered together in Christ as brothers and sisters, we thank
and praise God for his many blessings. We ask him to hear
the prayers we make for the good estate of the Church and
its healthy adaptation to new situations.

Intentions
1. For zeal, enthusiasm and dedication in Church leaders and
people.
2. For imaginative initiatives in using the media to present
Jesus and the good news of the Gospel to the world.
3. For all oppressed by anti-Christian laws, for all who are
deprived of freedom of worship, for prisoners of conscience,
and persons deprived of civil liberties.
4. For vigilance and courage in protecting the defenceless, the
weak, the poor and the exploited.
5. For enterprise, vision and daring to experiment in our
parish and courage to break out of routine.

Concluding Prayer
Father, hear the prayers of your suppliant people. You know
our needs. Grant our requests. Keep us always in your love,
loyal and true in the service of your Son. Bring all Christians
together in unity and mutual respect. We present our prayers
in the name of Jesus the Lord.

THIRTY-FIRST WEEK OF THE YEAR: SATURDAY

Introduction
My brothers and sisters, we are gathered together to celebrate

the mystery of our salvation in Jesus Christ. Let us ask our Father to open our minds to the beauty of his truth and to enrich us with a firm grasp of Christian values.

Intentions

1. That the Church's attitude to money be one of detachment and independence, that the Church may be seen to be the friend of the poor.
2. That money be used for the service of people and never be a priority over human need.
3. We pray for the victims of unscrupulous moneylenders, for those oppressed by debt, for the victims of fraud, deceit and criminal conspiracy.
4. We pray that we may never judge people by their possessions nor use money as a measure of our esteem of others.
5. With Mary and Joseph we pray for families and those preparing to marry. May their love and their happiness increase.

Concluding Prayer

Father, hear the prayers of your suppliant people. You know our needs. Grant our requests. Keep us always in your love, loyal and true in the service of your Son. Bring all Christians together in unity and mutual respect. We present our prayers in the name of Jesus the Lord.

WEEK 32

THIRTY-SECOND WEEK OF THE YEAR: MONDAY

Introduction

Let us pray with faith and confidence to God our Father that we become more alert and single-minded in his service.

Intentions

1. May all Church members be faithful, loyal and responsible witnesses to the Lord Jesus, cost what it may.
2. May Christians respond to the expectations of the world

community as peacemakers and bridge-builders.
3. May public representatives be tireless promoters of justice, integrity and brotherhood.
4. May the hurts caused by scandal be healed; may the victims of graft and corruption be supported.
5. May brotherly love and mutual esteem grow in our local community. May the love of Jesus draw us closer together.

Concluding Prayer
Almighty, ever living God, you will all mankind to come to the knowledge of your truth. Shape us to be your docile instruments. Let your Church enjoy peace and joy as it proclaims the good news to the ends of the earth. May harmony prevail, unity grow and true brotherhood flourish. We ask this through Christ our Lord.

THIRTY-SECOND WEEK OF THE YEAR: TUESDAY

Introduction
My brothers and sisters, as God's chosen people we pray for fidelity in his service, for humility in one another's service, for generosity in our approach to all humankind.

Intentions
1. For a humble and servant Church, open to the needs of people, working for unity and reconciliation.
2. For those who exercise power: that they may listen to the cries of the hungry, the weak, the neglected.
3. For a deeper involvement by civil servants and tv people in promoting the poor and the helpless.
4. For a generous readiness on our part to share what we have with the poor nations and the underprivileged masses.
5. For a delicate sensitivity to the presence of Jesus in our parish community and in our families.

Concluding Prayer
Almighty, ever living God, you will all mankind to come to the knowledge of your truth. Shape us to be your docile instruments. Let your Church enjoy peace and joy as it pro-

claims the good news to the ends of the earth. May harmony prevail, unity grow and true brotherhood flourish. We ask this through Christ our Lord.

THIRTY-SECOND WEEK OF THE YEAR: WEDNESDAY

Introduction
My brothers and sisters, let us ask God to make us a truly eucharistic community, giving thanks for the blessing of life and friendship.

Intentions
1. May Christians grow in their appreciation of the Church and be constantly alert for God's love and providence.
2. May the gospel principles be a yardstick of public administration, respecting human dignity always.
3. May the sick be comforted by our concern, may prisoners be helped, may the dispossessed experience our care.
4. May our parish community witness to its Lord by the quality of our personal prayer, our public worship and our care for one another.

Concluding Prayer
Almighty, ever living God, you will all mankind to come to the knowledge of your truth. Shape us to be your docile instruments. Let your Church enjoy peace and joy as it proclaims the good news to the ends of the earth. May harmony prevail, unity grow and true brotherhood flourish. We ask this through Christ our Lord.

THIRTY-SECOND WEEK OF THE YEAR: THURSDAY

Introduction
My brothers and sisters, the kingdom of God is among us. Let us pray that it may be realised among all those for whom we pray today.

Intentions
1. For the Church: that it may become more and more the

realisation of the kingdom of God's love in our midst.
2. For our own local community: that it may build up in its midst the kingdom of justice which flows from love.
3. For ourselves in our individual lives: that we may realise that the kingdom of God is within us.
4. For those who like the Son of Man are suffering to bring the kingdom of God about.
5. For joy in our service of the kingdom, the joy which comes from perfect giving.

Concluding Prayer
Almighty, ever living God, you will all mankind to come to the knowledge of your truth. Shape us to be your docile instruments. Let your Church enjoy peace and joy as it proclaims the good news to the ends of the earth. May harmony prevail, unity grow and true brotherhood flourish. We ask this through Christ our Lord.

THIRTY-SECOND WEEK OF THE YEAR: FRIDAY

Introduction
We have come into the Lord's presence that we may be healed. Let us pray that we may become his instruments of healing and grace to one another and to the whole world.

Intentions
1. May we take to heart the Lord's warnings to us in the disasters which strike our world.
2. May we listen to the voice of the Lord in the wonders of creation, in the upheavals of nature.
3. May we watch and wait as his faithful servants until he comes.
4. May we generously share with those who are smitten by continuous drought and by shortage of the essentials of life.
5. May we be healed of all our fears and preoccupations as we listen in faith to his word.

Concluding Prayer
Almighty, ever living God, you will all mankind to come to the knowledge of your truth. Shape us to be your docile

instruments. Let your Church enjoy peace and joy as it proclaims the good news to the ends of the earth. May harmony prevail, unity grow and true brotherhood flourish. We ask this through Christ our Lord.

THIRTY-SECOND WEEK OF THE YEAR: SATURDAY

Introduction
My brothers and sisters, faith gathers us together. We beg our Father to hear our prayers, to keep us in his love, and to endow us with the spirit of unceasing prayer.

Intentions
1. Enrich people and priests with a prayerful spirit and a humble readiness to hear the gospel.
2. May public authorities show respect for the name and worship of God.
3. Give perseverance and persistence to those who champion the oppressed and the deprived.
4. Open our hearts to the urgent needs of our hungry brothers and sisters.
5. Fill us with a practical concern for the growth in unity of this local community.
6. May Mary, queen of justice and peace, bring our prayers for the harmony of nations before the throne of heaven.

Concluding Prayer
Almighty, ever living God, you will all mankind to come to the knowledge of your truth. Shape us to be your docile instruments. Let your Church enjoy peace and joy as it proclaims the good news to the ends of the earth. May harmony prevail, unity grow and true brotherhood flourish. We ask this through Christ our Lord.

WEEK 33

THIRTY-THIRD WEEK OF THE YEAR: MONDAY

Introduction
With the persistence of the blind man of Jericho as an example, let us turn to God our Father, entreating him to have pity on us and to hear our prayers.

Intentions
1. Let us pray that the Christian community continue to make Christ vividly present for the people of our time.
2. For all peoples: that they come to recognize Christ in their midst.
3. We pray for the needy of this world: that they find in us listening and generous hearts.
4. That we in our locality come to a greater consciousness of our responsibilities towards the poor and the oppressed.

Concluding Prayer
Loving Father, look with favour on these petitions, which we your people bring before you in faith and confidence. Through Christ our Lord.

THIRTY-THIRD WEEK OF THE YEAR: TUESDAY

Introduction
Turning to our merciful Father, let us bring before him our needs and petitions.

Intentions
1. We pray for the Church: that she keep constantly in mind the mission of her Lord and Master to seek out and save the lost.
2. That a spirit of forgiveness be evident among the nations of the world in their dealings with one another.
3. That those with plenty be more aware of the plight of the needy.
4. For ourselves: that in our everyday lives we demonstrate greater love and understanding towards one another.

Concluding Prayer
Loving Father, look with favour on these petitions, which we
your people bring before you in faith and confidence.
Through Christ our Lord.

THIRTY-THIRD WEEK OF THE YEAR: WEDNESDAY

Introduction
God our Father has already blessed us with many gifts.
Confident that he will hear us, let us come before him with
our petitions.

Intentions
1. That all who hold office in the Church exercise it dili-
gently, under the guidance of the Holy Spirit, for the good
of all the faithful.
2. For those who find themselves in positions of authority in
society: that they use their power in a spirit of service to
others.
3. Let us pray that the talents of doctors, scientists and other
experts be used in helping the poor, the needy and the sick
of this world.
4. That each of us, in our local situation, use our gifts in love
and service of our brothers and sisters.

Concluding Prayer
Loving Father, look with favour on these petitions, which we
your people bring before you in faith and confidence.
Through Christ our Lord.

THIRTY-THIRD WEEK OF THE YEAR: THURSDAY

Introduction
As obedient children of a loving Father we come to God in
confidence with our concerns and requests.

Intentions
1. We pray for the leaders of the Church: that they be ever
sensitive to the voice of the Spirit in the signs of the times.

2. That all recognize the value of peace and strive to attain it in our world today.
3. For our children: that, as they face and confront the world, they find in us adults the support and the example they need.
4. Let us pray for on another: that we recognize the opportunities of grace offered us by God each day.

Concluding Prayer
Loving Father, look with favour on these petitions, which we your people bring before you in faith and confidence. Through Christ our Lord.

THIRTY-THIRD WEEK OF THE YEAR: FRIDAY

Introduction
Gathered together in this house of prayer, let us with confidence bring our needs before our loving Father.

Intentions
1. We pray that the Church throughout the world continue to grow in faith and love.
2. That respect for human rights be evident among the nations of each continent.
3. Let us remember those afflicted by addiction of any kind: that they allow the healing touch of Jesus into their lives.
4. For all the people of our parish and especially parents, as they seek to lead their children to God.

Concluding Prayer
Loving Father, look with favour on these petitions, which we your people bring before you in faith and confidence. Through Christ our Lord.

THIRTY-THIRD WEEK OF THE YEAR: SATURDAY

Introduction
Knowing that our heavenly Father gives good things to those who ask, let us bring before him our prayers.

Intentions
1. Let us pray that a greater number of Christians play a more active role in Church life.
2. That our present age be not deprived of the voice of the prophet.
3. For the underprivileged in our community: that they be recognized as the brothers and sisters of Jesus and treated accordingly.
4. For ourselves: that as a parish we grow closer together in the Lord.

Concluding Prayer
Loving Father, look with favour on these petitions, which we your people bring before you in faith and confidence. Through Christ our Lord.

WEEK 34

THIRTY-FOURTH WEEK OF THE YEAR: MONDAY

Introduction
With trust and confidence let us come before God our Father, praying for the needs of all his people.

Intentions
1. Let us pray for all who exercise a service of leadership in the Church: may they follow the example and teaching of the Lord Jesus by carrying out their task with humility, patience and kindness, without arrogance or favour.
2. Let us pray for all who work in social services: may they show compassion and courtesy in their dealings with the needy, and help to bring about a caring community.
3. Let us remember in our prayers all widows: may we always be concerned for them in their loneliness and neglect, and help them in their most felt needs.
4. Let us pray that we may not count the cost in our giving: may we remember that it is not the value of the gift that counts but the generosity of the giver.
5. Let us remember all whose work is dangerous, those who

risk their lives for others, and all victims of violence: may they experience the support of our intercession and know God's merciful love in their lives.

6. *Year 1:* Let us pray that we may remain faithful to the practice of our religion: may we be loyal to Christ and his teaching when we meet contempt, ridicule or indifference.

6. *Year 2:* Let us pray for perseverance in our Christian lives: when death calls us may we be found without fault and considered worthy to join the saints in heaven.

Concluding Prayer
Father, hear the prayers we make as we wait in hope for the blessed coming of our Lord and Saviour Jesus Christ who reigns with you for ever. Amen

---

THIRTY-FOURTH WEEK OF THE YEAR: TUESDAY

Introduction
Christ promised to be with us even until the end of time: with him let us pray to the Father, being mindful of the many needs of his people.

Intentions
1. Let us pray for the gift of discernment in the Church: that we may seek the truth in love and not be deceived by false signs and prophets.
2. Let us remember all those caught up in the effects of wars and revolutions (especially in . . . .): that we may render help and comfort to the sick, the homeless and the hungry.
3. We pray for daily courage and patience in our lives, frightened as we may be by the threat of war and violence: we pray that we may always be makers of peace in the place where we live.
4. Let us remember that human achievements, wealth and power are passing things; we pray that we may so work for the advancement of mankind that we may not forget the building up of the kingdom of God.
5. *Year 1:* We pray for trust in God's power supporting the Church in a changing world: that we may be a people of praise forever blessing the works of his hands.

5. *Year 2:* We remember that God will judge not only individuals but also communities and nations: let us pray for energy and enthusiasm in our work for social justice and peace.

Concluding Prayer
Father, we make these prayers in faith and trust. Hear all our desires and help us to do your will. We ask this through Christ our Lord.

THIRTY-FOURTH WEEK OF THE YEAR: WEDNESDAY

Introduction
We believe in God's active presence in our world. Let us ask him then to support us in our daily needs.

Intentions
1. For Christians throughout the world: that they be not afraid of persecution, treachery or death for the sake of Jesus' name.
2. For prisoners of conscience in all countries of the world: that they may not feel isolated from all men of good will nor lose their interior freedom.
3. For all facing personal difficulties: that they may have courage, and be helped by the thoughtfulness of those they meet.
4. For each one here present: that through the problems and difficulties of this life the hope of the kingdom of God may be a support each day.
5. For the dying: that they may not fear death but see it as achieving true life through their perseverance.
6. *Year 1:* For all here present: that we may work to the best of our abilities so that on the day of judgement when weighed in the balance we may not be found wanting.
6. *Year 2:* For our friends and relations who have died: that they may join with the angels in singing the wonderful works of God.

Concluding Prayer
Father, listen to our many needs some of which we have put

before you this day. Your Son gave us the confidence to ask for all we need. May our asking always be a sign of our faith in him who lives and reigns with you for ever and ever.

THIRTY-FOURTH WEEK OF THE YEAR: THURSDAY

Introduction
Let us pray to God whose love is eternal and whose mercy is from age to age.

Intentions
1. That all Christian people may live in high expectation of the day when the Lord Jesus Christ will come with power and great glory.
2. That we may be moved to practical concern for the refugees and the homeless in those countries desolated by war and civil disturbance.
3. That we may have the wisdom to recognise the shortness of our lives: may we use the time given us in greater service of God and neighbour.
4. That, being detached from persons and places, from power and wealth, we may be able to give an example of true freedom.
5. That the sick may have the comfort of Christ's presence to relieve their distress, remove their fears, give them peace, and restore their health.
6. *Year 1:* That all nations may come to know the kingship of the living God who saves, sets free, and works signs and wonders in the heavens and on earth.
6. *Year 2:* That our celebration of Mass may fill us with joy in the hope of heaven when we shall share in the wedding feast of the Lamb.

Concluding Prayer
Father, hear our prayers as we wait in hope for the blessed coming of our Lord and Saviour Jesus Christ who reigns with you forever.

THIRTY-FOURTH WEEK OF THE YEAR: FRIDAY

Introduction
United in Christ who told us to ask the Father for all our needs, we now pray with trust and confidence.

Intentions
1. Let us pray for all who teach and preach the word of God: may they do so with confidence in the everlasting power of that word.
2. Let us pray for all who work for the survival of this generation: may we support all efforts to eliminate the threat of nuclear holocaust.
3. Let us pray for the people of this country: may we share prosperity rather than seek private gain, may we work for peace and reconciliation rather than self preservation.
4. Let us pray for those who work for the preservation of endangered species of animal and plant life: may we take personal responsibility for love and care of God's creation.
5. Let us pray for the gift of prophecy: may we be open to the signs of the times, and not blind to the work of the Spirit in the lives of individuals and communities.
6. Let us pray for a courageous and peaceful mind: may we be lifted above our anxieties and fears, and go forward with trust in God.
7. *Year 1:* Let us pray that one day our names may be written in the book of life: may we always keep in mind that the Lord will judge us according to our way of life.
7. *Year 2:* Let us pray that we may be ready to meet the Lord when he comes on the clouds of heaven: may we always keep in mind that he will judge us according to our way of life.

Concluding Prayer
Father, we make these prayers in faith and trust. Hear all our desires and help us to do your will. We ask this through Christ our Lord.

THIRTY-FOURTH WEEK OF THE YEAR: SATURDAY

Introduction
Let us come before the Lord who made us for he is our God
and we are his people. He cares for us and listens to our
prayers.

Intentions
1. We are to stay awake praying at all times.
   We now pray for all who lead the Church in the ways of
prayer: through them may we find strength to persevere to
the end.
2. We are to watch ourselves lest our hearts be coarsened.
   We pray for all who seek to escape the challenges of life
through the abuse of alcohol and sexuality: may we help each
other by our concern and example.
3. We are not to be weighed down by the cares of life.
   We pray for parents, for the unemployed, for those
who struggle to make ends meet: may we always be grateful
for what we have received.
4. Our prayer of hope is to be, "Marana tha – Come, Lord
Jesus".
   We pray for all on the later stages of their pilgrim
journey, the elderly and infirm, the seriously ill and the
dying: in all the trials of flesh and spirit may we support each
other in prayer and work.
5. *Year 1:* We have been shown the vision of God's servants
at the river of life.
   We pray for all our friends who have died recently: may
they and all the faithful departed see God face to face in true
light.
5. *Year 2:* In heaven the spirits and souls of the virtuous give
glory and eternal praise to God.
   We pray for all those who have recently died: may they
and all the faithful departed join in the unending hymn of
praise.

Concluding Prayer
Father, listen to our many needs some of which we have put
before you this day. Your Son gave us confidence to ask for
all we need. May our asking always be a sure sign of our faith
in him who lives and reigns with you for ever and ever.

FEASTS AND SOLEMNITIES

JANUARY

Solemnity of Mary, Mother of God

Introduction
We are children of God and co-heirs with his Son who was born of Mary. Let us make our needs known and call upon the blessing of God.

Intentions
1. That this New Year which begins today may bring peace to our broken world, a peace which only God can give.
2. That we too may hear the word of God and respond to it as Mary did.
3. That our leaders of Church and government may guide us this year with wisdom and truth.
4. That Mary, who treasured in her heart the mystery of the birth of God's Son, might inspire us to become men and women of deep prayer.

Concluding Prayer
Lord God, you sent your Son among us born of Mary. May our response to your word be deep and true so that we might make him known in our day, for he is Lord for ever and ever.

St John Bosco

Introduction
The Father made his priest John Bosco a sign and bearer of his love for young people in his Son Jesus. As we keep his memory today we turn to God in prayer.

Intentions
1. May we respond more generously to the friendship God

gives us in his Son Jesus and work actively to make other people his friends too.

2. In the spirit of St John Bosco may we see our daily duties as our first and surest path to holiness and joy.

3. May we become like St John Bosco signs and bearers of God's great love for young people, in the good example we give them, in the welcome we extend to them, in the trust we show them, and in the zeal we display to help and save them.

4. May all those involved in the Christian education of young people, parents, teachers and youth workers, find inspiration in St John Bosco and try to lead young people into real joy in this life and along the ways that will lead to the endless joy of heaven.

Concluding Prayer
Father, in the great love which you have shown us in your Son, and in all his friends and saints, we ask you to hear the prayers which we have made in faith as we remember your priest St John Bosco. We ask this through Christ our Lord.

FEBRUARY

1 FEBRUARY

St Brigid
Ireland

Introduction
Today we ask the help of God in the name of St Brigid, Mary of the Irish, whom he gave to us as patron and intercessor.

Intentions
1. May God stir up in our hearts the zeal that St Brigid showed in her heart for the good of the Church.
2. May the governments of the world, as Brigid did, remedy the injustices inflicted on the poor.
3. May we make our own Brigid's way of life: to feed the poor and exercise mercy towards all in misery.
4. That we may have true love for Ireland and the Christian heritage of which Brigid herself is part.

5. May Mary's mantle be over our dead, guiding them safely into the eternal presence of God.

Concluding Prayer
Father, fill us with the spirit of St Brigid, so that we may follow your Son always in this world in the guise of our neighbour, through Christ our Lord.

---

1 FEABHRA

Naomh Bríd
Éire

Réamhrá
Iarraimid cabhair Dé inniu trí impí Naomh Bríd ós é a thug dúinn í, Muire na nGael, mar éarlamh agus mar idirghuítheoir.

Achainí
1. Go músclaí Dia inár gcroí an dúthracht a bhí i gcroí Bhríde ar son leas na hEaglaise.
2. Go bhfóire rialtais an domhain ar leatrom na mbocht mar a rinne Naomh Bríd.
3. Go nglacaimid chugainn ardchuspóir Bhríde: sásamh na mbocht agus trua do lucht na hainnise.
4. Go raibh grá fíor againn d'Éirinn agus dá hoidhreacht Chríostaí.
5. Brat Mhuire go raibh ar ár mairbh, á seoladh slán isteach i láthair Dé go síoraí.

Paidir Scoir
A Athair, líon sinn de fairsing Bhríde, chun do Mhac a leanúint go dlúth ar an saol seo i gcló ár gcomharsan. Trí Chríost ár dTiarna.

Presentation of the Lord

Introduction
My brothers and sisters, as we listen to the words of Simeon and Anna today, may we too be filled with wonder in the presence of Jesus; and may that wonder lead us now to pray.

Intentions
1. We pray for the Church: that, inspired by the Holy Spirit with wisdom and knowledge, she may follow the example of Simeon and Anna in making Jesus and his mission known to the world.
2. We remember those in authority: that they may be conscious of the responsibilities of their vocation as a call to love and serve as Jesus has shown us by the example of leadership.
3. For the children of the world: that they may be cherished and loved by their families and the societies in which they live.
4. For those who are confused and bewildered: that in the darkness of their turmoil they may have the courage to turn to Jesus, the light of the world, and find in him new vision and hope for the future.
5. For elderly people: that as they age they may not be resentful of the passing of youth: but, like Simeon and Anna, may they entrust themselves to the Lord in prayer.

Concluding Prayer
Heavenly Father, in the name of Jesus your Son, the light of the world, we give you glory and praise. May you hear our prayers at the intercession of Anna and Simeon, Mary and Joseph. Through Christ our Lord.

Our Lady of Lourdes

Introduction
Let us pray to our heavenly Father that the message of Lourdes may be a comfort for all his people.

Intentions
1. We pray that the Lourdes call for penance and prayer may be heeded throughout the Church.
2. We pray for the healing of the nations through reconciliation and love.
3. We pray that those who have recourse to the Virgin conceived without sin may experience her motherly care.
4. We pray for those who travel to Lourdes, for those who organize pilgrimages, for the people of the town itself: that they may all know the healing grace of Christ.
5. We pray for the sick throughout the world: that they may receive healing and come to fullness of life and inner peace no matter what their illness may be.

Concluding Prayer
Heavenly Father, we thank you for the revelation of your Son, Jesus, born of the Immaculate Virgin; hear these prayers which we confidently make with her intercession and in the name of Jesus, your Son and our Lord.

MARCH

1 MARCH

St David
Wales

Introduction
Saint David, patron of Wales, endeared himself to many by his example of cheerfulness in holiness, by the eloquence with which he preserved the Church from error, and by the open-handed charity he showed to all in need. We pray that his

patronage may ever prosper the true teaching of Christ's
Church and the kingdom of his grace.

Intentions
1. We pray that God may keep us true to that faith which
Saint David upheld by the guidance of the Holy Spirit, and
which he left us as a holy legacy.
2. May we imitate him by the happiness with which we
celebrate the holy mysteries and share the Sacrament which
makes us one in faith and love.
3. May the monastic life, by means of which the faith was
once spread throughout Wales, be preserved among us; may
it find new vocations and be an example of holiness to all.
4. Following the example of Saint David, may we turn
promptly and generously to every call on our charity, and be
ready to serve God especially in those who are homeless,
distressed, or disabled.
5. We pray for that unity which will enable the world to
recognize Christ's kingdom by the love that unites his
disciples.

Concluding Prayer
Heavenly Father, may the intercessions we have offered
through your servant, our patron Saint David, enable us to
present our holy gifts with joy, to receive your sacraments
with reverence, and to share your grace with all men in love.
Through Christ our Lord.

1 MAWRTH

Dewi Sant
Cymru

Rhagymadrodd
Yr oedd Dewi, Nawddsant Cymru, yn annwyl i'w bobl an iddo arddangos sancteidddrwydd llawen, huodledd a waredodd
yr Eglwys rhag gau athrawiaeth, a haelioni cariadus tuag at
y rhai anghenus. Gweddïwn y bydd ei nawdd yn hyrwyddo'n
gyson wir athrawiaeth Eglwys Crist a Theyrnas ei ras.

Diysiadau
1. Gweddïwn bydd Duw yn ein cadw'n deyrngar i'r un gred a gynhaliai Dewi Sant drwy arweiniad yr Ysbryd Glân, ac a draddododd, yn etifeddiaeth sanctaidd, i ninnau.
2. Bydded i ni efelychu Dewi yn ein dedwyddwch wrth ddathlu'r dirgeleddau sanctaidd a chyfranogi o'r Sagrafen sy'n ein gwneud yn un mewn ffydd a chariad.
3. Bydded i'r bywyd mynachaidd, yr ymledodd y Ffydd drwyddo yng Nghymru gynt, aros yn ein plith i fod yn batrwm sancteiddrwydd i'r byd a bydded iddo gynyddu drwy alwadau newydd.
4. Gan efelychu Dewi Sant, bydded i ninnau ymateb yn hael i bawb sy'n ymofyn cymwynas, gan fod yn barod i wasanaethu Duw yn arbennig yn y rhai sy'n ddigartref, mewn trallod neu'n fethedig.
5. Gweddïwn am yr undod a fydd yn galluogi'r byd i adnabod teyrnas Crist trwy undod cariadus ei ddisgyblion.

Gweddi Olaf
O Dad Nefol, bydded i'n hymbiliadau drwy eiriolaeth dy was, ein Nawddsant Dewi, ein galluogi i gyflwyno'n llawen ein rhoddion cysegredig, i dderbyn dy sagrafennau yn wylaidd ac i gyfranogi o'th ras gyda phawb mewn undod cariadus. Trwy Iesu Grist ein Harglwydd.

---

8 MARCH

St John Ogilvie, Priest and Martyr
Scotland

Introduction
As we remember, affirm and celebrate the life of St John Ogilvie, we turn to the Father who is present to his Church gathered for worship.

Intentions
1. We pray for the Church: that she may sustain and nourish the whole life of God's people in her proclamation of the acceptable year of the Lord.
2. We pray for our leaders: may they seek to unite with others

of good will to work for a new international order, based on human dignity and values.

3. We pray for those who witness to the Gospel in difficult times: may they, like St John Ogilvie, continue to declare the saving mission of Christ in the world today.

4. We pray for the sick, the lonely and the bereaved: may we unite with them in practical love and hope.

5. We pray for our local needs: may we realize the necessary place of forgiveness and reconciliaton in individual and community growth.

Concluding Prayer
God our Father, receive our prayers and grant us your help as we pray to St John Ogilvie, and make us all to be courageous and caring followers of Christ your Son our Lord.

---

12 MARCH

The Novena of Grace (Final Day)

Introduction
On this day of grace, which sees the conclusion of our nine days of prayer, we gather together all the petitions of those who have made this novena and we present them to the Lord through the intercession of his servant, Francis.

Intentions
1. For the grace of faith: that the Lord would confirm us all in the truths of the Gospel and especially in the conviction of his mercy and love.

2. For the grace of hope: that the Lord would deepen within us our confidence in his love and the strength to turn from sin and to seek only his will.

3. For the grace of charity: that the Lord would set our hearts on fire with something of that love for God and man which he gave to his servant, Francis.

4. For the grace of repentance: that the Lord would accept our penances this Lent as an earnest of our contrition, and

that we would learn to grieve for our sins because they offend his love.

5. For all our needs in body, mind and heart: that the Lord would help all here present and those for whom we pray, the poor, the sick, the lonely, the weak; that we might learn again this Lent to bear the cross with Christ so as to have an even greater share in the consolation of Easter.

Concluding Prayer
Almighty God and Father, you have been pleased to work countless wonders through the intercession of Francis Xavier. Grant by his merits and prayers that we learn to love and cherish not only the gifts of God but the Giver through whom they come, Jesus Christ our Lord.

17 MARCH

St Patrick
Australia, England and Wales, Ireland, Scotland

Introduction
Patrick's faith expresses itself in his writings through his practice of prayer to his heavenly Father. Let us now direct our own prayer to the Father in the same spirit of faith and with the same personal conviction.

Intentions
1. For our bishops, priests, teachers, and all who speak in the name of the Church: that they may lead us into the deeper understanding of the teaching of Christ which is required by the needs of our times.
2. For our public representatives at home and abroad: that they may be an example of Christian living to all whom they meet and with whom they work.
3. For those who strive to bring our people together, whatever their race or creed: that by the power of Christ they may heal the wounds of fear and history.
4. For our own local community: that we may give witness to our faith by our kindness to those who need our help, the

old and the young, the sick and the lonely, and those who are
deprived in any way.

5. For all of us gathered here to honour Saint Patrick: that
our love for our country may arouse in us a stronger commitment to Christ and to his Gospel which our forefathers have
handed down to us.

Concluding Prayer
God our Father, hear the prayers of your people. Guide us
on our way to you, inspired by Patrick our national apostle.
Through Christ our Lord.

---

17 MÁRTA

Naomh Pádraig
Éire

Réamhrá
Nuair a léimid scríbhinní Phádraig, feicimid mar a chuir sé
a chreideamh in iúl do Dhia agus é ag guí. Cuirimís ár
bpaidreacha féin in iúl dár nAthair ar neamh mar a chuir
Pádraig, go bríomhar, dóchasach, duthrachtach.

Achainí
1. Guímis ar son na n-easpag, na sagart, na múinteoirí, ar
son gach duine a labhraíonn thar ceann na hEaglaise: go
dtugaidis tuiscint níos doimhne dúinn ar theagasc Chríost
mar is oiriúnach i saol na linne seo.
2. Guímis ar son ár n-ionaidithe poiblí i gcéin agus sa bhaile
in Éireann: go dtugaidis dea-shampla ina mbeatha gach áit a
dtéann siad agus do gach dream dá mbuaileann siad leo.
3. Guímis ar son na ndaoine a oibríonn go dian ar mhaithe
le muintir na hÉireann a thabhairt le chéile: go n-éirí leo trí
chumhacht Chríost creáchtaí na heagla agus na staire a
leigheas.
4. Guímis ar son ár bpobail áitiúil féin: go neartaí ár
gcreideamh sinn i dtreo is go mbeimid níos cineálta do
dhaoine atá i gcrua-chás, do dhaoine aosta agus do pháistí,
do dhaoine atá breoite agus in ísle brí, agus go gach duine a
luíonn an saol go trom air.

5. Guímis ar son a chéile atá bailithe le chéile anseo in onóir Naomh Phádraig: go spreaga ár ngrá tíre grá pearsanta do Chríost ionainn agus grá dá Shoiscéal a bhronn ár sinsear orainn.

Paidir Scoir
A Dhia uileachumachtaigh, éist le guí do phobail. Treoraigh sinn ar ár mbealach chugat 'le cúnamh ó Phádraig. Trí Chríost ár dTiarna.

---

19 MARCH

St Joseph, husband of the Blessed Virgin Mary

Introduction
We turn to God in whom all fatherhood has its origin and pray with confidence as to-day we honour St Joseph.

Intentions
1. Joseph watched over the Son of God. We pray for all priests and ministers who serve in the body of Christ and who feed God's people with his body and blood.
2. Joseph was upright and honourable. We pray for all in public office: that they may guide our people unselfishlessly and with wisdom.
3. Joseph cared for the family of Nazareth. We pray for all heads of families and for single parents: that they may have joy in their children.
4. Joseph was a simple carpenter. We pray for all workers: that they may have fulfilment in their jobs. We pray for those who cannot work or are unemployed: that they may find strength, courage and personal dignity.
5. Joseph walked in faith. We pray for ourselves: that we may know the guidance of God in all our affairs.

Concluding Prayer
Eternal Wisdom, loving Father, you teach us profound truths in the simple home of Nazareth; may our minds be always opened to your way, and our hearts ready to follow Jesus, your Son and our Lord.

The Annunciation of the Lord

Introduction
My sisters and brothers, we recall today with great joy the sacred moment when, graced by the Holy Spirit, Mary accepted her unique vocation in God's plan for all men and women, and conceived in her womb God's only Son, the Saviour of the world. May our prayers, united in the sacrifice of Jesus, bear fruit in our lives.

Intentions
1. We pray for the Church: that by her acceptance of the will of the Father, Jesus may be conceived in the hearts and minds of all peoples.
2. For those elected to govern the nations of the world: that, as they make their decisions for the welfare of their people, they may, like Mary, listen attentively to the word of God and allow themselves be guided by it.
3. We pray for expectant mothers: that they may accept the children they carry with love and joy.
4. We remember all women: that they may see in God's graciousness to Mary the dignity of womanhood and motherhood.
5. For all present: that as we try to follow Mary's example we may be strengthened by the power of the Holy Spirit.

Concluding Prayer
God our Father, you chose Mary to be the mother of your Son and graced her with gifts given to no one else. In our days you call us too and grace us. May we, through the intercession of Mary, respond to your call to bring Jesus into the lives of all people. We ask this through Christ our Lord.

APRIL

St John Baptist De La Salle

Introduction
In the spirit of Saint John Baptist de la Salle, let us offer our prayers, mindful of our needs, of the needs of Christian education, and of those who serve Christ and his Church in the instruction of others.

Intentions
1. All wisdom is of God. Let us pray that all that is taught and learned in our schools may be seen in the light of the Gospel and its values, and that our young people may be led into the way of truth.
2. We pray for those deprived of education through poverty or discrimination. May the Spirit of Christ the Teacher inspire all of us to ensure that all men receive the equality that is their due.
3. Saint De La Salle showed a firm and resolute attachment to the Chair of Saint Peter. Let us pray for the grace to be attentive to the voice of the Spirit, as expressed through the pope, the bishops, and our spiritual leaders.
4. As we recall the radical commitment of John Baptist De La Salle to the Christian message, we pray that the Lord may grant us the grace to follow generously in the way of love and the Gospel maxims.
5. For parents and teachers; let us pray that God may grant them the grace to educate the young according to Gospel principles.
6. For all religious communities, especially those engaged in the great apostolate of Christian education: we pray to the Lord that they may be zealous for his glory and follow faithfully in the footsteps of their founders.

Concluding Prayer
Father, look favourably upon the prayers we offer. Through the intercession of Saint John Baptist De La Salle, Patron of all Teachers, grant that all educators of youth be nourished

by your divine word. We make our prayer through the Word of Life, Christ our Lord.

---

23 APRIL

St George, Martyr, Patron Saint of England
England and Wales

Introduction
Today we venerate St George, our patron saint, who triumphed over the wiles of Satan by 'his good deeds which are known only to God' and by the witness of his martyrdom through the precious blood of the Lamb. Relying on his patronage, we make our needs known to our heavenly Father.

Intentions
1. Let us pray for the Church in our land, our bishops, clergy and lay people: that we may witness to our faith in Christ and, like St George, reap a rich harvest of good works.
2. We pray for our Sovereign, N.N., and all the royal family together with the government: that they may be guided in all their decisions by the right principles of peace, justice and love.
3. Let us pray for the young people of this country, the true hope of the future: that they may be true to God and to themselves and stand firm amidst the temptations of this life so that they may win for themselves the crown of life.
4. Let us pray that all our people may live together in true peace and harmony, that they may understand their own responsibility towards the less fortunate, and be found watching and ready at the Lord's second coming.
5. We pray for all who have died in defence of their country and for all who have departed this life: that they may all come, together with ourselves, into the glorious light of God's presence.

Concluding Prayer
Abba, Father, today we give you thanks for the protection of St George whom you have given to us as our patron. Through the merits of his martyrdom we ask you to listen to

our prayers. Grant that we may imitate your Son who has taught us by word and example to love one another as he has loved us and so come one day to that kingdom where he lives and reigns with you for ever and ever.

MAY

---

4 MAY

The Beatified Martyrs of England and Wales
England and Wales

Introduction
By his Spirit God our Father gave strength to our martyrs to enable them to bear witness to him in their sufferings. With confidence in the prayers of those who stood firm to the end, we make our petitions to our Father in heaven.

Intentions
1. Let us pray that, as spiritual descendants of the martyrs, Christians may bear witness by their lives to the Son of Man now in glory.
2. We pray for an end to strife and disharmony in our society.
3. We pray that all Christians may work and pray together so that soon there may be one flock and one shepherd.
4. We pray for all who are victims of injustice and ill-treatment: that they may be released from their sufferings and bear no malice against their persecutors.
5. Let us pray for all who have fallen asleep in the Lord: that they may see the glory of God and Jesus standing at the right hand of the Father.

Concluding Prayer
God of glory and Father of our Lord Jesus Christ, listen to the blood of the martyrs and to our prayers that we may all serve you in peace and love. We ask this through Christ our Lord.

24 MAY

Mary, Help of Christians
Australia

Introduction
Through her who is the refuge of sinners and the hope of the afflicted, let us make our needs known to the God of all consolation.

Intentions
1. For the Church: that she may truly image Mary, and be a source of help in time of need to all God's children.
2. For peace in our world: may she who brought forth the Prince of Peace be a beacon light to all the peoples of the earth.
3. For those who are suffering for their faith, and those who are threatened with persecution and death: that they may experience Mary's protecting hand.
4. For the Islamic peoples of the world: that we may seek to understand their faith, wisdom and endurance.
5. For all who are suffering in body and in mind: that she who is the help of all Christians may visit them with her motherly care.
6. For parents who are overburdened: that they may learn from the faith and courage of Mary.

Concluding Prayer
Lord our God, as we celebrate this feast day of Mary, Help of Christians, grant that we may be inspired by her example and encouraged by her prayers for us. We make this prayer through Christ our Lord.

St Bede the Venerable, Priest and Doctor of the Church
England

Introduction
God raised up St Bede to be a 'light of the Church, lit by the Holy Spirit.' Inspired by the same Spirit, we approach with confidence to the throne of grace to ask God's help.

Intentions
1. We pray for all engaged in the ministry of teaching: that they may be filled with the Spirit of understanding and be upright in purpose and in learning.
2. We pray for all who follow the Lord in the religious life: that they may ever find their delight in his company.
3. Let us pray that Christians in this land may be as the salt of the earth and the light of the world so that, seeing their good works, people may give the praise to their Father in heaven.
4. We pray for young people, the hope of the future: that they may learn to know about Christ through the Gospels and to know him in prayer.
5. Let us pray for all who have died: that the Lord may grant them their heart's desire and happiness for ever in his kingdom.

Concluding Prayer
Lord God, you made St Bede worthy of all honour. Through his intercession, we ask you to listen to our prayers and to make us less unworthy of your love. This we ask through Christ our Lord.

31 MAY

The Visitation of the Blessed Virgin Mary

Introduction
My brothers and sisters, as we remember today Mary's visitation to her cousin, we marvel with Elizabeth at the wonderful gifts God has given her and confidently, through her intercession, offer our prayer to him.

Intentions
1. We pray for the Church: that she may rejoice in God her Saviour, ever thankful of the mighty deeds he has done in human history.
2. We pray for governments and national leaders: that they may selflessly serve their people with mercy and compassion, conscious of the dignity and value of human life.
3. We pray for the more wealthy nations: that as they enjoy an abundance of the good things of this world, they may share willingly what they have with those who lack the basic necessities of life.
4. For religious consecrated to Mary: as they fulfil their mission in the Church, may they be inspired by Mary's generosity and total dedication in responding to God's plan for her.
5. We pray for the community gathered here: as Mary believed the promises made her by the Lord would be fulfilled, may we, prompted by the Holy Spirit, follow her example of constancy in faith and joyfulness in hope.

Concluding Prayer
Father Almighty, you honoured Mary, one of our race, with the motherhood of your Son. As we too claim her maternal care, accept our prayers mindful of your mercy. Through Christ our Lord.

JUNE

---

9 JUNE

St Columba (Colum Cille)
Ireland, Scotland

Introduction
May God our Father give us the grace this day to take his living word to heart as Columba did. May the life and teaching of the word made flesh, Jesus, God's Son, sustain us in the trials of this earthly pilgrimage as it inspired Columba in the contradictions, exile and pains of the suffering earth.

Intentions
1. St Columba was a powerful living witness to the Gospel in an age of conflict and confusion. May all of us gathered to honour his memory be conscious of our Christian witness in this age of comfortless sounds.

2. Columba's love for his native land occasionally blurred his vision of Christ's universal kingdom of peace. We pray his guidance on all who experience the conflict of patriotism with Christ's teaching of justice and peace.

3. Like countless thousands of others from Derry and Donegal in recent centuries, St Columba was an exile. We pray for all who have left their native land and, through the prayer of the exile saint, may they too spread the good news of Christ's Gospel to a war-weary world.

4. In times of clan conflict, exile and opposition, St Columba was supported by his constant contact with God. May we too remember that God will be our guide in times of stress if we turn to him daily in humble prayer.

5. We pray that his love for Derry and Ireland will draw his blessing on a country still searching for that elusive peace and harmony in a world which needs the witness of a Christian nation.

6. We pray that his love for Iona and Scotland will bless the land of Andrew.

Concluding Prayer
Father in heaven, be with us in our days of joy and sustain us in our nights of sorrow. May the inspiration of St Columba, a native of our land, be with us as we strive to live out the Gospel in the ordinary days of everyday living. Through Christ our Lord.

---

9 MEITHEAMH

Naomh Colm Cille
Éire

Réamhrá
A Dhia, a Athair dhil, tabhair de ghrásta dúinn do bhriathar beo a thaisceadh inár gcroí mar a rinne Colm Cille. Go raibh beatha agus teagasc do Mhic, ár dTiarna Íosa Críost, fíor-Dhai agus fíor-dhuine, mar thaca againne mar a bhí ag Colm Cille, trí chruatan, ainnise agus pianta ár ndeoraíochta abhus.

Achainí
1. Ba fhianaise bheo bhríomher é Colm Cille ar an Soiscéal in aimsir achrainn agus mearbhaill. Agus sinn le chéile anseo á onorú mar naomh, go dtuigimid nach foláir dúinn féin an fhianaise Chríostaí chéanna a thabhairt an aois seo na nglórtha duairce.
2. An grá a bhí ag Colm Cille dá thír dhúchais, tháinig sé corruair idir é agus a thuiscint ar ríocht na síochána a bhunaigh Críost do chách. Iarraimid ar an naomh a bheith mar threoir ag cách a bhraitheann deighilt idir an tírghrá and teagasc Chríost ar an gceart agus an tsíocháin.
3. Dála na mílte eile ó Dhoire agus ó Dhún na nGall le roinnt céadta bliain, bhí Colm Cille ina dheoraí. Guímid ar son na ndaoine uile a d'fhág a dtír dhúchais. Trí impí an naomhdheoraí go leatha siadsan fosta dea-scéal Chríost ar fud an domhain seo atá traochta ón gcogadh.
4. Lena linn féin, d'ainneoin choimhlint idir treabhchais, deoraíocht agus cur ina aghaidh féin, bhain Colm Cille neart as a shíorchaidreamh le Dia. Bíodh a fhios againne fosta go

gcabhróidh Dia linn in am an éigin ach iompú go umhal chuige gach lá inár gcuid urnaithe.

5. Guímid go dtiocfaidh rath Dé ar Éireann de bharr an ghrá atá ag Colm Cille do Dhoire and d'Éireann, óir táimid i gcónaí ar thóir na síochána agus an mhuintearais agus iad ag síoréalú uainn, fad tá an saol mór ag súil lena leithéid uainn mar thír Chríostaí.

6. Guímid de bharr ghrá Cholm Cille d'Í and d'Albain go dtiocfaidh rath Dé ar an tír sin Naomh Aindrias.

Paidir Scoir

A Athair neamhaí, bí linn in am na lúcháire agus cuidigh linn in am an bhróin. Go raibh sampla Cholm Cille, ár gcomhthíreach féin, dár síorneartú agus sinn ag iarraidh ár mbeatha a chaitheamh go leathúil de réir an tSoiscéil. Trí Chríost ár dTiarna.

---

22 JUNE

Sts John Fisher, bishop, and Thomas More, martyrs
England and Wales

Introduction
God raised up these two great martyrs and gave them courage to stand firm to the end. As their spiritual descendants, we rely on their intercession and make our prayers to the one true God, our merciful Father.

Intentions
1. Let us pray that the Spirit of the Lord will grant courage and strength to Christians in this land so that, while serving their country, they may serve God first.
2. We pray for our Sovereign, N., and all the royal family: that they may be preserved from all harm and danger.
3. Let us pray that the people of this land may come to know the one true God and Jesus Christ whom he has sent, and may thus receive eternal life.
4. Let us pray that our young people may be inspired by the example of the martyrs to give themselves unreservedly to the service of God and the Church.

5. We pray for an increase of charity so that we may be known as the true followers of Christ by the love we have for one another.

Concluding Prayer
Lord God, strength of the martyrs, we ask you to listen to our prayers and to grant that we may give an example of nobility and a record of virtue to all whom we meet. This we ask through Christ our Lord.

---

24 JUNE

The Birth of St John the Baptist

Introduction
As we rejoice with the whole Church at the birth of John the Baptist, let us pray that his life and preaching may prepare us for the coming of the Lord.

Intentions
1. That the Church may always experience great joy in encountering the Lord Jesus, and share that joy with men and women everywhere.
2. That the leaders of the Churches be faithful to their calling as prophets of God the Most High, and proclaim the way of God without fear or favour.
3. May all children be received as gifts of God, and, with the watchful help of Mary, may their birth be attended by rejoicing and marked by signs of promise.
4. May parents and children be at one in seeking and doing God's will: that, in their differing ways, they may be sensitive towards each other's needs.
5. May we, and all God's people, walk in the ways of justice and peace, assuring to those in need a life that befits their dignity and fulfills their aspirations.

Concluding Prayer
May the prayers of John, whom your Son called greatest of the sons of women, be heard on our behalf, O Lord, that

Christ may increase in our life and thoughts, and be glorified in all we do. Through the same Christ, our Lord.

---

29 JUNE

Solemnity of Sts Peter and Paul

Introduction
In honouring the blessed apostles Peter and Paul we celebrate the origins of our faith. Let us ask God to strengthen us in that faith.

Intentions
1. Peter's faith in Christ, the Son of God, was the Father's gift to him. May we always hold fast to our faith in Jesus, in spite of our weakness and our sins.
2. Both Peter and Paul experienced vividly what it is to be forgiven by the Lord. May sinners draw strength from their example and return to the Shepherd and Guardian of their souls.
3. The care of all the Churches rested heavily on Peter and Paul. May the pope and the bishops of the Church receive light and strength in continuing that arduous mission.
4. May all the ministers of the Gospel be convinced that the first requirement of their ministry is a deep personal love for Christ and for his flock.
5. Let us pray for persecuted Christians: may the example of Peter and Paul be for them a beacon of hope and a pledge of their reward.
6. May the sick, the bereaved and the lonely take comfort from the sense of the unity and fellowship of the Church which we joyfully celebrate on this festival.

Concluding Prayer
Father, you raised up Peter and Paul, men of varied gifts and contrasting talents, to work together in the service of the Gospel of Christ. Grant that we may likewise gladly labour for the spread of your kingdom on earth. Through Christ our Lord.

JULY

St Benedict

Introduction
Let us pray to God our Father in thanksgiving for the life and teaching of Saint Benedict.

Intentions
1. At the intercession of St Benedict, the man of prayer, teach us how to seek you by prayer.
2. Help us to follow St Benedict's example of work, and to finish the works you give us to do.
3. May St Benedict, as Patron of Europe, raise the hearts of the people of Europe to the things that are above.
4. We pray for all Benedictine monasteries, and for those committed to their care.
5. We praise you, Lord, for the beauty of creation: teach us how to live for your glory.

Concluding Prayer
Rekindle, Lord, within your Church, that Spirit whom St Benedict followed and obeyed. Filled with that same Spirit, may we love what he loved, and live as he taught us. Through Christ our Lord.

Our Lady of Mount Carmel

Introduction
On this feast of our Lady of Mount Carmel, let us pray to God for our needs so that, like Mary, we may respond generously to God in our daily lives.

Intentions
1. We pray that the word of God which Mary treasured in her heart may continue to be a source of nourishment in the life

of the Church.

2. We pray that many people today may come to discover personal prayer as a source of strength and serenity in their lives.

3. We pray for the wisdom to realise that we have not here a lasting city; amid the passing things of this life may we keep our hearts fixed on the joys that will last for ever.

4. We pray for all mothers: that they may have the spirit of Mary, and show compassion and understanding in caring for their children.

5. We pray for all members of religious congregations: that they may be strengthened in their vocation and find time to be with the Lord in prayer.

6. We pray for those who have died, especially for those who have touched our lives in any way: that the Lord may overlook their sins and give them a home with him for ever.

Concluding Prayer
God our Father, we present these needs to you, together with all the other unspoken requests of our hearts. We do so with confidence, because we know that you love us. We make our prayer through Christ our Lord.

---

31 JULY

St Ignatius Loyola

Introduction
On this feast of St Ignatius, a man of the Church and a man of prayer, let us rise to pray for the Church and the world through the merits of his life.

Intentions
1. Let us pray for the people of God throughout the world: that, through the prayer of St Ignatius, they may always think with the Church and grow in love of the faith entrusted to the saints.

2. Let us pray for peace and harmony among the nations: that mankind may enjoy the benefits of good government and that justice may grow in the affairs of the world.

3. We pray for priests and religious and for all engaged in pastoral ministry: that they may be renewed in their zeal for the Kingdom of God and may be generous in the service of faith and justice.
4. We pray for the young people in our schools and parishes: that they may come to know and love their Lord and Saviour and not be deaf to the call which he gives to each.
5. Let us pray for the people of this community: that, following the example of St Ignatius, they may seek God in all things and be blessed by the gift of prayer, and that they may grow in their love of the Mass and the Blessed Sacrament.

Concluding Prayer
Almighty God and Father, listen, we beseech you, to the prayers of your people, and through the merits of our Lady, St Ignatius and of all the saints, strengthen us in faith and hope and love through Christ our Lord.

AUGUST

1 AUGUST

St Alphonsus Maria Ligouri

Introduction
My brothers and sisters, on this the feast of St Alphonsus Liguori, let us pray to God our Father, that all of us in the Church today may witness to the universal compassion of the Redeemer.

Intentions
1. That the Lord may always be with his Church, especially with its leaders, in showing compassion to all people.
2. That our leaders, especially in countries where there are deep divisions and warring factions, give courageous and enlightened leadership.
3. That the Lord may continue through his Church to bring good news to the poor and proclaim liberty to those captive in sin.
4. That the Lord will send many zealous labourers into his

harvest.
5. That all of us might learn to turn away from the ways of selfishness that divide us, to the way of the Redeemer who seeks to bring all men into communion.

Concluding Prayer
Father, we thank you for the gift of St Alphonsus and for the congregation he founded; help us, like him, zealously to work for the salvation and redemption of our world. We ask this through Christ our Lord.

---

6 AUGUST

The Transfiguration of Our Lord

Introduction
As we have been brought together and formed by the word of God's Chosen One, let us now pray with confidence to be granted all the gifts of God's kingdom.

Intentions
1. That Christians everywhere may recognize the glory of Christ in the poor and deprived, and may be moved to offer love and hope.
2. That our world may be transformed so that the new law of love will put an end to fear, injustice and division.
3. Let us pray for all who labour to build up and conserve the gifts of creation: through their efforts may the splendour of God's handiwork become ever more clearly visible.
4. Let us pray for the sick, the lonely and the oppressed: may their faith prove to be a lamp shining in the dark places of their lives.
5. Let us pray for ourselves, for the courage to listen with attention to the words God addresses to us, and to accept both suffering and joy.

Concluding Prayer
God of unchanging glory and light, be pleased to accept the prayers of your people gathered in the name of your Son. Direct and govern our hearts and our bodies in the ways of

your law, so that our lives may be transformed by the presence among us of your Chosen One, our Lord Jesus Christ, who lives and reigns forever and ever.

---

8 AUGUST

St Dominic

Introduction
Saint Dominic's own way of prayer was to express his devotion with gestures, first bowing deeply before the presence of Christ. Even when travelling, he would steal sudden moments of prayer, unobtrusively. With his example to guide us, we now bring the many concerns of our lives and our world into the presence of God.

Intentions
1. For the Church throughout the world: that, constantly renewed by the spirit of truth, it may bring light and hope to all.
2. For all who believe in Christ, the Word made flesh: that they may come to that unity of love and faith which will enable them to join in the one Eucharist.
3. For all who work to establish justice and peace in the world: that their efforts may be sustained and brought to fulfilment under God's grace.
4. For all the members of the Dominican family: that, like Saint Dominic, they may proclaim the Gospel at all times by their words and by their lives.
5. For all who seek after truth: that God may grant them wisdom, insight, and the grace to welcome the word of God with open hearts.
6. For all the deceased members and friends of the Dominican Order, and for all the faithful departed: that they may enjoy the vision of God's glory in heaven.

Concluding Prayer
Father, recalling Saint Dominic's dying confession that he had always done your will with joy, and relying on his promise to watch over his family from heaven, we ask you to accept

our prayers, and through his intercession to build us up in love and hope and in faith in the Word of life, your Son our Lord Jesus Christ, who lives and reigns with you and the Holy Spirit one God for ever and ever.

---

26 AUGUST

St Ninian, Bishop
Scotland

Introduction
As we celebrate the feast of St Ninian, who was among the first to pronounce the word of life in our land, we remember our dependence on the all-pure God and ask for his help.

Intentions
1. Let us pray for the universal Church: that she may boldly proclaim the message of salvation and the reign of the Spirit.
2. Let us pray for those in public life: that they may be constant in building proper structures of justice and caring.
3. Let us pray for those who go out to preach the Gospel: may they speak the language of the modern world and address its problems.
4. Let us pray for those who are enduring troubles of any kind: may they be given the rich, more abundant life promised by our Saviour.
5. Let us pray for ourselves gathered here today: may we as a holy community practice honesty and integrity in our daily lives.

Concluding Prayer
Eternal Father, grant us your grace in abundance in honour of St Ninian whose feast we keep. As we recall his time here on earth may we merit to join him one day in heaven. Through Christ our Lord.

St Augustine

Introduction
The glory of the saints is the fruit of the death and resurrection of Christ. Therefore, as we celebrate the feast of Saint Augustine, we celebrate the generosity of God. Relying on this generosity, let us pray to him.

Intentions
1. Let us pray that God may make the Church more perfectly the Body of Christ and more clearly the continuation of his life on earth.
2. Let us pray that God may bless the work of theologians and inspire them to love the investigation of truth.
3. Let us ask God's help for all who pray: that their words may be in harmony with their actions, their lips with their hearts, and and their lives with their petitions.
4. Let us pray for all who seek God: that they may be humble and sincere in their searching, and successful and happy in their finding.
5. Let us pray to God for an increase of faith, hope and charity, that we may have in us the same sentiments as are in Christ Jesus.
6. Let us pray for all sinners: that they may find God and themselves in true conversion of heart.
7. Let us pray for a deeper understanding and appreciation of Christ's sacraments, which are truly his action among us.
8. Let us pray for the dead: that they may find perfect rest in God.

Concluding Prayer
O God, you enabled Saint Augustine to live by your wisdom in the faith, hope and love of your Church. By his prayers, may we grow in holiness and attain the rest of perfect conversion which you offer us through your Son, our Lord Jesus Christ and in the Holy Spirit.

SEPTEMBER

---

3 SEPTEMBER

St Gregory the Great
England

Introduction
Through the sending of his mission to the English people, St Gregory handed on to us the good news of God's merciful love. Confident in that merciful love, we make our petitions to our heavenly Father as his sons and daughters.

Intentions
1. Let us pray for our Holy Father, Pope N., the successor of St Gregory, and for the leaders of the Christian Church in this land: that they may be as devoted and as protective towards their flocks as a mother who feeds and looks after her own children.
2. We pray for all who do not know Christ: that the good news may be preached to them above all by the example of Christians in this land.
3. Let us pray that the gates of hell may not prevail against us and that the Spirit of truth may inspire all to recognise Jesus as Lord.
4. Let us ask the Lord to inspire many young men and women with the courage to proclaim the good news even in the face of opposition.
5. We pray for all who have died in the peace of Christ: that they may live for ever in the joy of God's kingdom.

Concluding Prayer
Lord God, by the teaching of St Gregory you revealed to the people of this land that Jesus is Christ, your Son. We ask you to listen to our prayers and to grant that your people may be ever more faithful to his Church, for he lives and reigns forever and ever.

14 SEPTEMBER

The Triumph of the Cross

Introduction
Today we honour the cross, the symbol of the Lord's victory over sin and death. We pray that the power of the cross may reach into our lives to heal us and bring us heart and hope.

Intentions
1. The Son of Man is lifted up on the cross. May he draw all people to himself.
2. Christ died to gather into one the children of God scattered abroad. May he gather into one all those who bear the name of Christ.
3. Christ hangs on the cross; may he give courage to all who are crucified by the trials of life.
4. The crucified Christ is our High Priest and King. May he enable us to offer our lives as a living sacrifice holy to his name.
5. With Mary who stood beneath the cross of her Son we pray for all who are in sorrow or in pain.

Concluding Prayer
Heavenly Father, we ask you to hear our prayers. Comfort those in need and enable us to share in the work of your Son's redemption. For you are Lord for ever and ever.

15 SEPTEMBER

Our Lady of Sorrows

Introduction
My brothers and sisters, as we celebrate the death and resurrecton of Jesus in this Eucharist, we remember Mary, the sorrowful virgin who willingly collaborated in the sacrifice of her Son. With confidence in her intercession, we offer our prayer to the Father.

Intentions

1. For the Church, mother of the afflicted: that, in imitating the sorrowful virgin, she may bring consolation to those in trouble and pour into their hearts that hope which does not deceive.

2. For civil and social authorities: that, aware of their duty to promote true progress, they may carefully imprint a spirit of Christian compassion on institutions and laws.

3. For those persecuted because of their faith: that like Mary they unite their suffering with Jesus in his passion, and so experience the liberating power of his death and resurrection.

4. For the unity of Christians: that as they look on their one Lord agonising on the Cross, they may be drawn together in the unity of the Spirit.

5. For all here present: that, as we look at Mary sharing in the passion of her Son, we may find the strength to face difficulties and sufferings of every kind.

Concluding Prayer

Father of mercies, accept the prayers of those whom you have called to stand with Mary on Calvary in union with your Son. Make us, like Mary, generous in sacrificing ourselves for the good of the Church. Through Christ our Lord.

---

24 SEPTEMBER

Our Lady of Ransom
England

Introduction

Mary once stood at the foot of the cross of Jesus on Calvary. She is with us now as we offer this same sacrifice. Confident of her maternal protection, we approach the throne of grace to make our petitions known to our heavenly father.

Intentions

1. We ask the Lord to strengthen and encourage our holy father, Pope N., the successor of Peter, through the obedience and love of his people in this land.

2. Let us pray that we may make a place for Mary in our

homes, so that England may once more be her dowry.

3. We pray for the leaders of the Church: that, filled with the Holy Spirit, they may guide their people as a shepherd leads his flock.

4. We pray for all who are engulfed in the darkness of sin: that they may be converted and live as sons and daughters of the Father.

5. Let us pray for all who are suffering for their faith and their principles: that the Lord will grant them courage and release them from their burdens.

Concluding Prayer

Lord God, you worked marvels for Mary, the Mother of your Son, and taught all generations to call her blessed. As we honour her today, be pleased to listen to our prayers and grant that once again this land may become her dowry and be ever obedient to the vicar of your Son who lives and reigns for ever and ever.

27 SEPTEMBER

St Vincent de Paul

Introduction

Let us acknowledge the love and mercy of God who hears our prayers and has pity on us.

Intentions

1. God sent his Son into the world to preach the good news to the poor: Let us pray that the Church may always be faithful in following Christ in this task.

2. The Spirit of God comes to renew the face of the earth: Let us pray that we may work together in our country to achieve justice, charity and peace for all.

3. St. Vincent de Paul worked for the training of holy priests in the Church: Let us pray for all priests, deacons and seminarians that they be faithful to their vocation, and care for the poor entrusted to them.

4. (a) Many have been inspired to follow the teaching and example of this patron of works of charity: Let us pray for

those who in his spirit serve the poor, the sick and the needy.
or

(b) Our Lord said: 'As you did it to one of the least of
these my brethren, you did it to me': Let us pray for those
who serve the poor, the sick and the needy in our parish;
remembering especially the Society of St Vincent de Paul and
those who support it.

5. 'Are not the poor the suffering members of our Lord?'
said St Vincent, 'They have been given to us as our masters
and patrons': Let us pray for compassionate hearts to seek
out the poor and needy, to comfort them with devoted care
and give them the help they need.

Concluding Prayer
Lord, you endowed St Vincent de Paul with a wonderful gift
of mercy. May we follow his example and experience your
mercy in our lives. Through Christ our Lord.

OCTOBER

1 OCTOBER

St Therese of Lisieux

Introduction
Let us praise God the Father who chose St Therese of the
Child Jesus to reveal the beauty of the gospel of his love.
Through her intercession we pray that the Lord may visit us
with his grace this day.

Intentions
1. Remembering that Therese of Liseaux revered the allness
of God and the littleness of the creature, we pray for the gift
of true humility.
2. The Lord made known to Therese the secret of spiritual
childhood. We pray that we may be led by the way of abandonment, simplicity and confidence.
3. Therese calls our attention to the holy face of ths suffering
Christ. May we bear our daily sufferings with tranquillity for
the salvation of the world.

4. Therese claimed that, if love were to fail, the Church would cease to function. May we realise in our lives that it is love alone that matters.
5. Therese has been declared patroness of the missions. May we have something of her great missionary spirit.

Concluding Prayer
Lord our God, as we remember Therese of the Child Jesus, we ask you to remember us in your love. For you are Lord for ever and ever.

---

4 OCTOBER

St Francis of Assisi

Introduction
God raised up Francis of Assisi to reveal afresh the beauty of holiness and the gladness which flows from living the Gospel. Let us ask for a share in his insight and in his joy.

Intentions
1. Let us pray for the Church: May her members learn once again how to live in simplicity and gladness of heart.
2. May Christian leaders follow Francis in renouncing earthly power and prestige so as to allow the figure of Jesus the Servant to shine forth more clearly in their ministry.
3. May Francis' love of all God's creatures be reflected in our care for our environment. May we see and reverence God's handiwork in the wonderful world which surrounds us.
4. We pray for all who suffer through sickness, addiction or abandonment. May the care shown them by their brothers and sisters be an extension of the care of God their loving Father.
5. May those who are close to death be strengthened to greet her as a sister, for she leads home God's children to the joy of the Father's house.

Concluding Prayer
Father in heaven, you have taught us in blessed Francis that it is in giving that we receive and in pardoning that we are

pardoned. Grant us, through his prayers, to follow Christ who became poor for us, and went through the gates of death to lead us to your kingdom, where he lives and reigns for ever.

---

7 OCTOBER

The Most Holy Rosary

Introduction
It is the mind of the Church that popular piety should draw from the riches of the liturgy and in turn lead back to it.

Intentions
1. Let us pray that the practice of the Rosary may increase our understanding and love of the Eucharist, and that our communion with Christ at Mass may enrich our experience of this much loved devotion.
2. At the heart of each Hail Mary is the holy name of Jesus. May each Hail Mary of our Rosary be an offering of Jesus to the Father and a communion with the Lord in the mysteries of his life, death and resurrection.
3. The Rosary has been called: 'The Gospel on its knees': As we meditate on the fifteen mysteries, may we come to know the mysteries of the kingdom, and imitate what they contain.
4. 'Rejoice, . . . do not be afraid,' the angel said to Mary. Let us pray for those who are troubled by their past, anxious about the present, or frightened of the future. May they experience the peace which comes from knowing that 'the Lord is with them', as he was with Mary.
5. 'I am the handmaid of the Lord,' Mary replied. May we be open to the word of God and be ready to serve as Mary was; yet know the different between serving a need and answering a call: Let what the Lord has said to each one individually find echo in our hearts.

Concluding Prayer
O God, whose only begotten Son by his life, death and resurrection has purchased for us the rewards of eternal life,

grant we beseech you, that, meditating on these mysteries in
the most holy Rosary of the Blessed Virgin Mary, we may
imitate what they contain, and obtain what they promise.
Through Christ Our Lord.

St Edward the Confessor
England

Introduction
In his providence God decreed that St Edward should 'serve
the people of this land by easing their burdens, by relieving
their necessities and by confirming them in their allegiance to
the faith.' Relying on his merits and prayers, we make our
present needs known to our heavenly Father.

Intentions
1. Let us pray that Christians may, like St Edward, take the
beatitudes as their rule of life and thus receive great reward
in heaven.
2. We pray for our Sovereign, N., and all the royal family:
that, following in the footsteps of St Edward, they may bear
witness to Christ by their lives.
3. Let us commend to the Lord all who are afflicted: that he
may comfort and strengthen them and raise up helpers to
minister to them in their hour of need.
4. We pray for all married couples: that they may be faithful
to each other and be blessed with happiness all their days.
5. Let us entrust ourselves and all we love to the providence
of God who watches over us with unending love.

Concluding Prayer
O God, our heavenly Father, you have given St Edward to
us as a model of trust in you. We ask you to listen to our
prayers and to assist us in our needs. Grant that we may find
happiness in devoting ourselves to your service and that of
the Church, and may one day, with Mary and all the saints,
rejoice in the kingdom of heaven where you live for ever and
ever.

St Teresa of Avila

Introduction
The Lord has continually raised up men and women full of love for him. United with all the saints and especially St Teresa on this her feast day, we present our prayers to the God and Father of all mankind.

Intentions
1. We pray that the people of God may continually offer themselves to God as a living sacrifice of praise.
2. We pray that those who are called to the contemplative life may respond with generosity and dedicate their lives for the salvation of all.
3. We pray that all those called to the priesthood and the religious life may unite themselves ever more closely with Christ so that everything they do may be filled with the love of God.
4. We pray that those who do not believe in God may sincerely seek the truth and open their hearts to receive it.
5. We pray that we here present may imitate Christ in his love for God the Father and all mankind.

Concluding Prayer
Father of all, help us to hear the call of Christ your Son who leads us into the way of perfection. Accept our prayers which we make in trust and love. We ask this through the same Christ our Lord.

St Paul of the Cross

Introduction
My brothers and sisters, as we joyfully celebrate the feast of St Paul of the Cross, founder of the Congregation of the Passion, we turn our hearts to God our Father and ask him to pour abundant graces on the Church and the world from

the treasury of Christ's passion and death.

Intentions
1. For the Church: that in the midst of persecutions and tribulations she may proclaim the death and resurrection of the Lord Jesus, and communicate to all men and women the power of the Holy Spirit.
2. For those who govern: that, inspired by Christ crucified, they may always work for the human development of peoples by striving for peace based on justice.
3. For those who share Christ's passion: that the Holy Spirit may make them strong in their trials and persevering in faith, so that they may fill up what is lacking in the sufferings of Christ.
4. For the Passionist family: that her religious, faithful to the charism of St Paul of the Cross, may live personally and communally their consecration to the passion of Jesus and in a great spirit of faith and charity proclaim to the world the infinite love of Christ crucified.
5. For all of us gathered here: that, through this memorial of the Lord's passion, we may gain the power to overcome evil and live in intimate union with God.

Concluding Prayer
Eternal Father, you called St Paul of the Cross to be a fervent apostle of the Gospel of the passion. Hear the prayers we make through his intercession that we may receive the gifts of your infinite mercy and love. Through Christ our Lord.

---

25 OCTOBER

The Forty Martyrs of England and Wales
England and Wales

Introduction
God raised up the Forty Martyrs of this land to witness to the power of his name by their lives and by their death. Relying on their intercession, we confidently make our petitions to him.

Intentions

1. We pray for ourselves, the Church in this land: that we may faithfully follow Christ and ever glory in the name of Christian.
2. Let us pray for all who hold authority: that they may sincerely serve the people of England and Wales and enable all to live in peace and justice.
3. We pray that all Christians may be known as the followers of Christ by the love they have for one another.
4. Let us commend to the Lord those who are searching for the truth: that they may come to know the one true God and Jesus Christ his Son whom he has sent.
5. We pray for young people, the hope of the future: that they may know the love of Christ and never be separated from him.

Concluding Prayer

By your strength, Lord, the martyrs of this land stood fast in their faith. We ask you to listen to our prayers and to give to each of us something of their strength so that we may, like them, be faithful to your Son, Jesus Christ, who lives and reigns for ever and ever.

---

25 OCTOBER

The Welsh Martyrs
Wales

Introduction

The martyrs of Wales set us two examples: a life spent in labour to advance Christ's kingdom in this land, and the same life laid down in perfect witness. We make our intercessions so that we may learn to share their zeal in the way that best befits our own circumstances.

Intentions

1. We pray for our Holy Father, Pope N: that, by confirming the faith of many brethren, he may make glorious that See of Peter, for which our martyrs shed their blood.
2. We pray for our bishops and priests: that they may give

witness to Christ by both holiness of life and fidelity to the teaching of God's Church, a witness raising up new and strong vocations.

3. May the blood shed by our martyrs be the seed of grace for parents and teachers, enabling them to bring up a new generation fit for the vineyard of Jesus Christ.

4. May we all become apostles, proud to confess our Lord before all men, and especially among our fellow Christians not of this fold.

5. May we be helped to preserve a love and reverence for the holy sacrifice by faithful attendance at Mass and a frequent and reverent reception of Holy Communion.

Concluding Prayer
Heavenly Father, may the commemoration of our martyrs be for us a strong reminder of those deep values that worldly standards constantly assail; make us proud to be their brethren, to inherit their faith, and to follow in their steps. Through Christ our Lord.

---

25 HYDREF

Y Merthyron Cymreig
Cymru

Rhagymadrodd
Patrwm deublyg a gawsom oddi wrth Ferthyron Cymru: oes o waith caled i hyrwyddo Teyrnas Grist yn y wlad hon, cyn rhoi einioes yn dystiolaeth berffaith. Ymbiliwn y gallwn ninnau etifeddu eu brwdfrydedd yn y dull addasaf i ni.

Disysiadau
1, Gweddïwn dros ein Tad Sanctaidd, Pab N.: fel, drwy gadarnhau ffydd lliaws o frodyr, yr anrhydedda Gadair Pedr y collodd ein merthyron eu gwaed drosti.

2. Gweddïwn dros ein hesgobion a'n hoffeiriaid: fel y tystiolaethant i Grist drwy fuchedd sanctaidd a thrwy ffyddlondeb i athrawiaeth Eglwys Duw, gan beri felly i eraill dderbyn yn eiddgar alwad i'w gweinidogaeth.

3. Bydded y gwaed a gollodd ein merthyron yn hedyn gras i rieni ac athrawon, gan beri iddynt fagu cenhedlaeth newydd a fydd yn addas i weithio yng ngwinllan Iesu Grist.

4. Bydded inni oll ddyfod yn opostolion, yn falch o arddel ein Harglwydd gerbron dynion ac yn enwedig ymhlith ein cyd-Gristnogion nad ydynt o'r gorlan hon.

5. Bydded inni gael gymorth i garu a pharchu bob amser yr Aberth Sanctaid drwy bresenoldeb ffyddlon yn yr Offeren Lân a thrwy dderbyn y Cymun Sanctaidd yn aml ac yn ostyngedig.

Gweddi Olaf

O Dad Nefol, bydded i ddathliad ein merthyron ein hatgoffa'n rymus am y gwerthoedd dwys yr ymosodir arnynt yn gyson gan safonau bydol; gwna ni'n falch o fod yn frodyr iddynt, o etifeddu eu cred ac o ddilyn ôl eu traed. Trwy Iesu Grist ein Harglwydd.

NOVEMBER

2 NOVEMBER

Commemoration of All the Faithful Departed

Introduction

Now that we have been comforted by God's holy word, let us pray for all the faithful departed: that they may be found worthy of the promises of Christ.

Intentions

1. That the Christian message of consolation and hope may strengthen us all, as we experience death among us.

2. That the crucified Saviour's consoling words to the repentant thief may be a reality for all those we prayerfully remember this day and through the month of November.

3. That the departed of our own families, especially those whose loss we feel deeply, may all be re-united in the communion of saints.

4. That all those who have served the Church as priests or

religious may now worship God in the eternal liturgy of heaven.

5. That those who have died through acts of violence and war may find a place of justice and peace in God's kingdom.

6. That those who have died alone, unwanted and unmourned, may be welcomed by the heavenly community and share in the light and joy of Christ.

7. That Christians may have faith to see God's love in our world, in spite of pain and suffering, separation and loss.

Concluding Prayer
Almighty, loving and caring Father, grant that those whose memory we recall today may find that fullness of peace that you alone can give. We make this prayer through Christ our Lord.

---

6 NOVEMBER

All Saints of Ireland
Ireland

Introduction
Today we acknowledge our debt to the generations who have gone before us in our country and who have handed down to us a way of life imbued with the spirit of Christ. We pray with them to the Lord that he will make not only our own country but the whole world more aware of the message of the Gospel.

Intentions
1. For the mission of the Church throughout the world: that in reaching out to the peoples of the world the Church may be sensitive to the history, the culture, and the native traditions of every race and nation.

2. For all the people of Ireland: that we may work hard to be faithful to our Christian heritage and to ensure that the living word of the Gospel is handed on to the next generation.

3. For those in positions of leadership in our country, the government, the civil service, employers: that their decisions

may be taken in the light of Christian truth and justice, and
be an example of Christian responsibility to all.
4. For parents and teachers of the faith to our children: that
they accept gladly their high calling to form young minds and
hearts in faith, hope and love.
5. For our own local community: that we may always be
outward-looking and ready to cope with changes which are
thrust on us; and that we see ourselves as part of the Church
in the modern world.
6. For our deceased relatives, friends and benefactors: that
the promise of eternal life may comfort us in our daily lives
and overcome the sorrow of separation and bereavement.

Concluding Prayer
Father, we believe that the saints of our land have gone
before us into eternal happiness. We believe that you will
answer these our prayers and bring us all together in heaven.
Through Christ our Lord.

6 SAMHAIN

Naoimh na hÉireann
Éire

Réamhrá
Tugaimid onóir inniu dár sinsear a chuaigh romhainn agus a
bhí dílis don bheatha Chríostaí ó ghlúin go glúin. Guímid in
éineacht leo chun an Tiarna go dtaga fás ar an bheatha sin
ní amháin sa tír seo ach ar fud an domhain uile.

Achainí
1. Guímis ar son mhisean na hEaglaise: go raibh rath ar
obair na misinéirí agus iad ag craoladh an tSoiscéil i bhfad
ó bhaile. Go dtuigidís an stair, an cultúir agus an dúchas faoi
leith a thugann a bhlas féin do gach treabh agus do gach
náisiún.
2. Guímis ar son mhuintir na hÉireann: go ndéanamis ár
ndícheall bheith dílis don Chríostaíocht a thugadh dúinn mar
bhronntanas; agus ár gCríostaíocht féin a bhronnadh beo
beathach ar an aos óg atá ag éirí aníos.

3. Guímis ar son ár gcinnirí náisiúnta, ar son an rialtais, an státseirbhís agus fostóirí na tíre: go raibh na socraithe a dhéanann said de réir na fírinne a thagann ón Soiscéal agus de reir chothrom na Féinne.

4. Guímis ar son tuismitheoirí agus na n-oidí a mhúineann an creideamh do pháistí na tíre: go nglacaidis go fonnmhar lena ngairm uasal chun aigní agus croíthe na bpáistí a mhúnlú sa chreideamh, sa dóchas agus sa charthannacht.

5. Guímis ar son ár bpobail áitiúil féin: go raibh dearcadh oscailte againn ar an saol. Go raibh níos mó misní againn agus sinn ag plé le hathraithe nach bhfuil smacht againn orthu. Go nglacaimis ár bpáirt sa choimhlint ar son na Críostaíochta i saol na linne seo.

6. Guímis ar son ár muintire, ár gcarad agus lucht ár gcúnta atá imithe ar shlí na bhfíréan: go raibh gealltanas na beatha síorraí ina ábhar suaimhnis againn inár saol leathúil agus go scaipe sé an cumha ón ár gcroí.

Paidir Scoir
A Athair, creidimid go ndeachaigh naoimh ár dtíre romhainn isteach sa síocháin agus sa suaimhneas síorraí. Creidimid go n-éistfidh tú leis na paidreacha seo agus go dtabharfaidh tú an t-iomlán againn le chéile ins na Flaithis. Trí Chríost ár dTiarna.

---

8 NOVEMBER

All Saints of Wales
Wales

Introduction
In this land of Wales, where almost every place is named after the saints who long ago built up Christ's Church among us, we remember our fathers in the faith, and under their protection seek the grace to be worthy again of such great beginnings.

Intentions
1. We ask God to foster in our hearts a warm devotion to the many saints who have enriched the history of the Church

in Wales; may they help us to build anew on the foundations they once laid.

2. May we be especially mindful of the saints who laboured in and about the place where we live, and proud to preserve and profess the faith they taught.

3. May we, like them, resist the inroads of false and foolish teaching and also the influence of careless moral standards. We pray that their intercession may protect our schools and young people.

4. We pray for all those who come to Wales to find rest and refreshment in the splendour of its mountains and the beauty of its coasts. May the memory of our saints preserved in the names of towns and villages proclaim to all the Gospel they professed.

5. We pray for all who have gone before us as priests, teachers, and parents, handing down the faith they received from the saints. May God reward them; may they rest in peace.

Concluding Prayer
Heavenly Father, through the intercession of all the saints of Wales, may we become worthy of them for the sake of the children who are to follow us. Through Christ our Lord.

---

8 PACHWEDD

Holl Saint Cymru
Cyrmu

Rhagymadrodd
Yng Nghymru, ein gwlad, y mae cymaint o'n henwau-lleoedd yn cynnwys enwau'r saint a adeiladodd ers talm Eglwys Crist yn ein plith; cofiwn felly ein tadau yn y ffydd, a chwiliwn dan eu nawdd am y gras i fod yn deilwng eto o'r fath ddechreuad mawr.

Disysiadau
1. Erfyniwn y bydd Duw'n meithrin yn ein calonnau gyfeillgarwch cynnes â'r lliaws o saint syddwedi cyfoethogi hanes yr Eglwys yma yng Nghymru; bydded iddynt ein

cynorthwyo i ail-adeiladu ar y seiliau a osodasant hwythau gynt.
2. Bydded i ni gofio'n arbennig y saint a weithiai yn ein hardal ni; byddwn yn falch o gadw ac arddel y ffydd a ddysgent.
3. Bydded i ninnau hefyd wrthsefyll anrhaith gau athrawiaeth ynfyd a dylanwad safonau moesol llac. Gweddïwn y gwarchodir ein hysgolion a'n pobl ieuanc drwy eiriolaeth y saint.
4. Gweddïwn dros bawb a ddaw i Gymru i gael gorffwys ac adloniant ym mawreddd ei mynyddoedd a glendid ei glannau. Bydded i enwau ein saint, sydd ar gof a chadw yn enwau ein trefi a'n pentrefi, gyhoeddi i bawb yr Efengyl a arddelasant.
5. Gweddïwn dros bawb a aeth o'n blaen: offeiriaid, athrawon a rhieni, gan draddodi'r ffydd a gawsant oddi wrth y saint. Gwobr Duw iddynt! Gorffwysent mewn tangnefedd!

Gweddi Olaf
O Dad Nefol, drwy eiriolaeth holl saint Cyrmu, gwna ninnau'n deilwng ohonynt hwy er mwyn y plant sydd i'n dilyn ni. Trwy Iesu Grist ein Harglwydd.

---

16 NOVEMBER

St Margaret
Scotland

Introduction
As we celebrate the feast of St Margaret, patroness of our country, we pray that through her intercession the Lord may remember his people.

Intentions
1. For the Church which St Margaret served with such fidelity: may it be strengthened in unity throughout the world.
2. For those who work in education in our country: may they be helped by the inspiration of Margaret who promoted education with such enthusiasm in her adopted land.
3. For the arts to which Margaret was so dedicated, for all

those who despite inadequate remuneration dedicate their lives to promoting art and beauty.

4. For all parents: like Margaret may they be concerned about the religious development of their children and enable them to grow in love of God and of country.

5. For all women: may they have the freedom of Margaret to become themselves.

6. For all of us gathered here today: may we, like Margaret, not allow themselves to be overwhelmed by the demands of life. May we find time for reading and prayer.

Concluding Prayer
Lord our God, we thank you for the inspiration of the woman who came as a stranger to our shores. May we emulate her example, especially in her love for the poor. We ask this through Christ our Lord.

---

21 NOVEMBER

The Presentation of Mary

Introduction
'Sing, rejoice, daughter of Zion, for I am coming, to dwell in the middle of you . . .' (Zeph. 3:14). We today are the daughter of Zion, as Israel was, as Mary was.

Intentions
1. Let us answer the divine command to sing and rejoice in the Lord. May all sadness and every root of bitterness be taken from us, as we magnify the Lord for the mighty things he has already done in and through each one of us.

2. 'I am coming to dwell in the middle of you — it is the Lord who speaks'. May we be a people of open minds, open hearts, open hands, so that God may find an open space where he may pitch his tent in the middle of us.

3. 'Stretching out his hand towards his disciples, Jesus said: "Here are my mother and my brothers".' May it be our glory to be the disciples of Jesus, and so enjoy the many-splendoured relationship with him of which the Gospel speaks.

4. 'Anyone who does the will of my Father in heaven, is my

brother and sister and mother.' May the example of Mary,
who so ardently sought the will of the Father, inspire us to
pray in every circumstance: 'Father, your will be done on
earth as it is in heaven . . .'
5. 'The Almighty works marvels for me; holy is his name.'
May we know how to glorify the Lord and seek first the
kingdom of God, trusting like Mary that he who is mighty
will not fail us, but do great things for us too in this our day.

Concluding Prayer
Father, the glory of your temple in Jerusalem is no more, but
we rejoice that you have built a temple of the Spirit in the
hearts of your people. May they know how to find you there
and ever live in your presence as Mary did. Through Christ
our Lord.

23 NOVEMBER

St Columban
Ireland

Introduction
Today we seek God's help through the intercession of St
Columban who earnestly cultivated holiness and spread the
word of God in Ireland and on the continent of Europe.

Intentions
1. May our holy father, in the words of Columban, follow
Peter and the whole Church follow the holy father.
2. May the rulers of the countries of Europe ever act, as
Columban demanded, according to the principles of the
faith.
3. For all those in Europe and throughout the world who are
suffering for their faith in Christ.
4. For Ireland: that she cling henceforth to the faith with its
inherited traditions that shaped Columban himself.
5. For Ireland: that she be, as was Columban, courageous
and missionary in her faith.
6. For our dead: that theirs may be eternal glory and joy in
the vision of the Trinity.

Concluding Prayer
Father, through the example and prayer of St Columban, may we live out our Christian daily life constantly and courageously. Through Christ our Lord. Amen.

---

23 SAMHAIN

Naomh Columbán
Éire

Reamhrá
Iarraimid cabhair Dé inniu dúinn féin agus don Eoraip ar fad trí impí Naomh Columbán a shaothraigh an naofacht agus a leath briathar Dé in Éirinn agus ar mhór-roinn na hEorpa.

Achainí
1. Go leana an pápa Peadar agus go leana an Eaglais ar fad an pápa.
2. Go ngéillfeadh rialtóirí thíortha na hEorpa do phrionsabail an chreidimh, mar a d'éiligh Columbán.
3. Ar son na hÉireann: go gcloífadh sí feasta leis an dúchas creidimh a mhúnlaigh Columbán féin.
4. Ar son na ndaoine san Eoraip agus ar fud an domhain atá ag fulaingt mar gheall ar a gcreideamh i gCríost.
5. Ar son na hÉireann: go mbeadh sí, dála Cholumbáin, misniúil miseanach ina creideamh.
6. Ar son ár marbh: go raibh siad ag caitheamh na glóire go síoraí sona.

Paidir Scoir
A Athair, trí shampla agus impí Cholumbáin, go saothraímid an bheatha Chríostaí go misniúil buanseasmhach gach lá. Trí Chríost ár dTiarna.

St Andrew, Apostle

Introduction
Today we celebrate the feastday of Andrew, apostle, and patron of Scotland. With confidence we pray.

Intentions
1. Andrew was sent to proclaim the good news: may the Church in our country be always the herald of the good news of joy to our people.
2. Andrew was one of the two who followed the Lord: may we follow him in courage and simplicity of heart.
3. Andrew was loved by the Lord: may we experience that love in all that we say and do.
4. Andrew rejoiced when he found the Messiah: we pray for all the disenchanted young people of our country who search in vain.
5. Andrew and Peter left their nets to follow the Lord: may we have the courage to abandon the nets of selfishness and sinful attachments.
6. As we celebrate the feast of Andrew, we remember especially to pray for all seminarians. May they learn from his courage and prepare to live heroic lives wherever they find themselves.

Concluding Prayer
Lord our God, may St Andrew your apostle continue to be the guardian of our country. May he build up our hope, and enable us to be a people faithful in good works. Through Christ our Lord.

DECEMBER

29 DECEMBER

St Thomas of Canterbury, Bishop and Martyr.
England

Introduction
God our Father gave to St Thomas the courage 'to die willingly for the name of Jesus and in defence of the Church.' Through his intercession we present our petitions to the same Father of mercies.

Intentions
1. We pray for the leaders of the Church in this land: that they may ever be true shepherds of the flock entrusted to their care.
2. We pray for our Sovereign N., and all the royal family: that the Lord will protect them from all harm.
3. Let us pray for the government of this realm: that in all their decisions and acts they ay be guided by the true principles of justice, peace and love.
4. We pray that we may stand by Christ faithfully and without fear in our trials and thus be less unworthy to receive the kingdom prepared for us from the foundation of the world.
5. We pray that each of us may understand our responsibilities towards those less fortunate than ourselves and may strive to relieve their burdens.

Concluding Prayer
Through your power, Lord, St Thomas changed from being 'a patron of play-actors and a follower of hounds and became a shepherd of souls.' We beg you to listen to the prayers we offer through his intercession. Help us always to be obedient to the vicar of your Son and loyal citizens of this realm. We ask this through Christ our Lord.

COMMONS

COMMON OF THE BLESSED VIRGIN MARY: ADVENT

Introduction
We turn to our Father who by his Spirit prepared the heart of Mary to welcome the eternal Son.

Intentions
1. That the Church may hear the voice of the Spirit saying "Come", and respond in faith "Come, Lord Jesus".
2. That those who come to others in work and kindly services may further enrich them by bringing also Jesus.
3. That those who are confused, as were Mary and Joseph, about God's will, may be open to the coming of the Holy Spirit to enlighten them.
4. That the sure coming of the Lord into each of our lives may deepen our hope and give us the freedom to love.

Concluding Prayer
Loving Father, let us come to your Son with hearts open to be guided by his Spirit, for you are Lord for ever and ever.

COMMON OF THE BLESSED VIRGIN MARY: LENT

Introduction
In this season of penance we ask our heavenly Father to support us in our trials and give meaning to our suffering.

Intentions
1. The sword of suffering pierced the heart of Mary: We pray for persecuted Christians everywhere: that they may stand firm in faith.
2. Mary mourned her Son: We pray for the bereaved and for all who feel no hope: that they may find comfort in the resurrection from the dead.
3. The shrines of Mary throughout the world teach with one voice a message of penance and prayer. We pray for the spread of this good news: that God's people may know the joy that prayer and penance bring.

4. The Holy Family bore the image of refugees and exiles. We pray for all who are uprooted from their homeland: that they may find caring and welcoming peoples.
5. The beloved disciple received Mary into his home. We pray for all Christians: that they may see the beauty of Mary and understand more deeply her role in God's plan.
6. Mary stood by the cross of Jesus as he died. We pray that the Church may preach the power of the cross, that its healing power may touch people's lives.

Concluding Prayer
Lord and Father, you pattern us by your Spirit into the image of your Son, crucified and risen; through Mary's intercession may we come to the surpassing worth of knowing Jesus, who is our Lord and Saviour.

COMMON OF THE BLESSED VIRGIN MARY: EASTERTIDE

Introduction
Since we are baptized into the risen Jesus, and are members of his Body, and have his mother to intercede for us, we pray with confidence to our good and kind Father.

Intentions
1. Mary sought Jesus anxiously. We pray that Christians may constantly find Jesus as risen Lord.
2. Mary said "do whatever he tells you". We pray that peoples may find peace and reconciliation through love and respect for human dignity.
3. Jesus and Mary enriched the marriage at Cana by their caring presence. We pray for all Christian marriages, for those that support them, and for all who do not have the comfort of a loving marriage partner.
4. Mary and Joseph did not understand the words of Jesus. We pray that we may ponder them in our hearts, and be led to know his truth and his Father's personal love for us.

Concluding Prayer
Loving Father, you sent your Son to become fully human; give us the wisdom to pattern our lives on the example of

Mary and Joseph, so that through the power of the resurrection we may be truly disciples of Jesus, your Son, and our Lord.

COMMON OF THE BLESSED VIRGIN MARY: GENERAL

Introduction
We bring to our loving Father the needs of the Church and the world. We rely on Mary's intercession to support these our prayers.

Intentions
1. Mary welcomed God's word: we pray that it may take deeper root in the hearts of Christians.
2. Mary heard the word of God: we pray that civil authorities and those at war may hear God's word of peace and justice.
3. Mary pondered the word of God in her heart: we pray for theologians and preachers that they may bring the message of God alive today.
4. Mary did the word of God and was happy to be his slave: we pray that we may put into practice the saving word that we hear.

Concluding Prayer
Father in heaven, we thank you for your plan of love for us: may the mother of Jesus through the Holy Spirit reveal her Son to us; may Jesus lead us to know Mary's motherly care for us all. We ask this in the name of your Son, Jesus, our Lord.

COMMON OF APOSTLES

Introduction
To mark our celebration of the feast of St N., Apostle (Ss Nn, Apostles), let us pray with faith and confidence for what we need.

Intentions
1. Let us pray for the Christian community throughout the

world: that, true to the heritage received from the apostles, it may remain faithful to the worship of God and the service of all the brothers and sisters.

2. For the leaders of the nations: that they may be enabled to judge wisely and govern with care for the people in their charge, and in particular for the poor.

3. For all who are engaged in care of the infirm and handicapped: that they may generously share Christ's love with those in their care.

4. Let us remember all Christians involved in the media of communications: may their voices echo that of Christ and may the images they project promote understanding, not prejudice.

5. Our thoughts turn, too, to those who suffer for their faith: may the example of the apostles be their inner strength in every crisis.

6. Let us pray that the newly-founded parish communities in our country (Nn) may draw inspiration and hope from the memory of the infant churches nurtured by the apostles.

Concluding Prayer
Lord our God, may the lives of your holy ones inspire us to greater endeavour in the service of your people and may our lives be abundant in good works. Through Christ our Lord. Amen.

COMMON OF MARTYRS

Introduction
As we rejoice to share with St N., the faith that he (she) professed at so high a cost, let us turn our thoughts and prayers to the needs of all people, believers and not.

Intentions
1. That the Church, corporate witness to Christ and all he stood for, may be united in courageously presenting to the world the good news of freedom from sin and death.

2. That world leaders might be inspired to set their hearts not on power but on every opportunity for service of the weak and oppressed.

3. For the Churches that persecution forces into silence: that their faith may realize that mustard-seeds, too, grow in silence.

4. Let us remember those who are tortured and de-humanized by instruments of violent power, the victims and the oppressors: that the sword may swiftly be returned to the scabbard and the wounds of hatred closed.

5. Our thoughts turn moreover to those who feel there is nothing worth living or fighting for: that on them Christ may shed a ray of his light to dispel that gloom and warm that indifference into love.

6. Let us implore God's protective and enlightening blessing on all organizations and persons who strive for the more effective preservation of human rights and personal and family dignity.

Concluding Prayer
Lord our God, may the lives of your holy ones inspire us to greater endeavour in the service of your people. May our lives be abundant in good works. Through Christ our Lord.

COMMON OF PASTORS

Introduction
The example of St N. is set before us today as we take up (rest from) our daily tasks and occupations. Let us pray with heart, therefore, and firm in trust.

Intentions
1. For all pastors, especially for bishops everywhere: that they may tend the flock entrusted to them with care, courage and perseverance.

2. For all who work in parishes, pastors, assistants and co-workers: that they may be agents of the Holy Spirit who leads the people of God into unity.

3. For priests and religious who engage in the work of Christ in difficult and trying situations: that their courage may not fail them in their hours of trial. May Christ the good pastor be their inspiration and joy.

4. For vocations to the priesthood: may the Lord call into his

harvest young men who will speak to the people of our time with insight and conviction.

5. For harmony among all who work for Christ: may petty factions not enter into their work for the kingdom of his love.

6. For those who have borne the burdens and toils of the years and who are now retired from active ministry: may God's peace dwell with them always.

Concluding Prayer

Lord our God, may the lives of your holy ones inspire us to greater endeavour in the service of your people. May our lives be abundant in good works. Through Christ our Lord.

COMMON OF DOCTORS

Introduction

The example of Saint N. is set before us today as we take up (rest from) our daily tasks and occupations. Let us pray with heart, therefore, and firm in trust.

Intentions

1. We pray for that wisdom which comes from the Lord. May we treasure it in our minds and hearts.

2. May we never hide wisdom's rules; may we realise its inexhaustible richness and share it with our fellow men and women.

3. May wisdom be our guide in all that we say and do.

4. The people tell of the wisdom of the saints; may that wisdom ever abide with those who lead God's people.

5. The Lord enlightened Saint N. with his heavenly truth; may he enlighten all those who are in darkness and in doubt.

6. May all those who are entrusted with teaching the young, not grow weary of this task; may they pass on to others the precious gift of wisdom.

Concluding Prayer

Lord our God, may the lives of your holy ones inspire us to greater endeavour in the service of your people. May our lives be abundant in good works. Through Christ our Lord.

COMMON OF VIRGINS

Introduction
Let us turn our minds totally to Christ once more, and on this, St N.'s day, pledge our allegiance to him in all our daily doings.

Intentions
1. For the Church, travelling in hope on the way of perfection: that all its members may be open to Christ's offer to come and abide with them.
2. For those who are devoting their lives to the service of the lonely and deserted: that they may themselves be strengthened for their ministry.
3. Let us remember all consecrated virgins the world over, and pray that their capacity to love and be loved might be enhanced through community life and service.
4. That we may all learn to be obedient to Christ's voice in the decision-making moments of our lives.
5. Let us pray that we may ever treasure Jesus as our true riches and delight, and not cling to temporary glitter and goods that are fleeting.
6. Let us pray that every Christian may know how best to develop and express his (her) own sexuality so as always to enhance and never to abuse so beautiful a gift of God.

Concluding Prayer
Lord our God, may the lives of your holy one inspire us to greater endeavour in the service of your people. May our lives be abundant in good works. Through Christ our Lord.

COMMON OF HOLY MEN

Introduction
The example of St N. is set before us today as we take up (rest from) our daily tasks and occupations. Let us pray with heart, therefore, and firm in trust.

Intentions
1. This holy man rejoiced to be part of the world-wide Chris-

tian community: we pray, then, for all who profess the name of Christ.

2. For all who inspire and are prophets in society: that they may serve the world's peoples in right judgement and leadership that is wise.

3. That we might be enabled to recognize God's gifts in others, rejoice in such blessings in our neighbour, and never outdo one another except in love and caring.

4. For teachers, and all who educate the young by their influence or by programmed courses: that they might kindle the growing flame of humanity that each young person is.

5. Let us remember the holy men of other faiths, the prophets who do not know the name of Christ: that the one God might be their inspiration too, and their guide.

6. May we never waver from our hope of joining this holy man, St N., in everlasting praise of Christ.

Concluding Prayer
Lord our God, may the lives of your holy ones inspire us to greater endeavour in the service of your people. May our lives be abundant in good works. Through Christ our Lord.

COMMON OF HOLY WOMEN

Introduction
The example of St N. is set before us today as we take up (rest from) our daily tasks and occupations. Let us pray with heart, therefore, and firm in trust.

Intentions
1. Let us pray earnestly for the Church, the mystical body of Christ: that our faith may be found worthy to rank alongside that of St N.

2. Let us pray, too, for all mothers and expectant mothers: that they may be filled with grace for their lives and vocations as mothers.

3. We pray for all families bereaved as a result of warfare and terrorism: that forgiveness, and not bitterness, might line their hearts.

4. And let us pray for good relations with our own

neighbours: that the faith we share may express itself in love and care for those who live nearest us in our avenues and streets.

Concluding Prayer
Lord our God, may the lives of your holy ones inspire us to greater endeavour in the service of your people. May our lives be abundant in good works. Through Christ our Lord.

MASSES FOR SPECIAL OCCASIONS

Introduction
My dear friends, Christ offered his life in sacrifice to gather into one the scattered children of God. With full confidence then we pray for the salvation of all mankind.

Intentions
1. Recognising the union with other Christians which is ours through our common baptism we pray:
   We thank you, Father, for the unity of the body of Christ, and we await with joy the day when we shall be perfectly one, so that the world may know that you have sent your Son, and that he loved us as you loved him.
2. We acknowledge that our sins and failings have created new obstacles between our fellow Christians and ourselves and left many older barriers untouched, and so we pray:
   Father, free us from our sins of prejudice and intolerance, forgive us our lack of courage; give us a new heart, put a new spirit in us, so that we may truly recognise you as our God, and live in harmony with one another as your people.
3. We pray for all those whose ministry gives them a special share in Christ's work of teaching, sanctifying and guiding his flock.
   Father, keep all pastors in integrity of life and tenderness of heart, so that, walking humbly before you, they may draw all who believe in you into one flock, with Christ as its chief shepherd.
4. Remembering the many non-Christian communities who acknowledge God's sovereignty and seek his wisdom we pray:
   Father, you have revealed yourself to mankind throughout the ages; give to the Jewish people, whom you first called to be your own, and to Muslims, Hindus and people of other living faiths, the fullness of revelation that comes from knowing you and your Son, our Lord Jesus Christ.
5. Divisions in society and discord between nations create suffering and want and pose threats to the very existence of

our civilisation. Let us pray for justice and peace for all mankind:

Father, by the power of your Spirit, give to us and all mankind a desire for justice and a love of peace. May the world be enlightened by your truth and transformed by your grace, so that, under the lordship of Christ, your kingdom may be revealed.

Concluding Prayer
Father, hear our prayers which we offer you through your Son, in the power of the Holy Spirit; bring us and all mankind into your kingdom where with the same Son and Holy Spirit you live and reign for ever and ever. Amen.

FOR THE EVANGELIZATION OF PEOPLES

Introduction
Father, from the beginning of time, you have revealed your love and invited us to respond. Awaken in our hearts a love for the truth that will set us free and may that same love motivate us to reach out to others as messengers of the good news of freedom, love and peace.

Intentions
1. May the light of Christ transform all who live in the darkness and selfishness of sin. May it help to break down the greed and destruction which divides, and create instead a climate of forgiveness and reconciliation so that our world can become a place of brotherhood, love and peace.
2. May the love of Christ create new bonds of brotherhood and sisterhood among the peoples of the world; may the forgiveness of Jesus heal the wounds of past misunderstandings and divisions, thus opening new avenues for universal love and dialogue.
3. May the hope of the risen Christ bring a sense of purpose and meaning to all those struggling for a better human life, for daily bread and a society marked by justice, equality and brotherhood.
4. May the joy of Christ touch the lives of those saddened by war, and hurt by the greed of multi-nationals. May it bring

to all our lives, whether oppressors or oppressed, a deeper awareness of the one God we seek to serve and the one people he wishes us to become in the kindgom he is creating on earth.

5. May the bread of Christ, broken for a better world, bring closer together all those estranged or divided in the name of religion, so that they may reconcile their differences and become one in the common search for the God of all peoples.

Concluding Prayer
Father, in this Eucharist we are gathered and united through the power of your word. May this word of life be proclaimed among all peoples so that we can grow and progress as one universal family. We make this prayer through Christ our Lord.

FOR PEACE AND JUSTICE

Introduction
God our Father, Creator of all good things, it is your will that people should live in harmony and peace and enjoy an abundance of the good things of our world. Help us to create the conditions through which these ideals will become attainable for more people.

Intentions
1. Create anew in your people, O Lord, a sense of unity and peace, conscious as we are today of the strife and division which can tear us apart. Reconcile us to one another, heal our wounds and help us grow beyond the differences that divide us.
2. Fill us with that generosity which will compel us to work for the betterment of all people, so that the gifts of creation may be more evenly distributed among the people of our earth.
3. Bring peace to our troubled world, especially to strained relationships, broken homes and war-ridden nations. Help us all in our various capacities to build bridges that unite and not barriers that divide.
4. We pray for industrial peace, especially in our own coun-

try, that workers and employers may treat each other with dignity and respect and work together for the common good of all our people.

5. Open our lives to your healing touch, O. Lord; calm the anger and bitterness which can divide and alienate; pour ointment on the wounds which time alone will heal. Help us to forgive and forget the past, so that we can begin to create a future of justice, love and peace.

Concluding Prayer
The bread of our Eucharist is broken and shared for all who come to receive, irrespective of race, colour, social or economic status. Grant, Lord, that all the other good gifts of our world may also be shared in a spirit of equality, justice and peace. Through Christ our Lord.

FOR THE STARVING PEOPLE OF THE WORLD

Introduction
Father, you gave manna from heaven to feed the hungry people of Israel. We pray today for the starving people of our earth (especially those afflicted by famine) that they may be nourished and relieved of their distress.

Intentions
1. Friend of the hungry multitudes, touch our selfish hearts that we, and all mankind, may share with our less-fortunate brethren the food our world produces for human joy and well-being.
2. Jesus, bread of life, give to all people, especially those afflicted by famine and hunger, food that will enhance their dignity and nourish their souls and bodies.
3. Bless those working among the poor and hungry — striving to develop local resources and thus improve the quality of life and health — especially missionaries, those associated with charitable organizations and lay volunteers.
4. Make us generous and ready to sacrifice something of our time and resources for the betterment of others through financial aid or personal voluntary service.

5. Guest at the wedding feast of Cana, providing wine in abundance, help us to receive with gratitude our daily food and drink and use our energy for the creation of a better world, where the goods of the earth are evenly and fairly distributed.

Concluding Prayer
Father, we offer in this Eucharist the bread of our world, the produce of our earth. Transformed into the Body of Christ, your Son, it becomes the Bread of Christ, your Son, it becomes the Bread of life. May it also be for the hungry people of our earth a source of nourishment, strength and hope. We make this prayer in the name of Jesus, the Lord.

FOR THE SANCTIFCATION OF HUMAN WORK

Introduction
The Creator of the universe entrusts to his people the cultivation and care of the earth we inhabit. We ask him to make us more responsive to his call and more conscientious in our creative task.

Intentions
1. The creative Spirit of God has entrusted the earth to man that he may enrich it through ingenuity of mind, intuition of heart and the labour of his hands. May he help us to realise the dignity of our stewardship, our call to be his creators in renewing the face of the earth.
2. The inventive Spirit of God awakens our imagination and inventiveness. May we create new possibilities for those whose lives are dulled by boredom and routine, and new openings for unemployed and redundant persons.
3. The productive Spirit of God makes fruitful our daily toil. May the goods we produce enrich the lives of our fellow men and women and bring them renewed strength in body and spirit.
4. The artistic Spirit of God blesses those who enrich our world with artistic skill, architectural design, musical composition and dramatic performance. May he awaken in all men and women those hidden talents which add radiance and

joy to human life.
5. The transforming Spirit of God works through those who bring healing and hope to the broken spirit of man. May he bless all those involved in the medical profession and those who care for our sick and elderly.

Concluding Prayer
Father, we bring to the eucharistic table the gifts of bread and wine, fruit of the earth and work of our hands. Transform us with the gifts we present that through them we may be nourished and renewed for the work you have given us to do. We make this prayer through Christ our Lord.

FOR REFUGEES AND EXILES

Introduction
The Father guided his people as they wandered through the desert for forty years. We pray today for all who are far from home, those who have no home to live in, and those forced to live in exile.

Intentions
1. May the Lord of mercy and compassion look upon the prodigal sons and daughters of this world. May he give them that peace which he alone can give.
2. We pray for those who feel rejected, who time and time again are told that there is no room at the inn. In the depth of their loneliness may they be saved from the bitterness that destroys, and may their hearts be open to the gentle touch of love and acceptance.
3. We pray for foreigners living in our own country: that they may find among us hospitality and supportive friendship.
4. We pray in a special way for the victims of war, particularly those forced to flee for protection from the aftermath of ruin and destruction. May the Lord bring healing and hope to their broken hearts. May he restore their strength and help them to build a brighter future for themselves and their dear ones.
5. May Christ be with all who travel in exile or alone as he

was with the bewildered disciples on the road to Emmaus. May he bring their journeys to a happy and fruitful end.

Concluding Prayer
Father, may Christ your Son, who gathered together his scattered disciples after rising from the dead and nourished them in the bread of the Eucharist, bring to all estranged or parted loved ones, something of his nourishment, strength and reassurance. We make this prayer through Christ our Lord.

ANNIVERSARY MASS FOR THE DEAD

Introduction
In the face of death, let us ask God our Father to often our sorrow, arouse our hope, and renew our confidence through his Son's victory over death.

Intentions
1. That Jesus, who is our resurrection and life, may give peace for ever to all who have died.
2. That all people of this world of ours may never lose sight of their eternal destiny.
3. That all those who have died this last year, especially N., whose anniversary now occurs, may be welcomed into the communion of saints, and share in the joy of heaven.
4. That all the bereaved and sorrowing may find comfort in the belief that death has no power over their loved ones.
5. That the eucharistic presence of the risen Lord may be our pledge and support as we journey through life, through death, to everlasting life.

Concluding Prayer
Almighty, loving and caring Father, help us to grow in faith and love so that we see death as our birth into the kingdom of heaven. Prepare our hearts to accept this truth. Grant that the faithful departed find that fullness of peace which you alone can give. We ask this through Jesus Christ our risen Lord and Saviour. Amen.

SUPPLEMENT FOR THE U.S.A.

St Elizabeth Ann Seton

Introduction
Trusting in God, whose providence guides every moment of our pilgrim journey, let us join together in prayer.

Intentions
1. That the Christian Churches may appreciate more and more deeply the great blessings they share in Baptism and in the word of God.
2. That teachers may never grow disenchanted of the challenge of helping young minds to grow in knowledge of the truth.
3. That widows may find acceptance, welcome and support within our community.
4. That God's blessing may accompany the life and work of the religious whose institute was founded by our saint.

Concluding Prayer
Lord our God, give us grace seriously to take to heart the challenge of being ever faithful to your word revealed in Jesus Christ your Son, who lives and reigns for ever and ever.

St John Neumann

Introduction
Let us pray on the feast of our saint, John Neumann. May his keen sense of God's call in our lives, his willing response to the challenge of the Gospel, his special love for those in need — may these graces and gifts of his touch us today in heart and mind, and make us better.

Intentions

1. Our saint left home and country for the love of God's people. We pray today for all those in exile and alone; and for all among us who live in loneliness or in a desert of the heart.

2. Our saint devoted his life to the education of youth and the building of good schools. We pray today for all those who teach and form the young: parents, teachers, preachers.

3. John Neumann died on the street as he went on his priestly rounds in the service of the sick and needy. We pray for vocations to the priesthood and the religious life, and for a generosity of heart among the young.

4. In his life St John was known as a man of extraordinary courtesy and repose of mind. We pray today, in our rushed and thoughtless time, for gentleness and mutual respect, and a decent quality of life.

Concluding Prayer

Lord, before you we place our prayers, spoken and unspoken. Through the intercession of our saint and of the Mother of God whom he particularly loved, may our prayers be heard and their fruit felt in our lives. Through Christ our Lord.

---

4 July

Independence Day

Introduction

Let us join together in prayer to the Lord from whom all blessings flow.

Intentions

1. That the Church of God in this land may seek first the kingship of Christ, his way of holiness.

2. That all who have the responsibility of government in this land may act always with justice and integrity.

3. For all who are oppressed by tyrannical authority: that they may achieve the liberation they need.

4. For all those throughout the world who are charged with framing new constitutions and laws: may their work be a source of justice, freedom and peace.

Concluding Prayer
Father of our Lord Jesus Christ, in whose image we seek to live, we pray you to fashion us together as one body witnessing to your justice and truth and to your love for all people. Through the same Christ our Lord.

FIRST MONDAY OF SEPTEMBER

Labour Day
Cf also pages 290 and 291

Introduction
Let us pray together to the God who fashioned the heavens and the earth and who knows all our needs.

Intentions
1. Let us ask God's blessing on all who commit themselves to bringing about justice and harmony in the work-place.
2. For those who have no work: that they too may be enabled to participate with dignity in the enjoyment of the blessings of creation.
3. That the Spirit of God may be present in all our labours, to make them fruitful and joyful.
4. That we may all appreciate more and more deeply that our work can be a sharing in God's creative action.

Concluding Prayer
Accept, O Lord, our prayers and our worship, and guide our work to cultivate and care for your world, making it for all your people a place to share the delight of your blessings. Through Christ our Lord.

---

13 November

St Frances Xavier Cabrini

Introduction
Let us open our hearts to the Holy Spirit of God who teaches us how to pray.

Intentions
1. That the Church, following the example of her Founder, may always recognise and serve the needs of the outcast and forgotten.
2. That our society may develop programmes to assure for the poor and the marginalised the dignity they need.
3. That all the children of our nation may be enabled to live in security and love.
4. That immigrants may always be assured of a welcome in our neighbourhoods.

Concluding Prayer
Guide our lives, good Lord, so that all we think and say and do may make your love to shine out in our world. Through Christ our Lord.

FOURTH THURSDAY OF NOVEMBER

Thanksgiving Day

Introduction
We do well always and everywhere to give thanks to God, but especially today as we join with our fellow-Americans in heartfelt gratitude.

Intentions
1. That we may be grateful for the natural riches and the beauty of this land of ours.
2. That we may be grateful for the gifts of grace and nature which God has given to our people.
3. That we may be grateful for the men and women who brought the Christian faith to America.
4. That we may be quick and generous in sharing with the less fortunate in our country.
5. That we may be quick and generous in sharing with the less fortunate nations of the world.

Concluding Prayer
God our Father, on this Thanksgiving Day we thank you, and we pledge ourselves to share with others the riches you have